DIVORCED FROM JUSTICE

DIVORCED
FROM
JUSTICE

The Abuse of Women and Children by Divorce Lawyers and Judges

KAREN WINNER

ReganBooks
An Imprint of HarperCollins*Publishers*

HarperCollins books may be purchased for educational, business, or sales promotional use. For information please write: Special Markets Department, HarperCollins Publishers, Inc., 10 East 53rd Street, New York, NY 10022.

FIRST EDITION

Designed by Laura Lindgren

ISBN 0-06-039184-7

96 97 98 99 00 ❖/HC 10 9 8 7 6 5 4 3 2 1

To Elissa West

To all the women who have found out the hard way that the law does not exist to protect women and children in divorce court.

These mothers have courageously fought the system to hold on to their children . . .

Anne Marie D'Angelo

Laura Grumney

Patricia Duchéne

Aliza Schwartz

and continue to fight in a brave effort to regain custody.

Tonya Pinkins

When I, the People, learn to remember, when I, the People,
use the lessons of yesterday and no longer forget
who robbed me last year, who played me for a fool —
then there will be no speaker in all the world say
the name: "The People" with any fleck of a sneer in
his voice or any far-off smile of derision.
The mob—the crowd—the mass—will arrive then.

CARL SANDBURG

CONTENTS

FOREWORD

THE LETTERS arrive weekly, like a trail of unpaid bills. They have come regularly since my involvement with the murder trial of O. J. Simpson, correspondence from all over the country, from men and women, black and white, waitresses and doctors, all of them frustrated by something they lump together as "the system."

Such people also seek me out to ask my advice on repairing this "system," which in their eyes is a thick soup of cynical and manipulative lawyers, unwise and unethical judges, and a glacial and impersonal bureaucracy.

Most of the people who write me don't work in the criminal justice system, yet their disgust and anger seem drawn from a far more personal place than the injustices they see on television and in the newspapers. It has become clear to me that they are disillusioned by more than just the O. J. Simpson case. More and more people are bumping up against some part of the court system themselves and coming away angry and distrustful.

In this powerful book *Divorced from Justice*, Karen Winner has pinpointed the place where most Americans have their first encounter with "the system." Family court.

It is a sad, well-chronicled fact that half of all marriages end in divorce. Unfortunately, these divorces are often just the beginning of the pain, antagonism, and suffering.

Ms. Winner explores divorce court the way too many people, especially women, encounter it—as a harrowing journey through deceit and incompetence, through uncaring and disbelieving professionals who are supposed to help but end up making things worse. *Divorced from Justice* provides a vital road map through the treacherous landscape of divorce, navigating otherwise powerless women through "the system."

I RECEIVE another kind of letter, mostly from women. They are difficult letters to read, vividly describing abusive husbands and boyfriends and the incredible strength it requires to escape such relationships. I meet women who have gathered the immense courage required to get out of marriages in which they were berated and beaten, victims of a predictable pattern of abuse.

Unfortunately, for many of the women who escape, there is another pattern of abuse they must survive—the one etched in the history of divorce court in the United States. "The trouble women have with securing their rights in divorce is not surprising given the history of marriage and divorce in the United States," Karen Winner writes. Indeed, the recent America in which women had no property rights is echoed today in the unfair settlements of many divorces.

Ms. Winner prepares women for the family court universe they might soon face: conflicts of interest, webs of politics, and the inbred, still-male-dominated world of lawyers and judges. Through anecdotes that are chilling in their familiarity, she exposes a system designed by judges and lawyers to serve judges and lawyers and not designed to help those hurt by divorce: a husband, a wife, and their children.

"Men treat divorces as business," Ms. Winner writes. The courts are replete with stories of men who hide their wealth and land on their feet while their ex-wives and children suffer economically. Indeed, children are often the currency in the business of divorce—mere bargaining chips for parents fighting over couches, cars, and bank accounts.

Custody battles can leave parents—men and women alike—feeling victimized by arbitrary rules and formulas, by unscrupulous lawyers and unfeeling judges. The examples in *Divorced from Justice*—such as the judge who called a mother "vindictive and manipulative" and returned a child to his father despite convincing evidence that the child was molested—are horrific. Unfortunately, most of us know a similar story.

There are too many unethical lawyers out there. As a prosecutor for sixteen years, I encountered my share in the criminal justice system, most recently in the prosecution of O. J. Simpson. *Divorced from Justice* reveals many of the same tricks—lying, obstructing, delaying—alive and well in the domestic-court system. At times, the entire process can seem like a game, one whose rules are unknown until it's too late. Of course, men are victimized by divorce, too. But Karen Winner has written a book for those most often left scarred by property fights and custody battles—women. She has identified in these women the same profound feeling that seeps from the letters I receive from women abused by their husbands and from people abused by "the system."

Powerlessness.

FOR ME, there are signs of encouragement every day. I teach law school, and I'm happy to see bright, energetic students who want to be lawyers and judges because they want to contribute to society, because they want to seek justice. There are—and always have been—good people out there: capable lawyers and honest judges.

Part three of *Divorced from Justice* provides another kind of anecdote: the example of women who are fighting back.

It also describes some simple actions that the government can take to begin remedying the system. From limiting the discretion of judges to establishing citizen oversight committees to applying consumer laws to lawyers, Ms. Winner makes suggestions that would make family court a place that actually provides help and guidance for families.

And finally, *Divorced from Justice* ends with a practical guide for women considering divorce. It is vital advice for someone about to embark on such a lonesome and frightening journey.

In the end, Karen Winner is pleading for the same thing we

all want from our system, the thing it should be designed to reach, the most precious and rare commodity in American courtrooms.

Justice. I believe this book is a start.

—Christopher Darden

ACKNOWLEDGMENTS

I AM DEEPLY GRATEFUL to Judith Regan, who believed in the need for this book and helped to bring it to fruition. Judith and her staff have been superb to work with, and I wish to thank Jennifer Hayes, Kristin Kiser, and Matthew Martin at Regan-Books and HarperCollins, as well as Nancy Peske.

There were numerous challenges involved in taking this book from idea to completion. I am deeply grateful to Barbara Seaman who wisely advised me to "keep your eye on the big picture." Barbara planted the seed in my mind to write this book and when the seed started sprouting, I often drew from her strength and insights along the way.

Given the subject matter of this book, the research was very labor-intensive and difficult to surmount. So much of what goes on in local divorce court is hidden from public scrutiny. So little can be taken at face value. Three things must be taken into account in any assessment: the acrimony between divorcing spouses; the lawyers' and judges' strongly entrenched custom of not reporting their colleagues' misconduct; and the secret workings of the lawyer disciplinary committees and judicial conduct commissions. The work of uncovering the facts requires extreme diligence. Many times there are no easy answers to questions, and it was a test of patience on the part of those on whom I relied for answers to so many questions. I am indebted to several people who gave generously of their time and legal acumen: Jeremiah McKenna, former counsel to the New York State Senate Crime and Correction Committee; Lillian Kozak, a certified public accountant and former Chairperson of the Domestic

Relations Law Task Force of the New York State National Organization for Women; Lynn Hecht Schafran, the Director of the National Judicial Education Program to Promote Equality for Women and Men in the Courts; Nancy Erickson, a lawyer and former staff member of the National Center on Women and Family Law, and Adria Hillman, a matrimonial lawyer and co-chair of the New York State Coalition on Women's Legal Issues (COWLI).

I wish to thank Ira Korner, who read an early draft of the manuscript and was extremely supportive, and Kathy Wood.

I am grateful to Law Professor John Elson from Northwestern University for his comments on part of the draft manuscript. New York University Law School Ethics Professor Stephen Gillers gave me permission at the initial phase of research to use the law library at New York University, and I wish to thank him.

Special gratitude goes to Brian Glasser, the owner of Computrs in Manhattan, who generously gave of his resources and equipment.

I want to thank all the women who contributed their stories to the book, particularly Monica Getz and Peggy Hammond.

INTRODUCTION

EACH YEAR MORE than one million marriages in the United States are dissolved in divorce court. Before these legal proceedings start, the husband and wife share one standard of living in their single household. Something strange happens, however, by the time the divorce decree is issued: the division of the household income between the two parties no longer remains equitable and the new arrangement is lopsided, almost always against women. These facts are startling to researchers because our country's divorce laws—known as equitable distribution and community property laws—were intentionally designed to financially protect women and children in divorce. Yet newly divorced women find that their standard of living has plummeted, on the average, by 30 percent, and mothers' and children's available income has fallen as much as 37 percent. Meanwhile, the standard of living for their ex-husbands has risen from 10 to 15 percent.[1] Why is it that divorcing women overwhelmingly face economic hardship after being processed through the legal system, while divorcing men prosper?

To understand this puzzling question I turned to a seemingly obvious place to look for answers: in the lawyer suites and courtrooms where women go for their divorces. Lawyers and judges control the main events in the legal process of divorce and determine what is in the woman's final divorce decree. I have found that while their behavior as advice-givers and decision-makers crucially affects the outcomes of women's lives after divorce, they are often strongly influenced by factors other than the woman's needs.

What emerges from my research is that the present divorce

court system is, in fact, a very lucrative industry run by lawyers and judges. This industry is buoyed by a fee-for-profit system benefiting lawyers and judges, often at the expense and welfare of clients. My findings show that practices specific to the divorce industry, and some others attributed to the legal profession as a whole, are cause for deep concern to divorcing women as well as for public officials. These findings are based on interviews with ethicists, jurists, lawyers, academicians, women's rights activists, and victims, as well as a review of divorce industry trade literature and court and government records.

To begin to understand the divorce industry and its hold over families in divorce, it is important to recognize that lawyers are in a different position from other professionals. What differentiates lawyers is that they exclusively control the public's access to the judicial branch of our government. For all practical purposes, a person cannot gain access to the court if she or he does not have enough money to afford a lawyer. The well-worn phrase that justice is for sale is as true in divorce as in other fields of law. Only the well-off can comfortably afford divorce lawyers; the rest have trouble getting through the courtroom door.[2] In civil court, lawyers aren't usually appointed, so the only way to obtain legal representation is to hire a lawyer. Services like Legal Aid, meant to provide a safety net for poor people, are so typically understaffed that in some places, such as New York City, long waiting lists cause them to shut the door on divorcing people trying to get help. There aren't enough pro bono lawyers, but with those who do there are problems too.[3] Technically speaking, anyone can represent herself, but she will be no match for an experienced lawyer.

We might expect poor and working-class women to have difficulty finding affordable, competent representation, but as these pages will reveal, well-off women who are at the end of their marriages may also find it hard to gain access to the court. That's because women, even professional, affluent women, typically don't control the family assets. Consequently, they often find themselves in the peculiar position of being cash-poor at the end of their marriages and at the beginning of the divorce process. This has a most dire consequence: If a divorcing woman can't afford a lawyer, she's left without representation or protection in a situation that will totally affect her life. There is no ceiling to lawyers' fees, but these women's resources (personal life savings, parental loans, etc.) are finite. That's just the beginning of an explanation of how formerly wealthy women find themselves impoverished through the process of divorce. Even worse, whether a woman can afford to hire a lawyer or not at the outset, all divorcing women stand an equal chance of being priced out of their lawyer. (There is much to be learned here that will be explained later.)

Injury piles on injury for those women thrust into divorce involuntarily. Not only may divorce be imposed on women by their husbands, but the legal apparatus and industry that are divorce court may force these women to face involuntary economic sanctions as well. The penalties start with the imposed high cost of having to hire a lawyer and culminate with having to abide by financial settlements in which the women's needs may not have been represented at all. The sad truth is that lawyers in the industry of divorce court use the woman's divorce as an opportunity to enrich themselves at her expense.

Several practices that are standard industry-wide enhance the lawyer's profit potential:

- Lawyers in most states are not required to provide clients with itemized bills, which makes it nearly impossible for the clients to know what they are paying for.[4] Even when the bills are itemized, it does not preclude common abuses such as fee padding.
- Lawyers are permitted to hold their clients' files hostage if the clients refuse to pay, which can make it extremely difficult for clients to pursue their divorces. There is an ethical prohibition against retaining the documents in the file if

damaging to the client's case, but this ethical code is poorly enforced.

- The legal establishment allows a judicial-selection process heavily tainted by politics.
- The legal establishment allows a judicial-selection process that does not screen applicants for psychological suitability for the job.
- Lawyers are allowed to use children as bargaining chips in the divorce to force mothers into giving up financial rights in return for gaining custody.
- Lawyers are allowed to charge legal fees that exceed the amount of the marital estates.
- Lawyers in many states are allowed to force the sale of the family home in compensation for legal fees even if this leaves family members homeless.[5]

As a result of these practices, women are subject to any number of economic and emotional assaults by their own attorneys, who may well collude with their husbands' attorneys to manipulate a settlement favorable to the lawyers. Vulnerable spouses are overcharged, coerced into trading off property rights for the right to keep custody of their children, and manipulated in various ways into conceding their rights.

Some of these practices, which will be described in detail, are unethical, others clearly illegal. There are also those vast, murky, gray areas that allow ethics and common decency to be evaded. On one hand, there are so many ethics rules, so many of them ill-defined and cast along such narrow technical lines, that what clearly seems like morally indefensible behavior to the layperson turns into a debate between lawyers over legal technicalities. Lawyers rest their argument on what's legal rather than what's right or wrong, unfair or equitable. For example, in a contemporary case, a matrimonial lawyer not only properly advised his affluent client that it was perfectly legal not to pay sufficient alimony if the judge agreed and ordered a low award, but then, when the client decided to adopt this option, the lawyer agreed to take the case. All the while, the lawyer knew that without sufficient alimony the woman would lose all financial security and become destitute. Contrast this to what Abraham Lincoln told a prospective client whose legal claim to $600 meant bankrupting a widow and impoverishing her six children. "Some things that are right legally are not right morally," Lincoln said, refusing to take the case, and adding: "I advise a sprightly, energetic man like you to try your hand at making six hundred dollars in some other way."[6] While appealing to common decency might sound naive or even laughable in these cynical times, Abraham Lincoln knew there was a court of higher justice, by which civilization need abide.

The situation for legal consumers in divorce is that the foxes are guarding the courthouse. Self-regulation of the legal profession by lawyers only adds to the problems for women. The present disciplinary system is seriously deficient. With a few very recent exceptions, consumer safeguards have been sorely lacking. Figures show that the state disciplinary agencies summarily dismiss most complaints. In 1992 (the latest figures available), 111,745 calls accusing lawyers of misconduct were made to disciplinary agencies representing forty-eight states.[7] Out of this total, less than 3 percent—3,102—resulted in lawyers either losing their licenses or having their licenses suspended—a pretty dismal rate.[8] The distinguished ethicist Geoffrey C. Hazard, Jr. surmises that a full quarter of all lawyers practicing are either incompetent or dishonest, or they aren't practicing full-time.[9] That would add up to around 200,000 lawyers, nationwide. Lawyers would point to the statistics cited above to back up their claims that most complaints against lawyers are negligible or dismissable and that lawyers are, for the most part, honest. The public, however, would look at the same data and rate of complaint dismissal and come to a very different conclusion—that lawyers can't be left to hold themselves accountable. Compare, for example, the rate of lawyer complaint dismissals with the record of the New York

City Department of Consumer Affairs, where 90 percent of the complaints are judged valid and legitimate.

Some lawyers dismiss complaints that are filed as mere revenge or hysteria on the part of disgruntled clients. In one damning declaration, Haliburton Fales II, Chairman of the Departmental Disciplinary Committee First Judicial Department, Supreme Court Appellate Division and Hal Lieberman, Chief Counsel, gave yet another reason for their agency's dismissing complaints. Fales said at a public hearing in New York that if the complaint were too complicated to prove because the agency lacked sufficient resources, it would be dismissed.[10] Without data that the public and legal community can agree on, the legal establishment cannot back up its claims that most lawyers are honest by using these statistics as proof.

As a result of this lack of protections, divorce lawyers can easily violate client rights in divorce court with impunity. For the most part, the disciplinary system for lawyers and judges maintains practices and policies that assure an environment in which consumer abuses can continue.

The women and men who are hurt by lawyers and judges are really hurt twice, first as consumers and second as taxpayers whose pocketbooks fund the same system that is harming them. Yet the legal establishment holds that taxpayers have no right to be involved in how the legal and court system should be run. Even though the government is supposedly for the people and by the people, citizens are denied the right to make rules guiding the practices of lawyers, including divorce lawyers. This one-sided system is the result. There is no citizens' review board for divorce court. In this system, laws regulating lawyer conduct are written mainly by lawyers. It should come as no surprise, then, that these laws favor lawyers over consumers. Similarly, the court process and procedures are managed by lawyers, and this forum is not consumer-friendly. It is designed to serve lawyers, primarily.

The one-sided features of the divorce court system extend all the way up to the highest court in the land. Equal protection under the law is supposed to be guaranteed for all. But when a divorcing woman's civil rights are violated by a judge, she has little chance to redress these wrongs in the federal courts, where violations of Constitutional rights are normally addressed. The reason is that federal courts have ruled—with few exceptions—that family issues belong solely in the lower state courts. In theory, individuals can have their Constitutional rights addressed in federal court, but as Lynn Hecht Schafran, director of the Legal Defense and Education Fund at the National Organization for Women (NOW), points out: "Realistically, you can't [get into federal court]. I suppose in some dream world you could. . . . But the federal courts absolutely do not want any part at all, under any circumstances, of anything having to do with domestic relations. So it is extremely difficult."[11]

Schafran's view is supported by case law precedent and, more recently, a 1992 U.S. Supreme Court decision in the case of *Ankenbrandt* v. *Richards*. In that case, the Supreme Court addressed this issue very plainly when the majority accepted the existence of a "domestic relations exception" barring spouses in divorce from federal court and held that this exception applies to cases "involving divorce, alimony and child custody."[12]

Even more recently, a 1994 law passed by Congress to curb domestic violence includes a provision to protect the civil rights of victims of gender-motivated violence, but the act specifically forbids civil rights violations in domestic relations cases from being heard in federal court. Under Subtitle C—Civil Rights for Women, the provision reads: "Neither section 1367 of title 28, United States Code, nor subsection (c) of this section shall be construed, by reason of a claim arising under such subsection, to confer on the courts of the United States jurisdiction over any State law claim seeking the establishment of a divorce, alimony, equitable distribution of marital property or child custody decree."[13]

Because of these rulings, Constitutional rights are not guaranteed. For example, when a state court or state agency wrong-fully removes a child from its parents, this is considered a violation of a parent's Constitutional rights. The U.S. Supreme Court has ruled on this matter, in the case of *Santosky* v. *Kramer* (New York, 1982), that the state courts "can't terminate rights without clear and convincing evidence. . . ." But when mothers try to use this ruling or other similar rulings to get into federal court, they may be turned away. As child rights activist Michelle Etlin explained: "I know of more than a dozen cases where the mothers suing for civil right violations perpetrated on them were kicked out of the federal courts in anywhere from fifteen minutes to two years, on the stated basis that domestic relations cases are not entitled to federal jurisdiction—even though the cases that sought federal jurisdiction were based on *Santosky* v. *Kramer* and *Duchesne* v. *Sugarman*."[14]

Without adequate consumer safeguards in place to curb the divorce industry and its culture, or the ability to address grievances in federal court, the most vulnerable are the first to get hurt. These are financially dependent spouses, predominantly women in long-term marriages who are uprooted by divorce, and mothers with children. These two groups are literally at the mercy of lawyers and the courts.

Each year a huge number of women are potentially affected by the present crisis: between one third and one half of all civil litigation in this nation involves family law issues. Divorce, child support enforcement, and domestic violence make up the bulk of these court cases, in which the woman must seek legal representation or go through legal proceedings to have her rights defended.

In this book I will give accounts of abuse that are typical nationwide. The universality of these stories is reinforced by the large number of complaints against divorce lawyers, as opposed to other kinds of lawyers, in states where statistics against divorce lawyers are kept (Illinois, Wisconsin, California, and New York). Still, the exact extent of lawyer and court-related abuse remains unknown. It is hard to quantify for a few major reasons. The divorce industry has not been examined until very recently, and there are only a few reports and government hearings dealing specifically with the ethics and practices of lawyers in family law. In fact, the first-ever report on this topic was one I wrote for the New York City Department of Consumer Affairs in 1992: *Women in Divorce: Lawyers, Ethics, Fees, and Fairness.* It dealt specifically with the mistreatment of women by their divorce lawyers.

The extent of the problem is also difficult to gauge because the abuse is often hidden, taking place quietly, routinely, and out of public view, without the input or awareness of citizens. Each woman who goes through divorce court tends to think her own experience, however painful or outrageous, is an isolated one, and she has no way of knowing otherwise. The environment that allows for abuses is so dominated by the foxes that the consumer who presses forward with her own complaint is doing far more than arguing the facts of her case. She is taking on the entire system. Consumers who attempt to draw public attention to the abuses in their own cases face the very real possibility of retribution from the court.

While numerical data on how lawyers treat women is lacking, plenty of evidence has been amassed that shows that the crisis for divorcing women is real and that indicates why women rather than men are disproportionately affected by divorce court abuse. We know, for example, that judicial discrimination against women is a major nationwide phenomenon. As of 1993, 38 states and the District of Columbia had gender bias task forces. Over 30 of these were appointed by the states' chief justices. These reports cumulatively show that judicial discrimination against divorcing women in all areas—custody, property rights, and alimony—is rampant. Although the state judiciaries recognize the prejudice against women, there is no overall indication that divorcing women are treated any better now than when the reports were written, or that judges have changed their attitudes. Lynn Hecht Schafran, the lawyer who is credited with having designed the studies, sounded doubtful in 1994, when she was asked if the system was making progress in addressing judicial discrimination against divorcing women. In 1996, Schafran sounded a little more optimistic: "I think there have been some changes but not enough—and every litigant is still subject to the vagaries of the judge before whom she finds herself." And as revealing as they are, these reports oddly do not raise the larger question of why judges are not held accountable when they violate their own laws.

Of course, not all judges are unfair. There are some judges who feel tremendous compassion toward the women and children who are suffering from mistreatment by officials in our judicial system. But even judges can be blocked and suppressed from exposing perceived wrongs, because they are up against the same system too. Kentucky Court of Appeals Judge Michael O. McDonald, now retired, is a hero to some women's advocates. He was one of the judges who reviewed a 1992 decision by a lower trial court judge who ordered the placement of a seven-year-old boy into permanent custody with his father—a lawyer— whom the boy accused of sexually molesting him (and whose claims were backed up by medical reports that showed anal scarring). Judge McDonald said in a telephone interview that he was shocked at all the irregularities he saw in the way the lower court judge handled the case, and sought to overturn the decision. ". . . The deck was stacked against her [the mother]. In a previous finding the judge said she was not believable. Then why was he hearing the case? He had already made up his mind." Judge McDonald wrote the dissenting opinion in the case, showing that the lower court judge was biased, but McDonald said he could not get the other two judges to go along with him. And so the lower court judge's order stood. Judge McDonald said he was further stymied when the other two judges would not even let him publish his dissent, which was highly critical of the lower court judge's actions. "When you see this stuff first-hand it makes you sick," Judge McDonald noted, adding that this case only helped to increase his motivation to retire in 1995.

Despite local variations in divorce laws, accounts of abuse permeate all local judicial systems and nearly all states. There is a familiar theme of intimidation and coercion running through these accounts, regardless of the client's resources or how much the attorney has already made for him or herself on the client's case. Consider the woman in Atlanta, Georgia, whose lawyer made a typical threat: "[He] actually threatened to take my home unless I paid him more money," she said. The attorney had already gotten $50,000 in legal fees from the woman and her husband.

Although women are more likely than men to be abused by the legal system, for reasons that will be explained fully in Chapter 1, men are vulnerable to exploitation too. If a man is isolated or emotionally vulnerable, he can be lured by the predator masquerading as the professional into the same financial traps as a woman can. A prominent professor on the graduate faculty of the New School for Social Research in New York painfully recounted to me how he was bilked of $212,000 by his matrimonial lawyer, Michael Erdheim.[15] The money had been in an escrow account that was for the professor's children's college education, but the professor discovered that Erdheim had appropriated the money for himself, claiming it as legal fees. Erdheim was later arrested and found guilty of defrauding some of his other clients. But the professor could not recover his money. He recalled that his lawyer isolated him by insisting that the professor not discuss the legal proceedings with his estranged wife. Erdheim also had a ruse for protecting himself, as his former client recalled. He had asked the professor to write letters on several occasions during the legal proceeding, saying Erdheim was a good lawyer and that he, the professor, was a satisfied client. "Erdheim contended he wanted these for prospective clients and to show his wife—informal, friendly letters," the professor said. "When I did turn to a lawyer to explore the possibility of getting my money back, Erdheim, in fact, said he had letters showing I was highly satisfied with his performance." Erdheim was disbarred in 1993 and went to prison for his crimes.

Some judges may treat men as harshly as women. One ex-policeman in New York recounted that several years ago the judge in his divorce made him pay alimony and child support to his wife even though she had abandoned the marriage and sent the children to live with him.

To begin the task of understanding how these abuses actually occur is the aim of this book. Toward that end, I will expose the clandestine environment in which these abuses flourish, in the lawyer suites and courtrooms across America. You will learn exactly how lawyers and judges subjugate an entire population of divorcing women and children to the interests of the divorce industry.

I am not a lawyer. My understanding of the problems women face in divorce court has evolved during an ongoing journey of learning. When I was working as an investigative writer for the New York City Department of Consumer Affairs and began the task of looking into complaints from women in the divorce court system, I wondered if the stories I was hearing were anomalies. I had never had any personal legal problems requiring the help of a lawyer. Perhaps the problem was limited to a few unscrupulous lawyers here or there. I was unfamiliar with the legal profession and had always regarded lawyers and judges with the guarded respect of a layperson. They were the official defenders of justice and truth, the upholders of our democratic ideals. This may sound "goody-two-shoes," but I think anyone would agree that if not for the lawyers who fashioned the U.S. Constitution, and those who then defended it through our country's tender years, democracy probably could not have taken root here.[16]

The legal profession bestows on its practitioners a wide and far-reaching power that can be used or misused for public gain or personal gain. Judges and lawyers have the power, in effect, to carry forward democratic freedoms or to advance the ugliest biases of a society. The contrast between the ideal and the way lawyers and judges function in the real world can be sobering.

In March 1991 I was at the New York City Department of Consumer Affairs, working for then-Commissioner Mark Green—a Harvard-educated lawyer himself, and now the Public Advocate of New York City. Four women in divorce turned activists, from a New York-based grass-roots organization, the National Coalition for Family Justice Inc., approached Commissioner Green's office asking for help. They said they didn't know where else to turn. They told of being abused in divorce court and complained that wives in divorce proceedings were being financially exploited by their lawyers.

Mark Green listened closely. He had written a couple of books himself on lawyer practices. He and his former boss, Ralph Nader, were well aware of the plight of the average person who could not afford the costs imposed on him by the legal system.

Mark Green handed the assignment to me, and so I began the very daunting task of investigating. It was a vexing challenge. In my research I found no prior documentation of this problem, but the more I heard, the more evidence verifying the women's complaints kept mounting.

Within a year I had interviewed at least 107 victims, jurists, lawyers, academics, and ethicists. What started to alarm me was the growing suspicion that these complaints were not anomalies at all. The cases were all beginning to suggest a much larger, horrible pattern of legal victimization. These women appeared to be the victims of abuse and exploitation by their own lawyers, and worse, their victimization appeared to be perfectly legal.

Yet lawyers I interviewed kept insisting that the problems were exaggerated and that the whole profession was being unfairly tainted by a few lone scoundrels. I began to feel myself bumping up against the myth that dishonest lawyering is the exception, not the rule. The report that I researched and wrote for the New York City Department of Consumer Affairs, *Women in Divorce: Lawyers, Ethics, Fees, and Fairness*, identified and catalogued lawyer deceptions that have been the routine behavior of lawyers in New York. When the report was released in March 1992, Consumer Affairs was deluged with letters and calls, mostly from women citing problems with divorce lawyers. Commissioner Green said the public response was bigger than anything he had seen as head of Consumer Affairs. "It was certainly the broadest and most emotional response to anything I've done in more than two years in office," he told *Crain's* magazine.[17] Clearly the issue touched a raw public nerve.

Divorce lawyers responded as might be expected, adopting a variety of defensive postures. "As a group we are not without blemish," Manhattan divorce lawyer Eleanor B. Alter told *Crain's*. "But we are not different from other lawyers."[18] "The Consumer Affairs Department, they're supposed to deal with meat and plumbers—they're not competent to deal with lawyers," Hal Meyerson told then-*Newsday* reporter Nina Bernstein.[19] "It's kind of a crock," Kenneth Raggio, a Dallas attorney, was quoted as saying. "It's lawyer-bashing, pure and simple."[20]

The effects of the Consumer Affairs report on lawyers were still reverberating two years later at the 1994 annual American Bar Association convention in New Orleans, when lawyers publicly denounced it as "an attack on lawyers." One lawyer told the group that his trade association, the powerful American Academy of Matrimonial Lawyers, was taking action in Florida by submitting their own rules to prevent any attempt at lawyer regulation by consumer groups. "We want to get on the books before the brother of Mark Green or one of his cousins or somebody comes down to Florida with a bunch of New York carpetbaggers and does to us Florida lawyers what they did to you in New York," the lawyer said, according to a tape recording of the meeting. The Consumer Affairs report, by the way, also got a new name—lawyers dubbed it "The Green Report" after Mark Green.

In response to one of the recommendations I made in the report, a blue-ribbon judicial panel was appointed by New York's then Chief Judge Sol Wachtler. It turned out to be one of his last noble actions in office, before his own legal troubles erupted and he was subsequently imprisoned for harassing his mistress. In the following months, the blue-ribbon panel of judges launched a statewide investigation into the charges the *Women in Divorce* report made. Among the committee's members was Judith Kaye, who assumed the state judiciary's top command after Wachtler was indicted.

When the Committee to Examine Lawyer Conduct in Matrimonial Actions was formed, however, it was not without controversy. The committee was made up entirely of lawyers and judges, with no one representing the interests of consumers. To make matters even more one-sided, when the committee began examining the findings of the *Women in Divorce* report, I was the only nonlawyer called in to testify privately. I publicly complained in an op-ed piece carried by *New York Newsday*. Mark Green complained too, as did advocacy groups like the National Coalition for Family Justice. The complaints obviously served their purpose, because a few weeks after the private hearing, the committee decided to hold three public hearings, which were hastily scheduled in the following weeks. Scores of women called in to testify. According to appellate court clerk Catherine O'Hagan Wolfe, who was counsel for the committee at the time, there were so many litigants wanting to testify that the commission could not accommodate all of them. In May 1993 the committee filed its report with the Chief Judge of New York, confirming the findings of the Consumer Affairs report. In August of that year Chief Judge Judith Kaye took one of her first major steps in office, enacting a cavalcade of new reforms to better protect clients in divorce based on my suggestions in the Consumer Affairs report. New York's reforms were touted by the *New York Times* as the most progressive in the nation. But as Chief Judge Judith Kaye put it two years later: "The rules were important and more still needs to be done."

Encouraged by New York's reforms, others elsewhere have begun speaking out about the injustices and exploitative practices of divorce lawyers in their parts of the country. Critics of the system say that hidden financial abuses and court manipulations of clients by divorce lawyers are nationwide because the free-wheeling divorce industry invites the opportunity for abuse. At the time of this writing, several developments have taken place:

- In Illinois in 1995, the state legislature held hearings to consider adopting the New York reforms.
- In Pennsylvania in 1995, a joint task force on divorce court abuse heard testimony from the public complaining of legal and judicial corruption.
- In New Jersey in 1993, judicial officials issued a scathing report assailing that state's lawyer disciplinary system and urged colleagues to read the findings in the *Women in Divorce* report.[21]
- In 1994, the *National Law Journal* carried a front page story penned by Northwestern University Law School Professor John Elson. "Investigations by the New York City Department of Consumer Affairs and the New York Court of Appeals recently confirmed what most lawyers and the general public have long assumed, that abusive fee practices pervade the practice of divorce law," Elson wrote.[22]

Elson went on to describe a litany of fee abuses and predatory practices he has seen—divorce lawyers who overcharge, misrepresent, or who don't advocate vigorously because of the husband's influence over the lawyer (as when the husband pays the wife's legal fees). As the assistant director of Northwestern University's legal clinic, he has represented many middle- and upper-class ex-housewives from the Chicago area in malpractice cases against their former attorneys. These women were subjected to all manner of fee gouging and misrepresentation by their own lawyers, and then left without sufficient funds to battle their former lawyers.

THE CHAPTERS

Chapters 1 and 2 guide the reader, from the divorcing woman's point of view, on a tour of divorce court and show what can happen when women are unprepared for the divorce and the battle that follows, not necessarily against a hostile spouse but against the court and legal system. Chapter 3 traces the historical background of the present crisis. Ironically, new laws that promised women more economic equality in divorce were the springboard for calamities and abuses. The new no-fault, equitable distribution, and gender-neutral custody laws created in the 1970s had the reverse of their intended effect: the more "equality" women got, the less they received from the courts.[23] The inequities that were banished on paper were guaranteed to be continued through judicially prejudiced rulings. The new laws also opened the door to financial exploitation and mistreatment of women by their own lawyers and the judges. Lawyers' fees, for example—as opposed to the needs of the clients—became a very important factor in determining the outcomes of cases.

Chapter 4 details how your husband's lawyer can hurt you. Corporations do battle in the civil courts using legal manipulations such as delay and excessive litigation to hurt their legal opponents and win. These same court tactics are now being used against women and children in family law cases, even though women aren't financially equipped to defend themselves against such assaults. As distinguished lawyer Whitney North Seymour, Jr., a former U.S. attorney in New York, explained: "The basic problem is that the strategy they use in commercial cases—to wear the other side out—is used in matrimonial litigation. A corporation with a deep pocket can wipe out a small business because they can't afford all the litigation expense, and this is exactly what is happening in matrimonial cases."[24] The economic stakes are much higher for a woman in divorce than for a corporation in commercial litigation. While a corporation can file bankruptcy or take the losses off its taxes, this same expensive, unnecessary litigation may cause a woman to fall into destitution and even be deprived of the means to support her children. Also, corporations have the benefit of internal legal counsel to advise them in their dealings with outside law firms. Women (or men, for that matter) do not have the benefit of legal counsel to advise or warn them of what is in their best interests with the attorney they are hiring. In Chapter 5 you will learn about the dirty tricks of your own lawyer. Chapter 6 explains why lawyers are allowed to get away with unethical conduct, how the profit motive works, and how the legal system protects lawyers who cheat.

Chapter 7 focuses on the role that judges play in the abuse. Those who run for judicial office are often not sufficiently qualified or are ill-suited for the important work of presiding over family law cases, yet as the chapters reveal, there are no checks and balances on their power. In Chapter 8 we see the court culture in which these abuses flourish. Lawyers and judges who engage in illegal or morally indefensible practices do not function in a vacuum. Instead, they are part of a tightly cohesive group, bonded together by their trade organizations, the local, state, and national bar associations. The way lawyers and judges operate the law has much to do with the political and social underpinnings of their culture and the power and control they exert over public policy in the courts.

Chapter 9 features two success stories of women who fought the system and won. Chapter 10 looks at the latest developments in divorce court and the future of divorce. The remaining chapters look at solutions that government can provide and suggests individual remedies for women who are either contemplating divorce or in the throes of the divorce proceeding, with troublesome cases and legal bills.

I take an advocacy approach and am openly critical of the system. This is not a dispassionate look. I believe that one can be accurate and feeling at the same time. To the best of my knowledge, I have not written anything that invades anyone's privacy, or that is libelous, and it is not my intent to harm any individual mentioned in these pages. If the reader is as alarmed by the content as I was when I learned the facts, that's good, because the facts are indeed alarming and the system is in dire need of reform. The bulk of my research was done in 1993–1994, and I've updated the information to the best of my ability. This book is not meant to be an exhaustive survey into the ethics and laws of every state, but rather as an investigative probe into the hidden practices and customs of local divorce courts. I hope that by exposing the illegitimate, inhumane legal practices in divorce court, I will help people understand that this is not just a "women's issue." This book is also for men who just want divorces and don't want their wives and children to be deliberately harmed by the proceedings.

From a broader perspective, the mounting danger is to our democratic processes, in which large segments of our population are routinely discriminated against and deprived of their liberties and rights in high-stakes cases involving their children, home, and property. The following pages are meant to activate Americans into understanding what is at stake.

PART ONE

THE PROBLEM

A GUIDED
TOUR OF DIVORCE

SOMETHING HAS gone wrong in your marriage. You drifted apart, or maybe you both didn't really know how to be in a relationship. Maybe it's just a plain clash of personalities. The breakup could be as simple as your husband wanting a new life with someone younger. Perhaps you got cancer or some other serious illness and your husband couldn't cope with it anymore and jumped ship. These are the "involuntary accidents of life," in the words of the distinguished legal ethics expert Geoffrey Hazard. Anything can happen. Suddenly you need a lawyer. The X marked *"You are here"* starts at the lawyer's office.

Most middle-class women in divorce experience conflicts with their husbands over children or money, and need lawyers. But how do you find a good lawyer? Most women have had little experience with the legal system or lawyers. The search is haphazard at best. You thumb through the yellow pages, or perhaps you obtain a recommendation from a friend. Maybe your husband has already filed for divorce and you are forced to make an emergency selection, so you call the local bar association for a referral.[1] All of these methods are fraught with risk, but you probably don't know that because you don't know how to ask the right questions and there's no one to tell you. You walk through the door of the lawyer's office like Little Red Riding Hood on the way to Grandma's house, only thinking of what you're bringing, not at all questioning what you'll find. What you don't know about divorce lawyers can hurt you.

You check out the attorney; he or she appears to be a professional. You feel good about your first impressions. You believe you are in good hands. The woman seeking a "good" lawyer places her trust in her lawyer precisely because of the appearance of prestige and professionalism. By dint of their professional personas, many unscrupulous attorneys are among the most prominent, the most powerful, and the most esteemed members of the matrimonial bar. In fact, the findings of an American Bar Association malpractice study analyzing claims against lawyers showed surprising results in the area of family law. The claims (over a four-year period from 1981 to 1985) revealed that the most experienced divorce lawyers had proportionally far more malpractice claims filed against them than the least experienced.[2]

The attorney wants to help you, but first he or she needs a substantial deposit to get started on the case. This deposit is called a retainer agreement and it can range anywhere from $500 to $25,000—or higher. If you're like most women, even if you work outside the home, you may be cash poor because your husband probably controls the family's money supply. You may have found that your husband cut off economic aid at the end of the marriage. What was once "ours" suddenly became "mine." You borrow the money and the attorney starts the legal procedures rolling. You're assigned a court index number. Welcome to the system.

Several months pass. Maybe years. The process has been long and arduous. You don't understand why things are taking so long. There are so many court hearings to attend. In fact, Pennsylvania divorce lawyer Elizabeth Bennett has counted up fourteen hearings that a couple has to go through in a fully contested divorce before the final divorce decree is granted. The nature of these hearings can be highly combative. Your husband and his lawyer seem to know how to play the game. To your shock, your husband and his lawyer are treating the proceeding like a guerrilla war. You may have to defend your fitness as a mother, even though you were never questioned about your fitness before the divorce began. You could be challenged to prove you were loyal to your husband, when he was actually the one who deserted the family. Lawyers call this the "the adversarial legal system." It pits two spouses against each other in a battle conducted by their lawyers. In the meantime, you are still without your divorce and your lawyer's bill has doubled, then tripled, and quadrupled, exponentially increasing with every turn of the divorce proceeding. You don't know what services you are actually paying for, and your lawyer has never fully explained. You are dissatisfied and you are not alone. In places like Chicago and Wisconsin, officials have at times received more complaints against lawyers practicing family law than any other category of law. Noted malpractice attorney Hilton Stein says his New Jersey office receives "by far" more requests from people wanting to sue family law lawyers than from any other area of practice.

THE COURTHOUSE
You are here: X at the courthouse. In these hallowed marble halls, you wait politely for justice to be dispensed. The commanding presence in the black robes doesn't talk directly to you, but speaks at length to your lawyer and your husband's lawyer. With the payment of a healthy deposit you have passed through the looking glass. You no longer have a voice. You are only allowed to communicate through the new middle man—the attorney. You are not sure what has happened, because so much of the proceedings seem shrouded in secrecy. You will learn that your lawyer and judge might not keep you very well informed, and you are kept out of crucial discussions concerning you, which seems incredible but is actually routine.

By the time you leave, you don't realize it yet, but like many other divorcing women you are on the verge of losing your middle-class status. Later, you will come to see how the lawyer and judge on your case had a lot to do with it. The judge, for example, has failed to award you your share of the marital property or alimony. All of a sudden you have no more medical insurance either, even though you were entitled to it. You may have been deprived of your share of your husband's pension benefits too. Maybe your lawyer didn't bother to figure it into the settlement agreement, or didn't know the law in your home state. Or the judge may have neglected to order it.[3] Again, you feel alone, but you aren't. At present, in thirty states, the highest courts have commissioned task forces which have documented judicial discrimination against women in divorce court.

By the time you exit the courthouse, sometime far in the future, you may be in deep debt to your attorney. The assets you thought were to be divided between you and your husband got split four ways instead, with the attorneys taking a large share of your life earnings.

LIFE AFTER DIVORCE

We are now passing the suburb where you used to live. There's the two-story brick family home where you raised your family. Wave good-bye to your neighbors, because you no longer live there. *You are now here.* X marks your new neighborhood, the one with the run-down buildings and broken glass on the street. You are not middle class anymore. According to researchers from Brandeis University, divorced women past age sixty-two have the highest poverty rates of any unmarried group including widows and never-married women.[4]

Post-divorce life for many older women becomes a continual struggle to keep from free-falling into poverty. You learn how to lie adeptly to debt collectors so your gas and electricity don't get shut off. You drive an old car, maybe twelve, fifteen years old, and cannot afford repairs every time the car breaks down. At times you are left stranded without transportation. Your new apartment is cramped; air-conditioning is now a luxury out of financial reach. In "The Divorce Over 40" national study, the authors found that half of all divorced women reported having trouble "keeping up payments on their home, making repairs, paying utility bills; and nearly two out of three lose the family home. Having further to fall, the affluent are often among the hardest hit."[5]

You can't get sick now, because your husband ended up with the insurance. Your former married life of comfort and security seems like a dream. You and your husband started from scratch. Now at the age of forty, sixty, or seventy, you are starting from scratch all over again. As a result of your new financial hardship, you can't spend with your friends the way you once did when you could afford to go to the movies or go out to eat. Despair and alienation are your new companions.[6]

Your husband, however, is even more financially comfortable than when he was married to you. According to the most conservative figures, while you and your child's household income plummeted by 37 percent following the divorce, your husband's income rose 10 to 15 percent.[7]

For mothers with children, the route from the lawyer's office to the courthouse now leads you to the dim halls of a poorly kept government building. *You are here.* X is where you stand in the welfare lines. In Oklahoma, Vermont, Alaska, Wyoming, or North Dakota, 25 percent of mothers and children will wind up on welfare after their legal separation or divorce. In Idaho and Maine, the figure is closer to 30 percent. In California, more than 600,000 mothers will need welfare after their separations or divorces.[8] It would be highly misleading to suggest that the courts or legal system were responsible for the plight of many of these women who were already on the margins of poverty before their divorces. Splitting up one household into two causes the poor to become poorer. But it would be just as misleading to ignore the welfare mothers who were once working or middle class and then were processed through the divorce court system only to end up on public support. Your numbers are also buried in the figures cited above. Your mate financially deserted you and the children; the courts, for a variety of reasons, did not protect your rights. Many of you tried desperately to obtain a lawyer, but no lawyer would take your case. There wasn't enough potential profit in it. You could not afford justice.

You think this is alarming? This is more common than you think.

Rita Hilsen from New York had spent years in court trying to get a judge to enforce a court order to compel her husband, a well-known Manhattan psychiatrist, to pay child support. She and her two children ended up needing food stamps, living in a mouse-infested apartment, while her husband lived less than a mile away in a fancy townhouse on over $1 million in earnings and assets. The judge presiding over the case refused to hold the husband in contempt for failure to pay the amount owed, telling a reporter that she has never jailed a delinquent spouse. Hilsen's phone was disconnected sometime in 1994, and since then her friends and acquaintances have lost touch with her and no longer know her whereabouts.

Perhaps Hilsen is in the welfare line where you too will learn to stand for hours on end so you and your children don't starve after the divorce or separation. You have suddenly joined the ranks of the traditional poor. From the safety of your husband's car you'd whiz past the impoverished people fanning themselves in the heat in front of their broken stoops. Now you are just like them. Escape back in your memory to the comfort of your carpeted, air-conditioned living room and sip a big, cool Coca-Cola. Remember how it was when you felt safe, away from the misery and poverty, and your thoughts would drift to putting that new deck on the house, or planning for the vacation on that pretty lake where you and husband conceived your first child. You had achieved your dream—a husband, children, a house, perhaps you even became a "Super Mom," handling a career too—before something went wrong, first in your marriage and then in the courts.

Your route now takes you to two points. *X marks* the homeless shelters and relatives' and friends' homes, which you shuffle between. You are an itinerant, looking for shelter. You may have been evicted through the legal wrangling of lawyers and judges in your divorce, or you may have succumbed through the war of attrition—your husband had more money. No one knows how many like you are out there, but researchers claim that half of women who became homeless did so after they sought escape from their batterers.[9] The legal system didn't protect you.

Now you go in another direction, toward the graveyard. *You are here.* X marks the spot for the murdered women, killed by their husbands and boyfriends. This is the sight of 10,000 graves dug over the past five or six years, representing the nationwide number of women killed by their boyfriends or husbands.[10] Under the flowers and gravestones are smashed faces, mangled torsos, women pummeled from head to foot. The dead don't talk, but researchers do. They have documented evidence across the country that the legal system has miserably failed battered women who pleaded for help before their deaths. More than half the state supreme courts in our country have documented the hell that battered women go through trying to get judges and lawyers to take domestic battery seriously.

Your route goes into the shadows now. There are no signs to follow. Only shadows and terror and lives lived in exile. X marks the spot for the fugitives—a small minority of women who are on the run from the system. Researchers have named them "protective mothers," those women whom the system has deemed vindictive or crazy for accusing a spouse of child abuse and who have gone underground to keep their children safe. According to one major study, only 2 percent of custody visitation disputes involve sexual abuse allegations, so most women will bypass these shadows.[11] But for those 2 percent, the system can turn into a terrible trap. Lawyers and judges who are not trained to handle these complex cases nonetheless have control over them, and if you are caught running, chances are the spouse accused of the abuse will be awarded custody of the child, according to legal experts.[12]

BACK TO COURT

Now your guided tour will head back. *X marks* the courthouse. You are being forced back to court after your divorce. Your route forms a zig-zag pattern that goes back and forth, back and forth, back and forth. You have to prove all over again why you should be awarded child support or alimony. You have to return every month to force collection of child support. Of the 5 million women owed child support payments in 1989, only half received what they were owed, according to government figures. One quarter got less than they were owed and the other quarter received nothing.[13] Resistance, delay, and obstruction by your husband and his lawyer, plus a judge who looks the other way, mark off years and years of your life. According to the federal government's figures, in 1989 alone 140,000 women would have been lifted out of abject poverty if they had been paid what was due them in child support.[14]

Jan Shaeffer, nineteen years old, spoke for thousands of children when she testified to the Pennsylvania state legislature in 1993: "Since the time of my parents' separation my mom has had custody of all six children. Even from the beginning my mom has always had to resort to legal means in order to get support from my dad. There have been many periods of time when my dad has not paid any support and at this point in time he owes my mom well over $10,000 in back support."

You are pleading for a lawyer to help you collect child support. Maybe you had a negotiated agreement, worked out over months with an expensive attorney. Everything looked great on paper. But your husband didn't honor the agreement. You are practically breaking down the courthouse door to get back in. Your access is blocked by an invisible barricade. You are not rich enough for the lawyer to profit on your case. You have no legal standing, even though you have a legal contract that is supposed to be legally binding. Thousands fall into this category. Others, including career-oriented and working mothers, are back at the court, having been forced into custody battles for their children.

"Judges are likely to award custody to the father when the mother works even though the father also works," according to law professor Mary Becker of the University of Chicago. A growing number of court decisions nationwide confirm this trend.[15]

If you haven't noticed by now, for many women the route from the courthouse is a steep downhill path into trauma, unnecessary loss, and financial decline. Not every woman ends up on this road. We all know someone who has fared well in her divorce. Some women are lucky enough to obtain caring lawyers and/or judges who show genuine concern for the welfare of their clients and constituents, through diligence, patience, and respect for the laws. But the phenomenon of women abused by the system is very real, and the statistics cited above give a good indication of the extent of the problem. Women who interact with the legal system for their divorces can face any number of minefields. This is not just the result of the system's passive failure. In the following chapters, it will become clear that the system itself becomes an actual trap, subjecting women to all sorts of legal, financial, and emotional abuse. Once the legal machinery is set in motion, you literally cannot exit of your own free will. You can't yell, "Stop!"

The grim scenarios described above come about because of problems that start with women's own attitudes about money, emotions, and divorce, which along with a host of differences between men and women produce an uneven playing field in the legal system. These differences and inequalities set the scene for the legal and economic bashing that takes place.

PSYCHOLOGICAL DIFFERENCES BETWEEN MEN AND WOMEN THAT GIVE MEN THE EDGE IN THE ADVERSARIAL LEGAL SYSTEM

Women and men experience conflict in psychologically different ways that are more advantageous to men in the current adversarial legal system. Men tend to react to marital conflict by wanting to fight, while women are more likely to react by

becoming depressed and insecure, turning inward instead of outward. As the authors of the national study *Our Turn: Women Who
Triumph in the Face of Divorce* point out, the woman has to fight
not only her husband but the entire adversarial legal system,
which is male-dominated and geared toward the way men think
and act—like the warriors of the species.[16] A Manhattan lawyer
argues that men seem to be more comfortable with being adversaries to their wives and are more likely to view the divorce as a
battle in which they will hire the best guns—the most aggressive
lawyers—to wage an all-out attack. In this legal battle, ironically,
some husbands are willing to spend more in legal fees than the
actual amount they are fighting over. Women, on the other hand,
initially are more likely to regard the system idealistically,
believing perhaps too literally in the image of the blindfolded
lady holding up the scales of justice. It is little wonder that so
many women made poorer by their divorces use the same words
to describe this misplaced trust in the system, saying, "I was so
naive—I was a babe in the woods."

Men tend to treat the divorce as a business and leave their
emotions behind, while women, on the other hand, dwell more
on their emotions—leaving concerns of their own financial welfare behind. "Being nice" to her husband during the divorce was
the main concern of Rae Logan, Director of the State Bond Commission in Louisiana. Logan concedes: "I was so concerned about
being nice. He got the Fiat, the savings account, and the girlfriend. I got the bills, the furniture, and the children. It was my
fault. I was so concerned with maintaining his image. I was concerned with not being seen as the stereotypical 'hysterical'
divorcée."[17] Many women, to their own disadvantage, are simply
not culturally geared to think about money at the time of divorce.

ECONOMIC DIFFERENCES BETWEEN MEN
AND WOMEN CREATE INEQUALITIES

Apart from the psychological differences, women are also usually
in weaker economic positions than their husbands at the time of

divorce, and not just accidentally. Men, thinking to protect their own financial interests, very often take control of the family's money supply for a very deliberate purpose. (In Chapter 4, I show how lawyers teach men to gain control of the marital estate furtively through skillful maneuvering when they are contemplating divorce.) The man who controls the family's money—and his wife's share—is in position financially and legally to overpower his spouse in the divorce proceeding. In 1991 Barbara L. Paltrow, President of the Nassau County Women's Bar Association, described the prototypical case in a letter to her peers: "He had access to high priced legal talent from the start, access to lawyers who knew how to use the system to great and often unfair advantage. The wife, on the other hand, quickly discovered that most lawyers would not represent her on the promise of getting paid, eventually, from family resources controlled by the husband. In order to have any representation these women had to exhaust their life savings, if they had any, and borrow to the hilt from family or friends. Even this was rarely enough to pay for the protracted litigation forced upon them."[18]

But there's an added wrinkle. Women often don't just need extra money to retain a lawyer, they need access to large amounts of cash because lawyer fees are customarily so high. Without hefty funding women cannot afford to hire the best lawyers, nor can they afford to defend themselves in a protracted legal battle in court. Despite these inequalities, the legal system treats women and men as if they were equal opponents on the divorce court playing field.

The inequality women face in the legal system is heightened because they still do not get equal treatment from society either. Women don't have the same earning power, job training, or career opportunities that men do, nor do they have access to affordable day care for their children. Women coming from the tradition of the 1950s homemaker, for example, cannot compete effectively in the workplace after being out of the job market for ten or twenty years. Mothers with young children are at a distinct disadvantage because they often cannot afford day care. With their duties divided between home and work, many sacrifice jobs with the potential for full-time career advancement.

As a result of these psychological and economic vulnerabilities, women face a Catch-22 when they are trying to protect their rights in the legal/judicial system. The divorce industry feeds off their vulnerabilities, and women become susceptible to many different forms of exploitation and mistreatment from within the legal/judicial system itself. Long after a woman and her husband stop talking, a whole cast of characters enters the scene. Lawyers, judges, sundry experts, and various professional people will become extremely involved in the woman's life. Of course lawyers and judges play the starring roles. Their actions, decisions, and dictates will affect how the woman and her children are treated during the divorce proceeding. These strangers make decisions throughout the woman's divorce proceeding that will to a large extent directly determine the quality of her future life. We will look at the dynamics of the system's *active failure* to protect women and children; the reasons involved; and what society can do now to stop the abuse of divorcing women by their divorce lawyers and judges. But first we will look at the stories of four women whose ordeals typify what can happen in divorce court.

A BATTLE CRY

IN MOURNING the loss of your relationship to your husband, you are emotionally caught up in your feelings and preoccupied by pain. You don't know yet that you can get even more badly hurt. If you don't understand how lawyers and the courts really work, things can go terribly wrong for you. By not being prepared for the battle in divorce court and by not staying on top of your case, you are making a big mistake that can have lasting repercussions. The legal system doesn't operate like normal people. In the realm of lawyers and laws, a tiny oversight can snowball into a huge catastrophe and trap you in ways you never thought possible. For example, if your attorney forgets to tell your husband's lawyer where you are going on vacation with your child, that may be all it takes to cause a major legal emergency and jeopardize your right to custody of your child. You could wind up living under a bridge like one formerly affluent wife from New York who couldn't meet her lawyer's exorbitant fee demands.

Women don't realize how ugly the battle can get. The stories of four divorcing women show what can happen when you are caught off guard. They trusted the lawyers and judges in their cases and believed that the justice system works fairly, never realizing that their trust was horribly misplaced.

COURT SHOCK

Ginger Martin was not celebrating Thanksgiving weekend in 1993. The judge in her divorce proceeding had just forced the forty-six-year-old ex-wife from her home. The soft-spoken working mom from Chesapeake, Virginia, looked dazed and seemed to be in shock. She didn't say much. Her brother and two sisters were scurrying around, transporting Ginger's belongings from her residence into another, temporary house. "It's terrible, it's just terrible," her sister Sylvia Deerfield told me during the aftermath.

Just a few years previously, Ginger had been living a comfortable life as Henry Martin's wife; they had been married for twenty-five years when he deserted her, according to Ginger's divorce complaint.

At the time the divorce was filed, Ginger, a mother of two, was earning $17,000 as a switchboard operator. Her husband, Henry, a real estate broker, had a net worth valued at more than $3 million.

Although Henry Martin and his wife, Ginger, had struggled for a quarter of a century to build their $3 million fortune, only a few months after the divorce proceeding began, Henry claimed that his real estate business was broke, and he filed for commercial bankruptcy. The commissioner took him at his word. He was never forced to make full disclosure of his financial assets. Nor would the commissioner allow Mrs. Martin to find out more about her husband's business holdings, which she believed had been co-mingled with his mother's.

Now Ginger's brother, Craig, was equally distressed. Craig Barkley had taken a very active role in trying to help his sister get a fair deal in court. Barkley, an ex-army colonel, was a Vietnam vet who had fought in the TET offensive. Duty and honor meant a lot to him. But Barkley's training as an army officer could not prepare him for what he saw happen to his sister in court. "I have not ever seen an institution of this nation so abuse a person as the court system, law enforcement system, and legal system attorneys have abused my sister. I have never seen that," he said, restraining his rage. "When the court can't protect you, you are past your last hope."

Barkley related how his sister's first attorney had walked off the case. Her siblings had sunk more than $30,000 into legal fees for the lawyer to defend their sister's rights in court, only to see him withdraw from the proceeding after his bill climbed to $70,000. He had already threatened to quit unless he got more money, so one of Ginger's sisters, a retired school teacher, had borrowed $23,000 on her credit cards to pay him to continue representing Ginger. They had also signed a promissory note. Despite these payments, the attorney dropped Ginger's case four months later. He had the judge's permission to do so.

Ginger Martin's second attorney, Stephen Comfort, took the case only to face a one-sided, bizarre response from the judge, who refused to allow him to look any further into Henry's assets. "It is this Court's opinion that to open up that can of worms and to hang that albatross around Mrs. Martin's neck, as you urge me to do, Mr. Comfort, is simply going to prolong the agony and the emotional upset that these parties have gone through for months and even years. And it is absolutely ridiculous to even consider doing that," the judge said.

Throughout the proceeding, the judges and commissioner who dealt with Mr. and Mrs. Martin seemed to ignore the merits of the case. According to legal briefs supplied to the court, Mrs. Martin's attorneys had to bring several court actions against Mr. Martin to get him to comply with the court orders to keep temporarily supporting Ginger. He was even jailed briefly for contempt. Ginger Martin remembers: "Every time we came in with legitimate motions he [my husband] would crowd it with frivolous motions. Where I was trying to get child support he'd come in with two motions to crowd mine. Every month I'd have to go to court to collect $600 a month. Each letter to the court was $25 dollars. It would cost $200 to go to court each time to collect."

In the end the court, in effect, rewarded Mr. Martin for his alleged financial evasions. In the final divorce decree, the judge awarded him all of the business holdings. The judge, who went along with the commissioner's report, also awarded the family home to Mr. Martin, despite the fact that Virginia is an equitable distribution state. All that Ginger received was a 1985 pickup truck, $1,000 a month in alimony, and securities already in her possession. She was also ordered from the family home, with the property awarded to Mr. Martin. By his one-sided ruling, the judge instantly pushed Mrs. Martin to the edge of poverty. Moreover, his decision left her completely uprooted, without any home to call her own. He had refused to make a ruling on the Martin's jointly owned vacation home in North Carolina because, he said, it was an out-of-state property, so the property was up for grabs. If Mrs. Martin tried to claim it, Mr. Martin could challenge her.

Considering the outcome of her case, Ginger Martin probably could have done as well with no lawyer at all. In 1994, she and her siblings had shelled out more than $50,000 to her lawyers, and Ginger was looking ahead to a very uncertain financial future. Of course, in the beginning, she couldn't have imagined what would happen to her in court.

No amount of money for legal fees had helped. Nor did the good faith negotiations by Ginger's brother, Craig. He had made three separate attempts to negotiate an agreement with Ginger's husband, through her first lawyer, but he always came up against a brick wall. "Every time we got to an agreement the other party reneged," he explained. "They'd come back with another offer, always less. Her own lawyer would say, 'It looks all right to me. Take it.' These were [offers like] $125,000 cash without the house and get out of my life. He [Ginger's first attorney] recognized that he was no match for the defendant's attorney and the defendant.

"An officer's word is his bond," Barkley continued, not understanding the amorality of divorce court. "Any officer who lies should be decommissioned. If his word cannot be taken he should not be entrusted to defend his country. He should not be entrusted to safeguard the welfare of 10,000 troops. . . . I have no confidence any longer in officers of the court. I have no confidence in this particular judge and another one who sat on this case at one time. . . ." Craig Barkley had an explanation for what he believed had happened to his sister: "The judge's response in this case has been a response to the well-established good old boy syndrome. I know good old boy syndrome. I know that you scratch my back, I scratch yours, but I also know it means compromising from time to time—integrity. I have seen it time and time again. More than I wish to admit, I see it here."

Ginger's brother and two sisters had witnessed much of the legal manipulations in the court that led to their sister's downfall. While people abused in court often seem "out of it," family members who try to help are often traumatized by the experience too. This is known as *court shock*, a term coined by child rights activist Michelle Etlin to describe the characteristic emotional response of victims who have been manipulated in court and then arbitrarily stripped of their property or legal rights by those people in charge of protecting their rights. The numbing, out-of-touch feeling is brought on not just by the violation of one's rights but by the Kafkaesque reality that officials entrusted to represent the legal/judicial system can act arbitrarily with no regard for human life.

Ginger's sister Sylvia Deerfield recalled that her sister's financially powerful husband had issued a warning one day early in the proceedings: "Henry just said to me, 'If Ginger tries to fight me she'll be sorry,' and then he referred to a business associate of his who had 'eaten alive' *his* wife in court."

Sylvia Deerfield was so upset by her brother-in-law's prediction that she literally tracked down the woman he was referring to. She found Jane H. (name has been changed) living in a garage apartment in a neighboring Virginia town. Jane H., in her mid-sixties, had also been wealthy and married to a real estate broker. She said she had paid for the couple's home with her own separate funds. Now that and all her other investments were gone. She was suffering from a nervous condition brought on by her divorce. Her voice shook as she talked, describing her ordeal: the way her husband had used her separate money to fund their real estate business and then deserted her, cutting off her access to their marital estate. Her own lawyer had refused to look into her husband's property holdings, she said. Moreover, the commissioner's report on Jane's divorce proceeding had been held up for more than a year because her husband refused to pay the commissioner's fees.

Sylvia Deerfield and Jane H. became friends through their mutual nightmares in the divorce court system, and had the same camaraderie one sees in war buddies. "I'm just going to have to go out and shoot the son-of-a-bitch," Jane H. would say in her wobbly voice, laughing.

But there was no time at the moment for black humor. The siblings had too much to do, getting their sister moved into her new temporary home. In the next two years there would be more legal entanglements over the remaining asset, the vacation house, and more court shock to follow. In 1995, however, events turned around for Ginger after an appellate court overturned her divorce judgment, saying her judge had erred, and ordered new court proceedings to find out the real worth of Henry Martin's marital estate. As of December 1995, she owed $40,000 to the new attorneys who were litigating the case.[2]

THE ANATOMY OF A FRAME-UP

Ginger Martin didn't know that some judges don't require husbands to make full disclosure of the marital assets, even though women are legally entitled to obtain this information, since a marital estate legally belongs to both husband and wife. As a result, Ginger was totally unprepared for what was to happen. However, with strong emotional and financial support from her family, she eventually prevailed in an appellate court, although the litigation back in the lower court is ongoing and the end result is still unknown.

While Ginger and her siblings were trying to get justice in Virginia, hundreds of miles north, in another state, another divorcing woman was learning how the court really works. She did not realize that in the current legal system, a woman cannot remain passive to attack.

Laura Preston (name has been changed) couldn't sleep. It was 3 a.m. and her husband was blasting the stereo at full volume in another room in the house. The loud pounding of the rock music would rob her of her sleep yet another night. This was part of his nightly campaign of harassment to drive her out of the house, Laura believed. She and her husband were in the process of divorcing.

She claimed he kept the heat turned down to 65 degrees in the dead of winter, freezing her and her child. Jim denied it to the judge. She complained of the nightly stereo blasting. Jim countered that if the music was so disruptive, it was not bad enough to make her miss work from lack of sleep. Then there was his alleged womanizing. Credit card statements showed lingerie and floral bills for presents he had purchased but she had never received. Female strangers brazenly called the house, openly asking for Jim. Laura claimed that on one occasion she even overheard her husband discussing with one of his girlfriends how he could get Laura out of the house so that the girlfriend could move in. At least two paramours had been identified in the divorce proceeding, which probably explains some of Jim's hostility toward his wife. She exposed his affairs. Jim was a lawyer—a public defender for the state courts—and this exposure embarrassed him publicly.

Laura's complaint charged her husband with extreme cruelty. After nearly six years of marriage, she wondered how she could have put up with her husband at all.

Most disturbing was Jim's inappropriate habit of leaving his robe open in front of the baby and female visitors. The babysitter was so unnerved by the sight of his exposed penis that she refused to go upstairs to the baby's bedroom in the mornings until after Jim left for work. In one incident, in the presence of the baby's godmother, Jim allegedly held Trina directly on his genitals rather than on his knee. The woman gave him a sharp look and he quickly fastened his robe. In Laura's mind, her husband was definitely a sick individual, despite his ability to function as a public defender earning $60,000 a year.

Laura felt she was being rejected by her husband, and that he didn't care about their baby either. She said in court papers that Jim never seemed to take a real interest in his child. For example, depositions show that Jim did not contribute financially to the bulk of the child's needs, even though he and his wife earned roughly the same amount. At the time, Laura worked as a manager at an insurance company, with $63,000 annual earnings, and she had to pay for most of the child's necessities with her own paycheck.

For two years Laura had been forced to live under the same roof with her husband as the divorce proceeding inched its way through divorce court. How could she have been forced into such a cruel situation?

Jim knew that if Laura didn't occupy the home, he could make the legal argument that she had willingly given up her rights to claim the home in the divorce. Laura knew it too. "It has been torture residing with defendant," Laura said in court papers. "He wants the house and for the past one-and-a-half years has been harassing to get me out. From the beginning he has stated that he wanted my baby and me to move out, then he would have the house appraised and then someday he would pay me something for my interest in the house deducting from my interest all of his earnings during the course of our marriage. I resisted him, remaining in the house so that no one would think I was giving up any rights to my home." If she moved out, her husband could claim that she abandoned her family, and she could lose possession of the house. Forcing a hostile couple to live under the same roof only increases animosity, but realistically, the legal system gave Laura no other choice.

Despite the fear that she could lose possession of the house, after two years Laura couldn't take the harassment anymore. She took their baby daughter and quietly moved out of the marital home to an apartment in another town about fifteen minutes away.

A year later, what Laura had feared came true. In a divorce settlement that she later claimed was coerced, she lost the house. On top of that, she did not receive alimony, even though she had lost her job after she went on maternity leave and even though her husband was now making $64,000 a year. He was required to pay child support of only $600 per month for three months and $550 per month after that, which amounted to 8.59 percent of his income. This departed from federal guidelines, which say a parent should pay about 20 percent of his or her income toward child support. During settlement negotiations, the judge justified this low amount because, he said, Laura "spends too much on her child."

Many women in divorce find themselves in Laura Preston's shoes. They get hurt by ugly war tactics, not realizing that they need to become warriors themselves to survive the divorce court system. It's not enough that the facts and the law are on their side. There are hidden land mines all around, and they must remain hypervigilant. Merrily Miller, a New York mother, learned that the hard way. She hadn't a clue that she needed to watch over her own lawyer to protect herself from him.

Merrily Miller, age forty-three, had to find a lawyer. For twenty-one years, the suburban housewife and mother of three had lived a comfortable upper-middle-class life with Ed Miller, a lawyer, until he deserted the family in 1985—leaving them virtually destitute, according to appellate briefs filed by Merrily's attorneys.

After divorce proceedings began, a judge ordered Mr. Miller to continue supporting his wife and their three young sons. But

Miller stopped sending checks after a few months. At the time, Merrily was working for a weekly wage of $75 as a part-time teaching assistant—clearly not enough to support herself or their young children. Merrily Miller had to find a law firm that would help her collect child support.

As the wife of a lawyer and also the daughter of one, Merrily was a savvy legal consumer. She was also highly educated, with a doctoral degree in education from Columbia University. After doing some checking around, she felt confident that her selection of the firm of Fink Weinberger et al in White Plains, New York, was the right decision. At the time, they were considered one of the finest matrimonial law firms on the East Coast. She instructed her lawyer at Fink Weinberger to get a child support award enforced, but after three years the law firm had not collected a single penny for her,[3] and she and her three young sons fell into desperate poverty. It was just weeks before the trial, when she was at her most vulnerable, that her lawyers told her to come to their office to sign a note, claiming that she owed $71,000 in legal fees. Merrily's common sense told her not to agree to the amount they claimed she owed. But when she refused they dropped her, abandoning her case. To make matters worse, they later sued her in court. A judge decided that their legal fees were too high and cut them in half—to $45,000. But Merrily's knowledge of her rights didn't prevent her lawyers from abandoning her case, or from financially jeopardizing her welfare. After they won against her in court, they froze her bank accounts. One of those accounts included her paycheck— another held her retirement funds. Then the law firm threatened to foreclose on Merrily's house. They charged her interest, plunging her into deep debt. Yet she never received any value in return for the 509 hours they said they had spent on the case. She had to hire a new lawyer to get her divorce. But the ruling by New York State Supreme Court Justice Vincent Gurahian only made matters worse. The judge forgave Merrily's husband the $88,000 he owed to Merrily in child support and maintenance and failed to award any alimony at all to Merrily, despite a twenty-six-year marriage. Additionally, the judge refused to order Merrily's husband to pay for any of Merrily's legal fees. Legally, the judge didn't have to explain his rulings; divorce judges seldom do.

Ginger Martin, Jane H., Laura Preston, and Merrily Miller thought they were just getting divorced, but instead they turned into victims of the legal/judicial system. All around the country, there are similar cases of women just like them. How did women get into this crisis?

None of these women's circumstances would have been possible if not for the radical overhaul in the divorce laws over the past thirty years, which ushered in the era of divorce court abuse. These laws—the no-fault, equitable distribution, and "best interest of the child" doctrines—were supposedly formulated to promote gender equality and make the laws more equitable between the sexes. But as exhaustive research has since borne out, these supposedly gender-neutral laws are being used as tools of discrimination and abuse against women, with a ferocity that seems unparalleled in modern American history. Women are now legally being ordered to give up their children, their homes, their economic security. The fact that the undermining of the laws' intent has taken place under the noses of the state judicial branches nationwide—and been openly acknowledged—makes this phenomenon all the more shocking.

We will look at these laws and their impact at length, but first we need to understand how our society's cultural attitudes concerning women and property and mothers with children came about, because our historical tradition is still influencing the way women are mistreated in the courts today.

HOW DID DIVORCING WOMEN GET INTO THIS CRISIS?

THE TROUBLE women have with securing their rights in divorce is not surprising given the history of marriage and divorce in the United States. Throughout the 1700s and long into the 1800s in our country, a woman had no legal rights apart from her spouse in marriage. An American woman literally had no right to control or own her own property during marriage—including what she acquired herself. Anything she inherited, was given, or bought herself was legally controlled by her husband. Historian Marylynn Salmon explains: "After marriage, all of the personal property owned by a wife came under the exclusive control of her husband. He could spend her money, including wages, sell her slaves or stocks, and appropriate her clothing and jewelry. With regard to real property his rights were almost as extensive. He made all managerial decisions concerning her lands and tenements and controlled the rents and profits."[1] In some colonies and states, a woman could own separate property—if and only if her husband consented, however.[2] Author Norma Basch writes: "This doctrine of marital unity not only mandated the wife's subservience to her husband, but it also held the distinction of obliterating her legal identity."[3]

This state of legal deprivation was called coverture. This doctrine was based on the notion that men were entitled to control women's property in return for men's protection and financial support of their wives. At root was our society's attitude that women are inferior—incapable of taking care of themselves, and that therefore they should not be entitled to the same privileges as males.[4] This law thus ensured that the male ruling class would maintain its political and economic power over women, and it forced women to be financially dependent on men.

This patronizing attitude can be traced back to English common law, which set precedents for the treatment of women. Under common law precedent in the early nineteenth and twentieth centuries, women were prevented from obtaining the right to vote, participating in certain professions, or serving on a jury.[5]

As a result of common law, men also had the absolute right to custody of their children, who like their mothers were without legal status. If the father chose to, he could deprive the child of contact with the mother, even during the marriage, according to Law Professor Mary Becker of the University of Chicago.[6]

But not all American women were subject to English common law. In some Native American tribes, women were the family's property owners. In the Pueblo culture of New Mexico, for example, the Zuni tribe was matrilineal, and Zuni women had far greater security than their European counterparts. According to Zuni rules, the house and corn stored within it belonged to "the women of the household—the grandmother and her sisters, her daughters and their daughters," famed anthropologist Ruth Benedict wrote in the 1930s. "No matter what may happen to marriages, the women of the household remain with the house for life. They present a solid front. . . . A man goes always, for all important occasions, to his mother's house, which, when she dies, becomes his sister's house, and if his marriage breaks up, he returns to the same stronghold."[7]

White American women who sought a divorce were worse off. They were without separate legal rights in marriage; at the

same time, they were expected to stay married. It was very difficult to obtain a divorce. They were faced with extremely limited
legal possibilities. In colonial times, only Connecticut and Massachusetts had laws allowing absolute divorce, as opposed to separation,[8] and some colonies refused to grant any divorces at all. In
the middle and southern colonies, the courts weren't set up to
handle divorces, according to a 1968 texbook on domestic relations law. As a result, divorce required a special legislative act.[9]
Sometimes a couple could make a private contract between
themselves, but most judges refused to enforce direct contracts
between husbands and wives unless they were made through
trustees, and some courts refused to honor the validity of these
contracts. If worse came to worst, the couple could go outside
the law and opt for a wife sale—a folk custom of early modern
England that made its way to the colonies, according to historian Salmon. After the couple agreed to separate, there would be
what Salmon describes as a "symbolic sale" of the wife, "usually
to a pre-arranged buyer who might be the woman's paramour or
a relative. . . . The procedure followed in a wife sale demonstrates with graphic precision the inferior status of women. . . for
in the most primitive instances the woman was led to market in
a halter and auctioned off to the highest bidder."[10]

Legal separations rather than absolute divorces were more
easily available, especially when the requests came from abused
or abandoned wives, according to Salmon. New York, Maryland,
and Virginia adopted formal policies for these type of separations. "Jurists reasoned that because the law gave men so much
power over women, it had an obligation to protect women when
husbands abused that power," wrote Salmon.[11]

REFORMATION OF DIVORCE LAWS

After the Revolutionary War, many states reformed their divorce
laws and formalized grounds for divorce. Separations could be
obtained for desertion of wives and for nonsupport. Divorces
could be obtained on certain grounds but these grounds varied

greatly from state to state. In Massachusetts, the grounds were adultery, impotence, and criminal conviction. In New York, divorce was extremely difficult to obtain. It was granted on one ground only—adultery—and the law remained that way all the way up until 1967.[12] But in other states, "cruelty was the ground most widely relied on . . . and was used in order to protect the spouse, usually the wife, from bodily injury."[13]

Very gradually, through the 1800s, women were granted the right to own separate property during marriage, but this was not achieved without a serious struggle. The Married Women's Property Act, fueled by the suffragette movement, was enacted in various forms throughout the states, giving women independent legal status and the right to own their own property for the first time. But some researchers point out that the laws did not benefit women nearly as much as they could have, because judges were interpreting these laws to favor men.

Even in their ideal form, the reforms wrought by the Married Women's Property Act could not change society's attitudes, which still confined women to the traditional social roles of mother, housewife, and homemaker, with the primary responsibility of ministering to their families' needs. Women, who were entering the labor force in droves as factory workers at the turn of the century, were told their place was in the home. Society expected them to be subservient, secondary to their husbands in status—and to like it.

A 1914 textbook, *Eugenics*,[14] printed for the benefit of newly marrieds, offers a good example of the culture's idealized vision of women's subservience. The book provided men with a list of characteristics to look for in their mate:

> A Cook—Again, the wife a man chooses should be a good housekeeper. . . . There are women who live in sentimental dreams, neglecting meanwhile the duties that lie close to their hands. Good breakfasts, dinners and suppers, good bread, good coffee—in a word, good house-keeping.

A Worker—One of St. Paul's special counsels for young women is that they be "keepers at home," as our common version renders it and that is good too; but in the Revised Version it reads "workers at home;" that is, the place of a young wife's most sacred duty is in her own home. No doubt women have a wide field for Christ-like usefulness in ministering to human need and sorrow outside; but in performing such ministry, however beautiful and noble, a wife should never neglect her divinest duties, which lie within her own doors.

Disposition—Another suggestion is that in choosing a wife a young man should look for a woman of sweet temper. Nothing else can take the place of love in a home, nothing else can supply its lack. There are many women who have so much of the spirit of love and gentleness that they fill their homes as with the fragrance of heaven and the calm and peace of God.

Companionable—In choosing a wife a wise young man will seek for one who will enter with zest into all his life, who will stand close beside him in the day of struggle and adversity and who will ever inspire him to noble and brave things.

Godly—Religion adorns and beautifies a woman's character, clothing it with tender grace. Even a prayerless man feels safer in his home if his wife kneels morning and night before God.

A woman's life was narrowly defined, her role prescribed according to these traditional patriarchal values, even down to the personal traits she should cultivate in order to make her husband happy. Today all these dictated functions would cost a fortune in the commercial marketplace. The woman was the cleaning service, child caretaker, cook, bookkeeper, hostess, party planner, dishwasher, waitress, advisor, guidance counselor, psychologist, sexual servant, all rolled into one, on call twenty-four hours a day, for ten, twenty, thirty years. She didn't get paid for any of these jobs: they were her duties. In response to her loyalty and fulfillment of her marital obligations, her husband was supposed to shoulder the burden of financial responsibilities and support them both.

These rigid sex roles defined the institution of marriage up through the 1950s, and the social and religious taboos against divorce remained strong. Divorce was viewed as a failure, and the laws reinforced this view by assigning guilt to the spouse who had broken the marriage vows. If the couple wanted a divorce, one of them had to prove that the other was cruel or adulterous or unfit for marriage. Divorce was always based on fault, so it was very difficult to obtain if the couple were simply unhappy together.

The advantage of the old law, however, was that it forced men to be accountable for their families' continued welfare. If a husband abused or deserted his wife, she was entitled to alimony, which could be awarded for a lifetime. Lenore Weitzman points out that although alimony awards were less common than people generally assume, there was a separate, but important, benefit generally overlooked: "But whether or not alimony was awarded, the innocent wife typically received a larger share of the property, especially if her husband's adultery or cruelty was flagrant or if the only family asset was the home."[15]

Linking property awards to fault, such as cruelty, had some important consequences, giving "the 'innocent party' a decided economic advantage. . . . [T]he innocent party had a powerful lever to use in property and alimony negotiations. Indeed in California the law required that the innocent party get more than half of the property."[16] With bargaining power, women could leverage good settlements in return for agreeing to divorce, thereby protecting themselves and their children from the effects of desertion. Although divorcing women were plagued by the still common stereotype of the vindictive wife—"I'll take him for all he's worth"—in reality, putting a price on the husband's desertion or infidelity served a useful purpose in the family's interest, according to Weitzman, who wrote that it, *discouraged divorce by making it costly* for men. Since it was most commonly the man who wanted the divorce, in practice men, especially middle- and upper-class men, often 'bought' their divorces by agreeing to give their wives more property (such as the family home) or alimony, or child support, or all of these."[17] Under the old laws mother and children also averted physical dislocation and disruption after divorce by being allowed to remain in the marital home.

The laws also reinforced the long-standing societal view that older women, divorcing after long-term marriages, should receive permanent alimony in return for their contribution to the marriage. Lastly, these laws promoted the cultural belief that young children belonged with their mothers because of the nourishing effect of the mother/child bond. By the end of the nineteenth century, most jurisdictions had replaced the father's absolute custody rights at divorce with a the view that young children needed nurturing and were best off in the custody of their mothers. "The best interest of the child, particularly for very young or female children, became increasingly associated with the mother," according to Mary Ann Mason, author of *From Father's Property to Children's Rights.*[18]

When traditional divorce laws were overturned virtually overnight in the 1970s, they ushered in a legal landscape rife with pitfalls and minefields that unsuspecting women could not avoid. And although some of the old stereotypes still linger, such as the vindictive "I'll take him for all he's worth" wife, the new reality for women is in stark contrast to the days before no-fault divorce. Women after divorce are fast becoming a new class of the impoverished. Besides sudden economic deprivation, women now face unexpected loss of custody of their children after the marriage is over.

RADICAL REFORMS OF THE LAST THIRTY YEARS
The Introduction of No-Fault Divorce
Traditional divorce law and the basic protections for women that were built into the old laws came to an abrupt end in 1970,

when California led the way by abolishing any requirement of fault as the basis for divorce.[19] By 1985, all but one state—South Dakota—had adopted some form of no-fault.[20] In some of the states, such as California, a no-fault divorce allowed a spouse to walk away from the marriage without consent of the other spouse. In other states, no-fault was optional, if, for example, both parties agreed to the divorce. Marital misconduct was no longer legally relevant as an issue in the divorce.

No-fault law dovetailed with the arrival of the birth control pill and the loosening sexual mores of the sixties; with the easing of restrictions against divorce, marital breakups dramatically increased in the 1970s and 1980s. Divorce rates climbed from 400,000 annually in the early 1960s to 845,000 in 1972, then 1,213,000 in 1981.[21] Nowadays, more divorces take place in the United States than in any other country worldwide, according to the latest figures provided by the United Nations. A comparison of worldwide figures for 1988 (the latest year available) shows that the United States issued 1,183,000 divorce decrees. The only country to come close to this figure was Russia and its respective territories at the time, which issued 972,010 divorce decrees.[22]

Contrast this to the divorce rates in the nineteenth century and early twentieth century, when Russia, Japan, and Egypt exhibited higher divorce rates than the United States.[23]

Nonconsensual divorce had another immediate impact besides increasing America's divorce rates. With the economic disincentives against divorce no longer in place, women lost their former bargaining power. Lenore Weitzman writes: ". . . Since 'guilt' and 'innocence' are no longer the issue, the erstwhile 'innocent' or unwilling party no longer has the power to prevent or delay a divorce, or to bargain for financial concessions in return for consent."[24] As Harry Krause, author of *Family Law in a Nutshell*, put it: "Today, with no-fault, 'unilateral' divorce the rule, no bargaining tool remains in the hands of the economically weak wife."[25] In 1992, Nobel laureate economist Gary Becker, who concluded that no-fault was "an experiment that failed," observed: "A woman with young children can't stop her husband from divorcing her, no matter how much hardship it might cause. If her consent were needed, she would have the leverage to strike a better bargain. . . . Since child-support payments are often meager, she faces a bleak financial future where she must work long hours or go on welfare just to make ends meet."[26]

When a man no longer had to seek his wife's consent for divorce, women lost their leverage in divorce settlements. In the opinion of Lillian Kozak, a well-known women's rights activist in New York, the resulting power imbalance in these negotiations can amount to blackmail: "No-fault has allowed a blackmail on the part of the powerful party to refuse to negotiate. He blackmails by withholding the money."[27]

Not everyone who has studied the no-fault laws holds the theory that the change was to blame for lowering the standard of living for women following divorce. U.S. Congressman Jerrold Nadler said he came to the conclusion that the evidence against no-fault does not hold up. "It's a false hypothesis," Nadler asserted, citing much evidence including a New Haven, Connecticut, study that looked at the lowered standard for women following divorce, before and after no-fault was enacted there. Nadler said the results of the study found that 85 percent of the women were the plaintiffs in the cases, and therefore the leverage or bargaining power that no-fault eliminated had no effect.

In Nadler's view the real blame lies with judges who obtained the discretion to eliminate permanent alimony. In 1990, when Nadler was serving as an Assemblyman in New York, he introduced a no-fault bill that would have eliminated judicial discretion. "Judges' discretion is terrible. It [my bill] would have said the judge would have to award attorney's fees in equal amounts and secondly . . . where her [the woman's] standard of living is less, then the judge must order permanent maintenence." Nadler said the bill was defeated by women's groups opposed to no-fault who were driven by the belief that bargaining power would be lost. "It's led the women's movement to make a terrible mistake," he added.

From Alimony to "Rehabilitation"

When the courts removed fault as a grounds for divorce, the blame so often assigned to men for breaking the marriage vows was no longer used as a standard for dividing property and awarding alimony. The new law no longer assumed that ex-husbands should be responsible for the financial support of their former wives, and its goal was to make the wife self-sufficient after divorce. Permanent alimony awards were replaced with time-limited transitional awards, known oddly as "rehabilitative" alimony. Homemakers with children were now supposed to immediately restore themselves as wage earners in the labor market. In 1985 when Weitzman studied California's system she found the average alimony award was for a period of about two years.[28] Weitzman's study revealed that middle-class women were expected to become employed right away and that the new legal norm was applying to the three groups that were supposed to be exempted from the new standards of self-sufficiency: mothers with young children, older homemakers incapable of self-sufficiency, and women in need of longer-term transitional financial support.[29] Weitzman also found that a judge's goal of making the wife self-sufficient even took precedence over the goal of supporting the parent who had custody of the children. According to her study, two thirds of the Superior Court judges who presided over family law cases in Los Angeles encouraged the ideology that "it was 'good' for a divorced woman to earn money instead of being dependent on her former husband. . . . Although the sex-neutral standards of the new law give priority to the needs of custodial parents caring for minor children, the judges' responses suggest that they are always balancing the interests of children against the father's interest in keeping his income for himself."[30]

In the past decade, other researchers have confirmed

Weitzman's findings. In 1988 Sally Goldfarb, a lawyer with the Legal Defense and Education Fund at the National Organization for Women (NOW), found that "the trend toward rehabilitative [temporary] alimony is affecting a huge number of women. Many of these women experience severe economic deprivation because of the absence of long-term spousal support."[31]

In 1990 Harry D. Krause, author of *Family Law in a Nutshell*, observed: "Invoking 'women's liberation' as a fait accompli, some courts have denied alimony altogether, except in cases of actual need and for a limited time. . . . A basic change in attitudes toward alimony is in the making, and the traditional judicial chivalry vis-a-vis the ('innocent') divorcing wife is being replaced with attitudes that, at least in some cases, are not free of vindictiveness."[32]

Who were the people behind these new no-fault rules? They were the National Conference of Commissioners on Uniform State Laws, a group that had been creating uniform policy issues in family law since the early 1900s. The Commissioners formulated recommendations for no-fault, calling it the Uniform Marriage and Divorce Act (UMDA). After they made their recommendations to the American Bar Association in 1972, the states began adopting them—but not without controversy over some of the potential implications.

Lillian Kozak recalled the feeling in New York: "All of the liberals, and women—everybody—felt no-fault was a big advance over the old fault laws. Why should you have to get a detective to take a picture at a hotel over a transom? It was all so ugly."[33] But Kozak, who was chair of New York NOW's Domestic Relations Law Task Force, was deeply concerned about the financial effects of no-fault divorce on women, and succesfully opposed a unilateral no-fault bill in New York. Many lawyers were also opposing no-fault for an entirely different reason. They feared losing money, believing that a less adversarial system would result in a reduced need for lawyers, according to Michael Wheeler, an early no-fault proponent who wrote the 1974 book *No-Fault Divorce*.[34]

The lawyers and legislators who conceived the laws that would cut off alimony were out of touch with the very real social and economic problems women face: women do not have an equal chance to succeed economically in the labor market, and quality day care is still expensive and hard to find. Sylvia Ann Hewlett, an economist and author of *When the Bough Breaks*, explains: "Not only is the typical divorcée faced with the lower wage rates typical of women's jobs (and year-round, full-time women workers still earn only 71 percent of the male wage) but often she is returning to the labor force after years of being a full-time homemaker. It is extremely hard to get a well-paid job if you are older or inexperienced. Add to this the fact that 52 percent of divorced women have custody of minor children. Inadequate and expensive child care provides a further constraint on the kind of employment a divorcée can get or accept."[35]

Oddly enough, while the notion of alimony was being eliminated for women, for the first time in modern history men became eligible for alimony, providing that they were in financial need, after the 1979 U.S. Supreme Court decision in *Orr* v. *Orr*.[36]

A Specious Change in Property Rights?

Property rights for women also changed under the new reforms. Both spouses were now entitled to property acquired during the marriage. The idea behind the new property law was that marriage is a financial partnership between a husband and a wife as much as it is a physical and emotional one. Previously under the law, the courts had awarded property and assets to whoever held title. The wife was not compensated for her unpaid work in the household. "Because wives rarely had assets in their own names and because few assets other than the marital home were jointly held, property accumulated during the marriage usually went solely to the husband after divorce," explained the 1986 report of the New York Task Force on Women in the Courts,[37] which assessed the changes wrought by the so-called equitable distribution laws. The new laws were supposed to take the homemaker's contributions into account as well as the length of the marriage and the future financial circumstances of the wife after divorce, among several other factors.

The equitable distribution laws, which called for a proportional split, and community property laws, which presumed a fifty-fifty split, *seemed* fairer to women. The acquisitions of marriage were to be divided like a business that is being liquidated, with both partners sharing the assets. But this arrangement has backfired for women and children. One problem that Weitzman found in California was that family homes were being sold upon divorce. While historically the tradition was to award occupancy of the family home to the wife, especially if she had custody of the children, by 1977, after the advent of no-fault in California, one in three homes were being sold upon divorce.[38]

The new property laws also carried a hidden penalty for women. In order for women to obtain their rightful share, first they had to prove that it was their share. Divorce proceedings became infinitely more expensive for women, who were forced to rely on exorbitantly expensive legal procedures to substantiate their claims to property and money that already theoretically belonged to them. The knowledge and evidence of the value of these assets were mainly with their husbands, and a major problem for women in divorce is the refusal of the courts to force disclosure from the party with the facts.

NEW DIVORCE LAWS CREATE BONANZAS FOR LAWYERS

As a result of the new laws, litigation became far more expensive than under the old procedures, too expensive for most middle-class women to afford. Lawyer fees became a major barrier blocking many middle-class women from access to court. Under the new equitable distribution and no-fault laws, divorce has become so expensive that only the most well-off women can afford lawyers. The key to lawyer riches is a password—EDL, the equitable distribution laws enacted over the past two decades in forty states. These equitable distribution laws were created to benefit women by requiring that all the assets acquired during the marriage be considered the property of both partners. Instead, the new laws turned out to be a financial bonanza for lawyers, with little practical advantage for most women. Because the new laws permitted the distrbution of marital assets to wives, the doors were opened for lawyer invasion of marital assets, which the courts have failed to control. Thus was created the opportunity for lawyer chicanery and financial exploitation.

What the EDL intended as a two-way split of the assets between spouses has in fact turned into a four-way split—with lawyers claiming a big share of the pie. For example, it is not uncommon for lawyers to win the woman's marital home—often the only marital asset—for her in the settlement and then feel entitled to force her to sell the home they saved so they can reap a big chunk of the proceeds as their legal fees. In Illinois, a woman named Susan Clabault had to pack up her personal belongings in November of 1995, after Judge Kenneth Abraham ordered Clabault's home sold to pay for $30,000 in divorce lawyer fees.[39]

The laws' lucrative benefits to lawyers actually became an inside joke among lawyers. "We called it ERA—the Economic Recovery Act for Lawyers, Accountants, and Appraisers," revealed Steve Liebman, a Court Referee at the New York State Supreme Court in Manhattan.[40]

The passage of EDLs drove up lawyer fees practically overnight. The *New York Times* reported: "Six months after major changes in New York's divorce law went into effect, many of the state's matrimonial lawyers say they are raising their fees because their work is now more complex and time-consuming."[41]

Lawyers follow the road to riches by accumulating hours—the key to lawyer profits. Divorce lawyers typically use an hourly billing system, and the new laws, with all their complications, drove up the potential for billable hours. Hourly rates usually start at $125 an hour but vary, depending mostly on what the market will bear. On both coasts, for example, top lawyers charge from $300 to $450 an hour. In small towns rates are lower, but for many women and men, even these hourly rates are unaffordable because in the context of the new EDLs, hours and fees can add up quickly in a divorce where money or children are involved. The client must also come up with a sizable down payment before the lawyer will even begin to work on the case. These down payments, called retainers, can range anywhere from $1,000 to $25,000 or higher. One wealthy professional in New York reportedly had to pay $75,000 up front to her lawyer.

NEW LAWS PUT THE BURDEN ON THE WOMAN TO PROVE HER CLAIMS

Billable hours increased as the division of marital property became more complicated under the new laws. Indeed, the procedures a woman now had to go through to obtain her property rights became hopelessly complex, notoriously ineffective, and laden with hidden costs. For one thing, the woman's lawyer has to track down her share of the estate and then she has to hire outside experts to prove the property's value. (Under EDL, all assets acquired during marriage are subject to distribution.) This process, called discovery, includes the valuation of stocks and bonds, real estate, pension funds, and the husband's business. All the outside experts have to be paid by the client. Every call or letter from a lawyer to an expert automatically boosts the lawyer's fees. But the cost of outside experts isn't the biggest problem.

Husbands usually control the money supply at the end of the marriage. If a woman's husband chooses to conceal assets, the discovery process can be dragged out for years, her lawyer charging fees every step of the way, in the effort to collect and assess financial information from her husband and his lawyers. The legal burden is on the woman to prove the assets she already theoretically owns as a partner in the marriage. She must pursue discovery or forfeit her rights.

The abuses in discovery are a well-documented problem

throughout the civil court system. In 1990, the results of a Louis Harris poll of more than 1,000 lawyers and federal judges were reported at a U.S. Senate hearing. The findings were astonishing: "Lawyers who abuse the discovery process" was the number one cause for unnecessary expenses and delays in civil court, according to the lawyers and judges polled.[42] Senator Joseph Biden Jr., then-Judiciary Committee chairman, declared: "When cases cost so much and take so long that some people can't use the courts at all, and those who can use them find their pocketbooks depleted at a record pace, we have a crisis of major dimensions."[43]

For many women, the process of discovery is much like cutting off an arm to save a finger. Commissioning experts to track down assets is a major expense. And the financial information the lawyer obtains from the husband and his attorneys doesn't necessarily help women in the courtroom, because the information often isn't reliable. Perjury is a major problem in divorce court (see Chapter 4). And even if the information that is presented in court is true, there's no telling how the judge will rule. Judges systematically lowball property awards to women. Alimony is based on judges' subjective opinions and personal value judgments concerning what women should get, rather than on what women deserve or need. In 1994, many of our state courts had documented this problem.

SOME OF US ARE MORE EQUAL THAN OTHERS

As early as 1978 a grassroots women's organization wrote to then New Jersey Governor Brendan T. Byrne of the financial devastation women started experiencing soon after the passage of EDLs. "Equitable distribution was established in the state of New Jersey without any specific guidelines as to division percentages," the letter stated. "This has caused extended and dragged-out litigation with unfair, low awards to women regardless of length of the marriage. Women receive, according to our statistics, at the most, one third of the assets excluding personal property. The Organization of Women for Legal Awareness has observed that women married as long as twenty, thirty, and forty years receive no more and usually less than one third of the marital assets."

The judge has the discretion to interpret EDL any way he or she wants. The laws were written in language that leaves broad discretion to the court. In New York, the legislature made sure the law would be intentionally open to judicial interpretation. Two weeks after EDL passed in 1980, the legislators changed a memorandum accompanying the EDL law that was given to judges. Judges often refer to legislative memoranda to find the intent of the legislature, according to Lillian Kozak, the former head of NOW's Domestic Relations Law Task Force. Where the first memo states that "modern marriage should be viewed as a partnership of co-equals," the second memorandum eliminated this language of equality, stating only: "Marriage in current times, is, in fact, a partnership which is not fully recognized under the existing domestic relations law." Kozak explained why the change in wording was of concern: "The first memorandum was circulated among the legislators to get them to vote for the bill. The second memorandum, which removed the language of equality, was issued after the bill was passed. By changing the memorandum, the courts in effect read an intent that was not there when the legislature passed the bill."[44] In substituting the word *equitable* for "a partnership of co-equals," the amended wording provided the court with unlimited discretion, which decisions show to be inequitable to women. Kozak added: "If judges were instructed to divide the property equally, the attorneys would have less room to complicate a case and drive up the fees. If the litigants knew the division was fifty-fifty, the woman would go in saying, 'I'm entitled to half.'"

EDL did something else besides force women to drain their resources to protect their rights—it gave lawyers direct responsibility for allocating women's property rights. Lawyers now have hands-on involvement with the family estates of divorcing women. The situation has created a wide opportunity for economic fraud and ruthless profiteering. It has opened the door to deceptive fee practices, such as fee padding and charging lawyer time for nonlawyer services; and coercive tactics, such as bullying women into signing liens on their homes. "Our hotlines ring continuously from 7 a.m. to 1 a.m.," stated the letter written by representatives of Women for Legal Awareness in New Jersey. "Something must be done [about] the mechanisms employed by lawyers to drag cases out in order to perpetuate exorbitant fees in matrimonial matters. . . ."

COMMUNITY PROPERTY

Those states without equitable distribution laws—Arizona, California, Idaho, Louisiana, Nevada, New Mexico, Texas, Washington, and Wisconsin—had community property laws. These laws are different from EDL in that they assume joint ownership of all marital property. Regardless of this theoretical equality, the woman has to prove her share of the assets, so she is subject to the same abuses in discovery and the effort to lay claim to her entitled share of the marital estate.

Still, the longer hours and bigger workloads of divorce lawyers caused by the new discovery rules could not alone account for the exponentially huge jump in fees. Fees have also been raised in uncomplicated cases. As I pointed out in the *Women in Divorce* report, in New York a divorce that used to cost $6,000 before the equitable distribution law now suddenly costs $50,000. In middle America in the mid-1990s, divorce can easily run to $30,000. Interestingly enough, lawyers had anticipated increased profits from EDL. Raoul Felder made this prediction to the *New York Daily News* in January 1980, before the law took effect: "Instead of just handling a divorce, the lawyer will be asked to help split up large amounts of money and property. When this happens, a lawyer becomes a kind of partner in the litigation and makes considerably more money."[45]

The new reforms extended the need for litigation in court

because they multiplied the number of routine court matters necessary to resolve various crucial issues. Each matter, of course, requires lawyer fees.

There are any number of routine services women regularly need during the preparation–trial–post-divorce phases of the divorce proceeding. The need to pay for all these services, such as court transcripts, depositions, and myriad appearance fees, stems from having to battle against custody and money issues that can arise at any time. While the vast majority of contested cases lead to settlement as opposed to trial, there are typically numerous court hearings leading up to the settlement. Because the rules have changed, the need for a lawyer can continue years or decades after the actual legal completion of the divorce because litigation can be triggered by practically any claim, false or real. Issues like property division can be dragged out or left in limbo if the judge does not see to it that there is compliance with his or her decisions.

Even if the litigation has no merit, the woman must respond. This point was made in *The Litigation Explosion*: "new rules, most formulated since 1970, make it possible to sue on almost any pretext, start the search for evidence only after a case has begun, and drag it out so long that opponents are well advised to settle no matter how strong the defense."[46] A woman who just wants her fair share and the divorce decree so she can get on with her life can be hit with not just one meritless charge but a veritable blizzard of litigation that she must be prepared to defend against.

SUDDEN CHANGES IN CUSTODY LAWS

With the emergence of the divorce reforms, new rules also suddenly sprang up throughout the country regarding custody. For the past century, custody of young children generally has been awarded to the mother, unless she was unfit. Our society took the view that young children belonged with their mothers. The best interest of the child was associated with the child's mother.

This later became known as the "Tender Years Doctrine." But with the new push toward gender neutrality, states began to abandon the old rule that young children up to the age of six automatically belonged with their mothers. Around 1970, states made a radical shift in their attitudes toward custody. The "maternal preference" rule was seen as discriminatory to men on the basis of their sex, so it was discarded. According to the new, gender-neutral legal standard, judges were supposed to evaluate each custody case individually and decide which parent seemed the most competent to receive custody. According to *Family Law in a Nutshell*: "Many states have amended their statutes to provide that 'no party shall be presumed to be able to serve the best interest of the child better than any other party because of sex' (Colorado), others have accomplished the same by judicial action. . . ."[47] As a result of this new neutrality standard, many states passed laws for joint custody, in which the child is shuttled between both parents' homes. Judges were now also routinely asking older children if they preferred to live with mom or dad.

The new gender neutrality rules have taken mothers nationwide by surprise. Even if the divorce is involuntary on the woman's part, or the man deserted the family, the children are suddenly up for grabs. A March 1995 *McCall's* article warned: "No mother should walk into a courtroom counting on the advantage a woman once had simply by virtue of being the mother. If a father wants custody, his chances of getting it are better than they've ever been—and a woman may have to be ready to defend her parenting skills. . . ."[48]

While it is true that most women retain custody of children, that is only because most men do not challenge their wives for custody. In cases where men challenge the women for custody, the best evidence shows that they obtain it 70 percent of the time, according to studies that have appeared in investigations into gender bias in the courts. In Massachusetts, the authors of that state's gender bias study, issued by the Supreme Judicial Court, found that "Refuting complaints that the bias in favor of mothers was pervasive, we found that fathers who actively seek custody obtain either primary or joint *physical* custody over 70 percent of the time."[49]

THE NEW LAWS CREATE A NEW DOUBLE STANDARD

The legal standard that judges are supposed to use to decide custody of the children is the "best interest of the child" doctrine, which is supposed to put the child's interests at the forefront of the judge's mind.[50] To some this doctrine seems fair on the surface, because some fathers are fine parents while some mothers are lousy parents. But to other observers, this doctrine defies reality and is more representative of a double standard than an attempt at gender neutrality. For example, one area in which the new standard discriminates is against working women. Custody issues have been seemingly complicated by the fact that so many mothers have been entering the labor force. Most women aren't stay-at-home mothers anymore. Often mothers have to work, due to sheer financial need wrought by changes in the national economy. The women's rights movement too has had a revolutionary effect, propelling other women into careers by choice. As a result of these changes, mothers are now losing custody because they work outside the home. Women are fearful, especially after two high-profile custody cases in 1994 that involved moms who work. During the O.J. Simpson case, Los Angeles District Attorney's prosecutor Marcia Clark found herself in a custody battle after her estranged husband complained that the long hours she was working on the Simpson trial were detrimental to their children. The claim, of course, did not take into account the relationship between Clark and her children in all the preceding years during which she was a prosecutor up until she started working overtime on this particular trial. In a second case, Jennifer Ireland, a twenty-year-old living in Michigan, lost her child because she planned to put her child in day care while she attended college. The judge awarded the child to the father, not because the father was willing and able to stay home with his child but because the father's mother could take care of the child in her home. This ruling was later overturned by a higher court in 1995.

While mothers are losing custody because they work outside the home, there is no evidence on the other side to suggest that men are losing custody of children because they work outside the home. In fact, the opposite is true. In many places, the man gains an advantage in court if he works long hours and makes more money than his wife because the economic superiority of the parent is one criterion some judges now use to decide custody cases. If the woman is not earning as much money as her ex-husband, the judge might classify her as not serving the best interest of the child.

Nor is there any indication that men have abandoned their careers to become homemakers or the primary nurturers of young children. Worldwide, men still assign to women the task of raising the children. Studies have shown that fathers do not spend significantly more time taking care of the children when mothers work outside the home.[51]

Professor Mary Becker's and others' research has found that mothers who had been the primary caretakers of their children before the divorce proceeding and who have to work outside the home afterward, are particularly likely to lose their children to their ex-husbands' new wives when the husbands remarry and their new wives don't work outside the home.[52] Working mothers who lose custody after the father remarries are common, according to the Nevada Supreme Court Gender Bias Task Force. As one lawyer testified: "God help her if Dad remarries a wife who doesn't work. . . . Modification of custody is filed. We get into a best interest of the home [situation]. There is a tendency in my opinion to award custody, change custody on the basis that you've got better care; the kids aren't in day care, they're not latchkey kids."[53]

For this reason Nevada's Gender Bias Task Force recommended that "a mother's economic circumstances (including the need or desire for full-time employment) should not be used as indication of 'unfitness,' or be the basis for an award of custody to the parent in better economic circumstances, when such discrepancy could be alleviated by more equitable child support, spousal support or property division awards."[54]

Using the gender neutrality legal standard, a judge who morally disapproves of a mother's lifestyle might also take away her children. If she has a boyfriend, or even worse, a girlfriend, a prudish judge might transfer custody, even if the woman is a responsible and devoted mother. But the custody rules are vaguely written, open to wide interpretation that allows judges to impose their own personal value judgments on the situation. In fact, thirty-one states and Washington, D.C., have developed statutes for custody guidelines, "[b]ecause of the great judicial discretion allowed, the vagueness of the best interests standards and the reluctance of the appellate courts to overturn a trial judge's decision. . . ," according to *Child Custody: Practice and Procedure*.[55] While these guidelines are welcome to help judges with these crucial decisions, most states *do not* require judges to give reasons for their custody decisions, because appellate courts "are most reluctant to upset trial court decisions that are based on facts and impressions that cannot easily be captured in written records," according to University of Illinois law professor Harry Krause.[56]

A devoted mother who took care of her kids for the length of the marriage could all of a sudden lose them at the point of divorce as a result of the new, vague legal standards. Judges and mental health experts who evaluate custody typically ignore the past relationship between a mother and child and often do not take into consideration the parent's time, such as who does the bulk of the caretaking and nurturing during the length of the entire marriage, or which parent the child is most emotionally connected to (called the "psychological parent" in legal parlance). In this way, the new laws are putting loving mothers at risk of arbitrarily losing their children. Custody has now been made an issue, for the sake of gender neutrality, where it never was in the past. In the words of the late Judge Lois Forer, the gender-neutral rules create "an artificial symmetry of neutrality"[57] because they ignore the very real differences between mothers and fathers at the time of divorce.

The new standard that calls for gender neutrality in custody decisions also ignores another fundamental difference between parents: the importance of the infant's nourishment through the mother/child bond. This new view presumes that mothers are no better than fathers in nurturing their young children, denying, according to Professor Mary Becker, the reality of caretaking—the "deep emotional ties that are formed during pregnancy, infancy and when the child is very young. It is during these periods that the relationship between the child and the caretaking mother is most emotionally intense. And it is precisely during these periods that fathers are least likely to caretake equally on even a physical level."[58] Thus, in ever-increasing numbers children are being deprived of the special quality of nurturing that mothers provide to infants, toddlers, and young children.

Curiously there is very little acknowledgment by the mainstream legal and medical establishment of the possible ramifications of depriving a child of its main parental attachment. In Professor Becker's experience, her peers remain silent about maternal feelings. She writes: "[A] conspiracy of silence forbids discussion of what is common knowledge: mothers are usually emotionally closer to their children than fathers."[59] Becker says female lawyers do not discuss the mother/child bond because they are trying to distance themselves from the possible career-limiting notion that women's biological destiny is motherhood. While career women have remained silent, men's rights groups make the argument that men can nurture as well as women can. Perhaps, but historically and in the present, according to all the available statistics, men rarely nurture small children. Men who win custody do not settle into new roles as primary caretakers of their children. They remain fathers and assign to the new females in their lives—their mothers or their new girlfriends—the primary duties of raising the children.[60] The view that fathers have less of a bond with their children is supported by evidence of thousands of fathers yearly who do not care enough about their children to support them economically after divorce.[61]

CUSTODY BECOMES A BARGAINING TOOL FOR FATHERS

The "best interests of the child" standard has not only been misused to create gender neutrality at the expense of mothers and children, but it has given rise to a widely acknowledged ongoing court abuse that terrorizes women. Rather than using the best interests of the child to determine custody, judges allow fathers to use custody as a financial bargaining tool. Lawyers often instruct fathers to threaten a custody battle to coerce their spouses into inequitable settlements. This tactic has been documented all over the country in gender-bias reports issued by the state courts. In California, a family law lawyer testified to the gender bias task force members. "I do suspect, though, and this may be a big part of the system, I think they're also being told by counsel, well, that's good [going for custody] because you know one of the results will be that your child support will probably go down if you're successful."[62]

The American Academy of Matrimonial Lawyers warns: "An attorney should not contest child custody or visitation for either financial leverage or vindictiveness,"[63] but as California lawyer Lawrence Moskowitz wrote, "Anyone who has practiced family law for a few years or more has come across at least one litigant who can be counted on to file repeated motions concerning custody or visitation. For such a party, the not-so-hidden agenda is to harass the other parent; usually the last thing he really wants is a resolution of the issue, even a favorable one."[64]

Retired West Virginia Chief Justice Richard Neely has written of the warped incentives this law has created for fathers in divorce settlements. Earlier in his career, when Chief Justice Neely was a divorce lawyer himself, he used this coercive tactic to help his own client win, as he candidly admitted in a journal article appearing in the *Yale Law & Policy Review*:[65]

> My client was a railroad brakeman who had fallen out of love with his wife and in love with motorcycles. Along the way, he had met a woman who was as taken with motorcycles as he. After about a year, my client's wife filed for divorce. My client had two children at home— one about nine and the other about twelve. Unfortunately for him, the judge in the county where his wife had filed her suit was notorious for giving high alimony and child support awards. The last thing that I wanted to do was go to trial. The wife had a strong case of adultery against my client, and the best my client could come up with was a lame countersuit for "cruel and inhuman treatment"—not exactly a showstopper in a rural domestic court.
>
> During the initial interview, I asked my client about his children, and he told me that he got along well with them. He also indicated, however, that two children were the last thing he wanted from his divorce. Nonetheless, it occurred to me in my role as zealous advocate that if my client developed a passionate attachment to his children and told his wife that he would fight for custody all the way to the state supreme court, we might settle the whole divorce fairly cheaply. My client was a quick study: That night he went home and began a campaign for his children. His chance of actually getting custody from the judge was virtually nonexistent, but that did not discourage our blustering threats.
>
> My client's wife was unwilling to take any chance, no matter how slight, on losing her children. Consequently, the divorce was settled exactly as we wanted. The wife got the children by agreement, along with rather modest alimony and child support. All we had needed to defeat her

legitimate claims in the settlement process was the halfway credible threat of a protracted custody battle. As Solomon showed us, the better a mother is as a parent, the less likely she is to allow a destructive fight over her children.

Neely concluded that "the everyday occurrence of children being traded for money should be sufficient in and of itself to prompt a reevaluation of a system that turns custody awards into bargaining chips. The fact that such trading also has contributed to the impoverishment of women makes the need for change still more urgent."[66] He wrote that in 1984. It is now 1996 and today this brutal legal practice is still alive and well.

Today, nowhere is baseless litigation more loathsome than in custody cases. Under the "best interests" standard, a vindictive ex-husband can bring a custody suit at any moment, and the mother's fitness will automatically be suspect, even if it has never been previously questioned. How prevalent is this despicable use of children as a bargaining tool? One divorce lawyer who testified at a public hearing on matrimonial cases in New York estimated that *only 5 to 10 percent of all custody cases are bona fide.*

FATHERS SEEK CUSTODY TO AVOID NEW CHILD SUPPORT AND PROTECTION LAWS

Under the gender-neutral law men could bring bogus custody challenges to intimidate their wives into settling for less, but now there is evidence that men are seeking and obtaining custody for a related reason. There is accumulating evidence that men are challenging their wives for custody of the children precisely because it is cheaper to keep them than to pay child support. This growing trend corresponds to new laws that require the noncustodial parent to pay for child support. Men are now being taught by their lawyers that to avoid child support they should obtain custody to force their ex-wives into paying child support instead.

In 1975 the federal government enacted the Child Support Enforcement (CSE) program. This, together with the Family

Support Act of 1988, required the noncustodial parent to pay support. These laws mostly affected fathers and required states to provide mechanisms for enforcement. While the mechanisms haven't worked too well (only 18 percent of all outstanding child support payments were collected in 1995), the laws nonetheless set a new legal threshold by which noncustodial parents are supposed to hand over about 20 percent of their earnings to ex-partners for child support. In 1995, President Clinton strengthened existing law with bold legislation that is expected to dramatically increase child support payments by taking away occupational and driver's licenses of parents who don't pay. (See Chapter 8 for a fuller description of the new law.) Fathers' rights groups have successfully argued that if fathers spend more time with their children, they should not have to pay as much support. As a result thirty-five states have gone along with that reasoning, as the *New York Times* reported in 1995. These new developments coupled with the vague "best interests" standard have given fathers both the financial incentive and the ammunition to challenge mothers for custody.

LAWYERS AND JUDGES HAVE NEW, DANGEROUS POWERS

Since the 1970s, equitable distribution, no-fault, and new child custody rules have caused a radical change beyond reinterpreting the legal rights of men and women in divorce.

The equitable distribution laws, no-fault divorce, and the "best interests of the child" standard were supposed to provide the cure for the inequities of years past. For men, the new laws eliminated the legal requirement to pay alimony. For women, the divorce reforms were supposed to guarantee they would be treated under the law as equal partners to their husbands. For children, the new laws supposedly took into account their needs for safety and nurturing. It all sounded good in theory; in practice the new system is terribly flawed. This is in large part due to the manner in which these laws are administered.

The inequities and injustices stemming from the uneven application of the laws have been addressed in two important books, *The Divorce Revolution* by Lenore Weitzman and *Mothers on Trial* by Phyllis Chesler. The findings accepted by most of our state supreme courts have also confirmed these problems. Even so, all of these changes in the laws—from EDL to custody— have two things in common that have not been sufficiently highlighted: the changes in laws have created a terrible unpredictability in the way the laws are applied, and these changes give lawyers and judges enormous, unprecedented, direct power and control over women's and children's lives. In earlier days the inequities were built into the laws themselves. Now the laws have changed, but not the attitudes of those who are supposed to apply the laws.

When a woman enters a divorce proceeding she doesn't know what the judge will decide, or how her husband's lawyer will act, and she can't predict if her own lawyer will become her advocate or adversary. She doesn't know if her divorce will be settled by virtue of an ethical rendering of the law or by dint of lawyers' and judges' prejudices and base motivations.

We urgently need to pass better laws that can definitely help limit the damaging effects of lawyers and judges, but more new laws in and of themselves won't necessarily help unless citizens first find a revolutionary new way of holding lawyers and judges accountable for their conduct and rulings.

PART TWO

THE
PROCESS

↭ 4 ↭

PROTECTING YOURSELF FROM HIS LAWYER'S DIRTY TRICKS

As we saw in Chapter 2, women often approach divorce with a naive faith that when they have their day in court, justice will prevail. They have faith in the system and do not approach divorce as a battle, pitting spouses as opponents, each with a hired gun (lawyer) to guard and advance his or her own interest. Without this battlefield mentality, women are often shocked by the number, audacity, and cruelty of the dirty tricks their husbands' lawyers play.

As the New York Committee to Examine Lawyer Conduct in Matrimonial Actions noted: "While some litigants and attorneys did complain of misconduct on the part of a judge or hearing officer, more often they reported instances of abuse committed by the other spouse or opposing counsel, which was tolerated by the court. . . ."[1]

Nearly every prominent attorney I spoke with has had experiences with lawyers who are all too willing to use unfair, deceptive legal tactics to gain strategic advantage in court. In 1991 the American Academy of Matrimonial Lawyers, a powerful divorce lawyer lobby headquartered in Chicago, issued rules advising lawyers not to use hardball tactics against spouses in divorce,[2] but this warning is for all practical purposes impotent. In fact when the rules were issued, then-president Sanford Dranoff told his colleagues at an 1991 seminar on ethics, "You can't be kicked out of the Academy if you don't follow this."[3] Needless to say, the rules go unheeded in daily practice.

Academy member Larry Litvac from Denver, Colorado, said that as an attorney he has had to deal with his share of abusive colleagues. He has dubbed them the "Rambos" and "Rambettes" of his profession. Says Litvac: "[These attorneys are] terrible to deal with. You can't trust them. You have to get everything in writing from them. They pick up [on the] animosity and anger of their clients which permeates negotiations and causes fees to become distorted."[4] For these kinds of lawyers, the end always justifies the means.

Lawyer Rambos and Rambettes are aggressive and ruthless in their approach to the opposition; their chief strategy is that of overpowering or undermining the opposition. They use "scorched earth" tactics, a term first used to describe the custom of General William Tecumsah Sherman in the Civil War of burning down everything in sight—including people and homes—to win his military objective. In divorce court, some lawyers use so-called scorched earth tactics against wives in a campaign to wear them down and starve them out. They attempt to outspend the wife by legally obstructing the proceedings and delaying an agreement until she finally runs out of money and patience and gives up. When that doesn't work, these opposing lawyers try to destroy the wife's credibility on the witness stand in front of the judge.

Besides destroying the woman's credibility in court, abusive attorneys set all kinds of dangerous legal traps for their clients' wives. Setting such a trap does not have to involve a conspiracy or collusion or a corrupt judge. The lawyer just needs to be willing to manipulate the law for his client's benefit, and if he's lucky, a prejudiced judge will blindly collaborate. The object of these legal traps? To damage the opponent—meaning the wife—without getting caught.

DISCREDITING THE WIFE

The husband's lawyer may use lies and deliberate distortions as a tactical weapon to discredit a woman's character. The goal, of course, is to convince the judge that the wife is an undeserving, bad person. The tactic is especially effective against women because it plays on the biases that many judges already harbor against them (which are covered in Chapter 7). When a man's lawyer uses character assassination as a weapon, a biased judge is all too eager to accept his claims at face value. And if this same woman who has been discredited claims that her husband is being unreasonable, the prejudiced judge will cynically assume that the woman is trying to frame her injured spouse. In divorce court, the lying that takes place in court papers and in oral testimony to discredit the woman in the judge's eyes has a very concrete purpose. Once the judge has a negative impression and believes the woman is bad or is malevolent toward her husband, the woman becomes a victim of the judge's disbelief.

There are only two people who really know what happened in any marriage: the husband and the wife. But even if drinking, infidelity, or physical abuse were involved, dramatic conditions such as these may be rendered irrelevant, minimized, or erased by the opposing side through careful twisting of the truth. Making the wife or mother look bad is the only way to win. The end justifies the means. The goal for the more economically powerful spouse—usually the husband—is to preserve what he has and give up as little as possible.

Of course, wives can set traps for husbands too, but women are more vulnerable than men to all kinds of dirty tricks. They are not on an equal playing field with their husbands in court. The more economically powerful spouse's goal is to preserve his money or his reputation. If women could be guaranteed vigorous representation by their lawyers, and if there were not so much domestic abuse against women or sexist bias against them, perhaps the discrediting of them and all the other dirty tricks that commonly take place in court wouldn't be as frequent. But dirty tricks affect women more because women are more frequently in a weaker position than their husbands.

Since all that counts is the appearance of the truth in front of the judge, the better performance the husband gives, the more likely the judge is to believe him. Sometimes the woman's own lawyer might believe the tainted picture the opposing lawyer paints. Dr. Phyllis Chesler found this to be the case in a study she conducted of women who were challenged for custody by their husbands. In her book *Mothers on Trial*, Chesler wrote: "Fathers' lawyers always routinely and falsely accused mothers of 'sexual promiscuity' or 'mental illness.' Mothers' lawyers believed or became 'worried' about such a accusations."[5]

In 1977, a Wisconsin divorce lawyer directed questions to his client on the witness stand suggesting that his client's wife, Jeanette Helmbrecht, was pregnant by another man and therefore did not deserve as much property as she was asking for in the divorce. In actuality, Mrs. Helmbrecht, who had given up a nursing career to raise five children, had undergone a total hysterectomy ten years previous to the divorce. She was also suffering from severe clinical depression at the time of the court date. When the judge called for a recess the two lawyers negotiated an agreement that Jeanette felt compelled to accept. The agreement deprived Mrs. Helmbrecht of her share of the property and reduced her child support to poverty level. The false information presented to the judge made it appear as if Jeanette had reason to give up her claims.

A wife who is put in a position of having to defend her credibility might get very angry at unfair attacks, and then her anger can be used against her by the husband's attorney and judge, as if she is being uncooperative. In Gloria Steinem's words: "For women or any other category of people for whom fair treatment would upset the social order, anger becomes the most punished and dangerous emotion."[6]

In the adversary process the truth does not matter, only the lawyer's ability to convince the judge or, in rarer cases, a jury, of what he wants them to believe. The divorce court system's very foundation of integrity is arguably shaky, because hearings and evidence so often rest on what appears to be the casual acceptance of lies and legal manipulations aimed at circumventing the laws.

PAID WITNESSES

The woman not only has to worry about the lies coming from her spouse and her adversary husband's attorney; she must deal with the husband's hired guns—accountants, mental health people, and other supposedly neutral experts—who may not be neutral at all.

The mental health of a mother is always a consideration in custody battles—even when it was never a consideration in the marriage or in any other aspect of her life. A woman faces a nightmare in the judicial system when mental health experts, who are actually hired by the father or are biased and acting as surrogates for the father, go on a mission to destroy the woman's character before the judge.

California lawyer Lawrence Moskowitz, who wrote the book *Unfair Tactics in Matrimonial Cases*, warns lawyers to beware of possible attempts to sway the court-appointed psychologist to testify in favor of one spouse. Moskowitz writes: "An overzealous opponent may attempt to influence the evaluator by repeatedly writing letters to the evaluator bringing up 'new' issues and complaining of recent behavior on the part of your client. If your client is not misbehaving . . . it will be apparent that opposing counsel is trying to prejudice the evaluator against your client and/or attempting to delay the investigation, thus lengthening the case and increasing his bill."[7]

Sometimes lawyers go even further than merely writing letters to the mental health expert in an attempt to influence him or her against the wife. In one case from New York, the mental health expert admitted under cross-examination that he had become a paid witness for the husband although he had been appointed originally by the judge as a neutral expert. According to the court documents, the mental health expert admitted that he had been asked to meet for several hours prior to the custody trial for a private session with the husband's attorneys. The private coaching session lasted four hours, for which the supposedly neutral expert was paid by the husband. At the subsequent hearing, the expert reversed his prior opinion, stated in his written report, which advocated joint custody, in favor of giving sole custody to the husband. The mental health expert said under oath: "I regret now that I didn't call the judge to say the [father's] attorney wanted to speak with me," and admitted that the private session with the father's attorneys created an appearance of impropriety. While this coaching seemed improper to the mother's attorneys, the judge on this case ignored any possible impropriety, and awarded sole custody to the father.[8]

PERJURY

When the husband swears to tell the truth and then lies under oath about his wife to damage her credibility or preserve his assets, he is actually committing perjury. Of course, there are strong laws on the books against perjury but they aren't typically enforced in civil matters. Perjury is a felony and punishable by a fine or imprisonment or both. But perjury is widely accepted as a courtroom tactic in divorce. According to many lawyers, it's an open secret—everybody knows but nobody talks about it. Julia Heit, a Manhattan criminal defense lawyer who specializes in appellate law, said she thought criminal court was "dirty" until she started doing divorce cases, when she discovered how common perjury was. "I couldn't believe it," she said, laughing at her own past naiveté. "I saw these people perjure themselves on the stand and I felt so bad, I thought, 'They're going to jail.' I didn't want them to have to go to jail. I wanted to give them a chance to purge themselves of the perjury [to admit the truth] so they wouldn't go to jail. But nothing happened to them."[9] Another New York lawyer whom I interviewed smiled sheepishly and admitted, "Everyone lies and everyone knows it. It's common practice in civil court."

Perjury is not confined to divorce proceedings; it is a widespread problem throughout the state civil and criminal court systems. The *New York Times* carried a story on May 7, 1994, about police perjury that reported: "Prosecuting people for perjury is unusual." Quoting Robert Baum, the citywide head of Legal Aid's criminal division, the newspaper went on to say, "the police regularly invent witnesses, tailor their testimony to meet constitutional objections, and alter arrest records. And prosecutors and judges wink at it."[10]

Divorcing women I have interviewed get a rude awakening when they realize that their husbands' lawyers have lied in the court papers, with the intention of presenting the women in a negative light to the judge. Cyndi, a woman from New York, put it this way: "You learn that everybody lies. I didn't understand that. The whole thing blew my mind. That their lawyers are there to represent his lies."

Cyndi, a working mother from New York, said the court papers were filled with falsehoods about her ability as a mother, which Cyndi had to defend herself against. She knew that in reality her husband did not want custody, because he had expressed little desire to care for the children. The father's real goal was to get out of paying child support. If he obtained custody, Cyndi, as the noncustodial parent, would be legally responsible for paying child support.

Cyndi's husband and his lawyer convinced the judge through false statements that she was not as good a mother as he was a father. The judge believed him and Cyndi lost custody. But not too long afterward, and unknown to the court, her ex-husband sent the kids to live with her. Cyndi is still paying her husband child support, even though she is now the de facto custodial parent. She told me she would rather keep her kids, even if it means paying child support too, because they mean more to her than anything. She fears having to go back to court to reopen the custody dispute, but adds that the current situation is also hard for her. If she does something to displease her ex-husband she knows that he can wrench the children away at any time, as their lawful custodial parent.

FALSIFYING FINANCIAL RECORDS

A typical complaint from middle- and upper-class women concerns husbands' misstatements to the court about the couple's finances. Divorcing husbands, often with the helpful advice of their lawyers, may hide assets to avoid having to divide them with their wives. Once the assets are concealed, the husbands' lawyers present the picture of a failing business or loss of income, falsifying information to the court.

First, their lawyers teach them how to take control of the assets when they are contemplating divorce, and some lawyers are all too eager to help. One slim tome published two decades ago openly advises men on how to take control of their marital estates by stealthy means. In *How to Divorce Your Wife: The Man's Side of Divorce*, author/lawyer Forden Athearn writes in the section "What to Do Before You Tell Her": "Once you have made the decision in favor of a divorce, the secret to success is *planning*." Before telling your wife, Athearn advises, you should:

1. Close joint bank accounts.
2. Take possession of the stocks, bonds, and other securities that are readily salable. "Removing these assets from a joint safe-deposit box or desk drawer removes the temptation [on the part of your wife] of running out and selling them."
3. Close charge accounts. "Notify—in writing—all of your credit companies and all stores. . . . Tell them that you will not be responsible for her charges after they receive this written notice. Again, this removes temptation."

In a seeming effort to justify this scheming, Athearn emphasizes to his readers that they are just taking "defensive action. You are not seeking to hurt your wife."[11]

Once the assets are hidden, false financial disclosures are then made to the court to protect the concealed assets. In one New York case, a woman testified to the state legislature that her husband used four different social security numbers in court documents, yet neither the woman's husband nor his lawyer were held accountable by the judge. Wealthy, self-employed men, including doctors, businessmen, lawyers, and real estate developers, who deal in cash and can keep their record books private, are especially prone to concealing assets. If they assume a corporation name, they easily co-mingle marital assets and hide them under the "front" of the corporation. For that reason, the American Academy of Matrimonial Lawyers warns: "Whether the client proposes opening up an out-of-state bank account or having a family member hold sums of cash for the purpose of concealment, the advice to the client must be the same: 'Don't do it.' "[12] Despite this advice, it is very easy to commit economic fraud in divorce. When the husband claims poverty in papers to the court and yet maintains a grand lifestyle, it is obvious that the court needs to do a reality check on the husband's stated claims. Yet the husband's lawyer may go along, pretending he or she is unaware of the husband's wealth, even if the lawyer is being paid at a rate that is out of sync with what the husband claims to earn. More states need to follow West Virginia's lead and subject lawyers and their clients to criminal penalties for the submission of false statements.[13]

FORGERY

Steve Liebman, a lawyer with the New York State Supreme Court in Manhattan, is a special referee who listens to divorce proceedings and then makes recommendations to the judge. He tells of an incident involving forgery that shows how casually this crime is committed, right under the nose of the court. A man wanted to hurry along the proceedings in an uncontested divorce from his wife, so he told Liebman his fiancée was pregnant, in her third trimester, and that they wanted to be married before the baby was born. In Manhattan's backlogged court system, any divorce usually takes between four and six months, even when there is no fight over money or custody, Liebman explained. The man then produced what was purportedly a doctor's note, indicating his fiancée's advanced stage of pregnancy. When Liebman saw it, he knew the doctor's signature was a fake. How? "First off," said Liebman, "the doctor's name was misspelled. Secondly, the doctor happens to be my father-in-law. The man and his girlfriend stole his stationery out of the office." Liebman said dryly, "I turned to the man and said, 'You just don't have any luck, sir.'" Liebman noted that the judge presiding over the case quickly granted the man the divorce anyway because his wife wanted it.[14]

Another case of forgery concerned a woman whose dentist-husband broke into the marital home and stole some bonds. The husband then signed her name to them but was so sloppy in his forgery that he actually misspelled her name. I called the District Attorney's office in Rockland County to find out why the office was not pursuing the forged bonds. One of the investigators told me that the amount the husband allegedly stole (about $2,000) was not large enough for the office to pursue. But two days later the wife called me to say that her husband had returned one of the bonds valued at about $1,000. The D.A.'s office had approached her husband following my call and told him they would have to arrest him for grand larceny unless he returned at least one of the bonds.[15]

OBSTRUCTION AND DELAY

Lawyers use many varieties of obstruction and delay tactics. For example, one lawyer tricks the other side by coming to a verbal agreement with the woman's attorney, say, to exchange financial documents, but then deliberately refuses to cooperate. Another favorite ploy is to deliberately stall.

Charlotte Bogart, age seventy-one, from Pennsylvania, had

been waiting thirteen years—since 1981—for the court to grant her portion of the financial settlement from her divorce from her husband, Donald. According to Charlotte, at the time of the couple's separation the marital estate was estimated at roughly a million dollars with considerable real estate holdings in several states—all of it controlled by her husband. There was little reason to believe that the divorce proceeding would be conciliatory. During the marriage, Charlotte had been a battered wife, with a broken leg and shoulder injury sustained in separate assaults by her husband. She was finally divorced in 1988, but she remained without her share of the estate after her husband's lawyer sought a *bifurcation*. This term refers to separating the divorce proceeding from the actual issues involved, like money, so that the divorce can be granted without the issues being resolved. Bifurcation put Charlotte's husband in a terribly advantageous position. Once he obtained the divorce, he had no incentive to settle financial issues. Why should he? He could keep the whole estate for himself by keeping it tied up indefinitely in the courts.

A letter dated January 6, 1986, from Charlotte's first attorney, who was resigning from the case, to her second attorney, who was just getting started, revealed all:

> Donald Bogart['s] threat. . . was repeated to me at least fifty times by Jack Howett [Charlotte's husband's lawyer] that, "they would appeal every single ruling as high as they could and delay the ultimate settlement for years."
>
> My greatest concern, as I expressed it to Charlotte on various occasions, was that if we couldn't reach a settlement, he would allow the properties involved to deteriorate substantially and use his funds to acquire other properties and assets. You might give this some consideration in view of the appeal because Charlotte related to me last year that he was failing to make routine maintenance [payments to her].[16]

Charlotte was without any financial support or assistance in paying her lawyer fees for fifteen years because of these legal delays and alleged obstructionism. She continued to support herself as a secretary while attempting to obtain her legal rights. Charlotte may have been at a disadvantage in court, but she knew very well how bifurcation had divorced her not only from her husband but from her rights. She complained high and low to the Pennsylvania legislature, where she became practically a permanent fixture at certain representatives' offices. In 1991, Charlotte Bogart was one of more than two dozen people who publicly testified to the state legislature that the Pennsylvania divorce court system was thoroughly corrupt. On September 12, 1991, she testified[17]:

Being a victim of the legal system and attempting to obtain support, alimony and/or an equitable distribution divorce settlement has made me very much aware that the legal/judicial system in this state is not based on justice and laws, but on an individual's pocketbook and the individual whims of some judges and attorneys. For many years I have listened to horrible stories in York, Lancaster, Main Line Philadelphia and Western PA; and many people have contacted me by phone and letter relating their own details of the cruel and at times sadistic treatment by the legal/judicial system which decent law-abiding citizens are receiving in the courts of PA. The stories sound more like the Dark Ages, not a supposedly civilized state.

The public hearings, although drawing some brief attention to the problem, have yet to improve anything for Charlotte Bogart or the others. A legislative bill was proposed in the Judicial Committee of the Pennsylvania House of Representatives that would have required a serious government investigation into charges of corruption, but in 1993 the proposal died without ever having had a chance of coming up for a vote on the floor.

In April 1994, despite having spent more than $100,000 on lawyer fees to get her case resolved, Charlotte Bogart was still fighting—and still without her rightful share of the property settlement. Then in late December of that year, she finally decided to throw in the towel. She accepted her ex-husband's settlement offer and gave up the legal fight in court. "They managed to put off the master's [surrogate judge's] hearing for eleven years and by then some of my witnesses were too old to testify," she said, explaining why she'd finally given up.

Strategic delays—each fruitless phone call, each missed appointment—cost the wife dearly. She still has to pay for her lawyer's time, even though nothing of value was accomplished, and even though the delay was not of her own making—in fact was out of her control. (One of the saddest cases on record took place in the Pennsylvania court system; the victim's 1991 testimony to the state legislature appears in Appendix III.)

There is virtually no defense against the dirty tricks described above. It is important to note, however, that dirty tricks are not limited to divorce law. Many of the manipulative tactics lawyers use in divorce cases are also used in commercial litigation. These findings were revealed in 1990 at a U.S. Senate Subcommittee hearing on the topic of delay and expense in federal civil court proceedings. A Louis Harris poll had found that of 1,000 experienced litigators and judges polled, *the majority blamed abusive attorneys for the unnecessary and exorbitant expense of litigation.*[18]

As a result of abusive litigation in divorce court, some women's lawyers advise them to give in, which is exactly the goal of the opposing attorney. Author Phyllis Chesler, who studied mothers caught in custody battles, found: "Several mothers described lawyers who tried to talk them out of alimony 'for their own good' and who urged them to consider joint custody 'for their own good.'"[19] Other women, like Charlotte Bogart, keep struggling for their rights, despite the aggressive tactics of the husband's attorney. Eventually many of these women get too worn out to continue the litigation and give up in this war of attrition.

As the previous pages show, the end justifies the means for some divorce lawyers. They represent lies, help to commit perjury, and devise means of delay and obstruction, to win for their clients. By virtue of their actions, they show no moral responsibility to the families who may be destroyed by their legal manipulations.

A woman's faith in the legal system leads to her belief that no matter what the other side does, her own attorney will at least look out for her welfare. Next we will see why this blind faith may be dangerous.

PROTECTING YOURSELF FROM YOUR LAWYER'S DIRTY TRICKS

W HILE YOU ARE busy watching out for your husband's attorney, you're not looking behind your back. You should be, because your divorce attorney may be taking advantage of you for his or her own gain. Of course, not all divorce attorneys are unscrupulous. But without adequate consumer safeguards in place for the divorce industry, you must beware and look out for these schemes. This chapter will help you determine if your divorce lawyer is your advocate or your adversary.

You can learn to protect yourself from the common types of fee abuses unscrupulous attorneys engage in by learning to identify these scams and understanding the means by which they actually occur. Fee-abusing attorneys are more dangerous than pickpockets or thieves because attorneys are in a decision-making role and control their clients' legal cases. As a result of their over-interest in fees, such attorneys' performance and judgment may suffer and hurt women's legal cases in multiple ways.

For example, a greedy lawyer may not bother to properly present the facts of the woman's case. In some instances the attorney may not even bother to learn the facts—facts that might be crucial to defending her custody rights or her property rights. Besides neglecting the case, the attorney who has gained confidence by committing fee abuse without detection is emboldened to follow with other types of deceptions or abuses against the client.[1]

The priority some unethical lawyers place on profit leads to another kind of "planned" neglect too: if the client refuses to comply with the lawyer's fee demands, the lawyer can hold the client's case hostage and refuse to provide any further legal help and protection. All the while, people won't know the woman is being victimized by her lawyer, because it appears she is receiving legitimate representation. The woman herself often remains unaware of what is actually happening.

At the first meeting, for example, the lawyer misrepresents himself or herself, or the facts, or deliberately misleads the unsuspecting client in order to attract business. During the course of the proceeding, the lawyer pretends to be on the client's side, and the woman has no reason to suspect otherwise. The lawyer's true intent, however, is to financially exploit the client. Even if her lawyer stands up for her in court, if in fact the lawyer is only serving his or her own interest, the lawyer is in truth the woman's adversary, leaving her unprotected and unrepresented in a court of law—in our country, it's illegal, a breach of the lawyer's fiduciary duty.

DELIBERATE EVASIVENESS

Many women hire lawyers in the expectation that they will work hard to obtain a good divorce settlement. But from the moment a woman walks into an attorney's office, she can be met with deliberate evasiveness meant to keep her from knowing her rights. The woman asks the lawyer a reasonable question like, "How much is this divorce going to cost me?" The divorce lawyer will probably say he or she doesn't know. Although they typically claim not to know how high their fees will run for your divorce, lawyers still can determine for themselves how much potential profit they can glean.[2] The lawyer will then ask the woman, "How much does your husband earn, and how big is your marital estate?" Lawyers ask this right away because whether they take your case or not usually depends on the financial worth of your marital estate. Some lawyers aren't above calculating how long to drag out the case, or how much to inflate the amount of time they spend on it, in order to collect maximum fees.

If the woman asks another pertinent question like, "How long will it take?" the lawyer may say, "It depends," but then doesn't explain how costs may accrue. Although these vague answers might be quite perplexing and distressing to the woman client, the divorce lawyer is not at all concerned or embarrassed, because he or she isn't legally required to tell clients anything about how high fees can climb, or how long the case may be prolonged.

At the first meeting, a lawyer may even go so far as to mislead a woman about her need to be concerned about fees. For example, the lawyer may tell the woman that her husband will pay the fees, when the lawyer has no intention of claiming the fees from the husband. A provision in the laws in all the states gives the "needy spouse"—usually the woman—the legal right to have the "moneyed spouse"—typically the husband—pay her legal fees in the divorce. So the lawyer might say, "I'll collect my fees by asking the judge to order your husband to pay my bill." But then the lawyer will deliberately fail to ask the judge to award fees and instead take the money out of the wife's share of the marital estate. By skimming fees from the client's share of the settlement, the attorney knows he won't have to disclose to the judge or the husband how much he is billing.[3]

DECEPTIVE BILLING TECHNIQUES

We all want to know what we are paying for, and consumer laws that regulate businesses generally require merchandising outlets to provide itemized receipts. But in the legal profession, lawyers are largely entitled to practice without any specific rules guiding or regulating their billing procedures (except in New York and a few other places).

Fraudulent billing is one of the most pervasive and blatant forms of legal deception. Particularly in large law firms, seasoned partners use inexperienced associates to do the research work and then charge the client for the time it takes the green associate to learn the law. *Wall Street Journal* columnist Russell R. Miller understands just how lawyers maximize their profits by "pushing down as much work as possible to junior attorneys to widen the law firm's profit margins."[4] Miller cites the tricks of the trade:

- The client is charged for the conversation in which he explains the problem to the senior partner.
- The client is charged for the senior telling the junior what the client told him.
- The client is charged for the junior calling the client to clarify some points.
- The client is charged for the senior reviewing the work of the junior.

None of this is ever itemized for the client.

It is important to understand that these practices are not at all limited to disreputable firms—they are institutionalized at many very reputable law firms. Take the quota system for billing. It's standard procedure at midsize and large law firms to impose annual billing-hour quotas on associate lawyers. They must bill clients a certain number of hours per year even when there's no work to justify that billing. Dana Susman, a twenty-six-year-old lawyer from Manhattan, says that one of the reasons she prefers working at a small firm to a large one is that she has seen how her friends who work as associates at large firms have to financially deceive clients to fulfill billing-hour quotas. "Everybody lies," Susman says. "There's no possible way to work all those hours. They [her friends] don't sit around and talk about it, but it's something they just do."[5] Northwestern University Law Professor John Elson noted in an interview with this author that those firms specializing in divorce practice are typically not large firms with quota requirements but small-sized firms where "the pressure is not to meet externally imposed quotas but to fulfill their own."

In addition to having to pay for senior lawyers teaching junior lawyers how to do their jobs, or getting overcharged by law firm associates pressured to overbill, there's no way for a client to determine if the legal task allegedly performed by a lawyer has been done—or if it's necessary.

No Way to Measure How Long the Task Should Take

No objective standards exist to gauge how much a legal service should cost, so clients have no way to measure and no way to know if their lawyers are overcharging or presenting an accurate reflection of real work. The Illinois appellate court in a 1988 decision confirmed that "the average client has little, if any, knowledge, regarding whether the services rendered by the attorney and time involved in performing them were necessary to the client's representation."[6] For example, there's no telling how long it takes a lawyer to prepare and produce a document for court. In the past several years the federal government has tried to curb fee abuses in the medical industry by establishing standards for the length of hospital stays and costs for routine operations. But legal consumers have no comparable standards. Consequently, lawyers can easily pad the costs of preparing legal documents. Computers now generate standard legal forms, which can be tailored to each client in a matter of minutes. The lawyer's secretary or paralegal merely inserts basic information about the client, such as name, property descriptions, etc., into a master information list. Then the computer automatically spits the information back into whatever document the court needs. As divorce lawyer Barbara Stark wrote in a trade journal article to her peers, "Most matrimonial attorneys have now developed a basic separation agreement form to be used in all cases and a computerized 'bank' of clauses to be inserted by paralegal staff to meet particular needs. The amount of attorney time in the production of the 'product' is significantly reduced and in an hourly fee system may result in reduction of the profit margin for the production of that particular product."[7]

How Many Lawyers and Staff Are Really Necessary?

Another legal but illegitimate way to boost fees in billing is to use two or more attorneys when only one is necessary. Sometimes the client is deliberately not told how many lawyers or staff personnel will be handling the case. Adding on more lawyers without getting the client's prior authorization is not considered ethical, but this practice happens every day.

The divorced wife of a multimillionaire in the insurance industry called for my advice one day. She holds a doctorate in psychology and is quite seasoned in finances, but still she could not understand why her divorce lawyer's bill was so high—totaling $50,000. I phoned Legalgard, a special accounting firm used by corporations to detect lawyer overcharging, and asked for their help in deciphering the woman's bill. Rosemary Patricelli, a lawyer with this Philadelphia-based firm, put the problem bluntly: "She's being financially raped," she told me. "Look at all these initials on the bill representing lawyers who are charging for their time." Indeed, I counted up initials representing six different lawyers charging her for various services, all involved in the divorce proceeding. Next, I called the woman at her home and asked her if she had authorized all these members of the legal staff to work on her case. She hadn't. I called her lawyer in New York and asked him to explain. In a very pleasant voice, he told me that he had been ill for three weeks and during that time, several lawyers in the firm had inadvertently duplicated the work in her case. I wondered why, if he knew that the bill was in error, he hadn't corrected it before mailing it to her, but I didn't say anything. I told him politely that she would like to resolve the bill as soon as possible. About an hour after this conversation, the woman called me. She said her lawyer had just phoned her and agreed to cut the bill in half—by $25,000.

In a postscript to this story, two years following this incident, the woman contacted me with the news that while her attorney was no longer claiming the original amount, the attorney's law firm had recently reinstated the attorney's original monetary claim and was demanding it in its entirety. Imagine. The lawyer admitted the work was unnecessarily duplicated, but after he left, the firm carried on as if its fees were legitimate and as if she were the wrongful debtor.

Double Billing

Former Associate Attorney General Webster Hubbell was convicted on a felony count of mail fraud in 1994 for, among other things, double billing his clients when he was a lawyer at an Arkansas firm. The news of his conviction for double billing was shocking to some lawyers, not because he did it, but because so many attorneys routinely double bill their clients and never get caught. In a newsletter for associate lawyers, called "The Rodent," a column was devoted to the practice of double billing. The column was pointedly sarcastic, showing how hypocritical the Hubbell conviction was in light of the fact that the practice of double billing is industrywide. The column revealed: "The fact that a fellow lawyer will be serving prison time for double billing is a devastating blow to the legal community. The Hubbell incident has taken a cherished and beloved law firm tradition and turned it into something offensive. . . . Traditionally, double billing has been held in very high regard at The Firm. Rather than being something to be punished for, lawyers strove to achieve double billing."[8] The column, "Double Billing a Bad Name" went on to cite some of the more common forms of double billing. They include:

- Lawyers who make court appearances for more than one client [without the clients being present] and bill each of them for all the time spent.
- Lawyers who bill a client for their travel time, while working en route on a file for another client.

- Lawyers who adapt documents from one client's file to fit a second client's case, and then bill the second client for the entire time required to draft the original documentation.

Padded Bills

Deceptive billing in the extreme involves out-and-out fabrication. Phony charges can range from the blatantly egregious to the seemingly trivial. In an example from New York, a well-known writer was billed about $850 for a conference with her divorce lawyer that she never attended. She later proved in court that she was out of town that day on a speaking engagement by showing a newspaper article that dated the day of her appearance. The bill was rescinded.[9]

A woman from a Cincinnati, Ohio, suburb was billed $31.25 for a fax of a witness list sent from one of her attorneys to her husband's attorney. The faxing supposedly took fifteen minutes. The woman was also charged $31.25 for a message her attorney left with her husband's attorney's answering service! It should be noted that the woman's lawyer's pettifoggery was not just billing for faxes and charging for dialing an answering service, but billing attorney time for nonattorney tasks that a secretary probably performed.

In New Orleans, a lawyer claimed he had obtained a court judgment to collect more legal fees from a woman client, who had already paid him more than $12,800. The lawyer actually printed the word *judgment* on his legal bills to fool her. But the woman knew the judgment was phony. She called his bluff and he backed down, as she recalled: "I caught him in it and he said it was a mistake and he'd credit me."[10]

Vague, Unclear Bills

Clients are often in for an unpleasant surprise when they receive their lawyer's first bill in the mail. Some bills are presented in a code as hard to decipher as hieroglyphics. Sometimes the charges aren't even presented in dollars and cents but in coded time-units. For example, .75 may represent three quarters of an hour, so if the lawyer bills at $150 an hour, the .75 represents $112.50. Some lawyers bill at fifteen-minute minimums for any work, even a thirty-second phone call. If the client asks the lawyer to clarify the bill, sometimes the client will be charged for asking. After the New York City Department of Consumer Affairs' *Women in Divorce* report came out, new court rules abolished this practice of charging for discussion of fees, but it is still too soon to know if this law is being enforced in New York. Meanwhile, the practice remains perfectly legal in many states.

Lawyer bills are also difficult to read, because the staff people working on the case may only be represented as initials and the itemized tasks may be vaguely labeled. "Legal research," for example, is a meaningless description. Legal research of what? Remembering the rudiments of the divorce law? Imagine charging a heart patient for time spent reviewing the arteries that lead to the aorta.

Sometimes bills arrive without any explanations or itemized charges at all: "For services rendered: $100,000. Please pay promptly. Thank you." As consumers, we expect even nickel items in the grocery store to be itemized, but in most states lawyers are not required to itemize their bills, no matter how high the charges. In those states that do require fee itemization in divorce proceedings, such as Illinois and New York, the only way to deal with a lawyer who refuses to itemize the bill is not to pay and then wait until he or she sues you. At this point you can challenge the bill in court. This is obviously an expensive proposition and requires either hiring a second lawyer to sue the first, or becoming your own lawyer by representing yourself against your former attorney in court.

WHEN THE CLIENT TRIES TO CHALLENGE THE BILL

Challenging a bill is sometimes extremely difficult, and lawyers are not always honest in their explanations. Lying to cover up apparently isn't all that uncommon among lawyers, according to Catholic University of America law professor Lisa Lerman. In a study she conducted she found that "when a client challenges a bill that is not entirely accurate, the lawyer often buttresses one lie with another."[11] One lawyer described to Professor Lerman what happens in her firm when the client questions a bill: "The client calls up . . . ask[s] about [the] bill, and you are saying, 'Oh, yeah, on 1/26/88 I spent X amount of time,' and you go through as if you had kept to the minute time records when in fact each week you've been fudging on them and padding them because you were required to have eighteen to twenty-two hundred billable hours [per year]. . . . This is so common. I have many friends working in large firms—it is the practice."[12]

When Carol Murray's divorce lawyer sued her for nonpayment of a $12,000 bill, this hard-working secretary and mother from Virginia Beach, Virginia, took apart her lawyer's legal bills with a fine-tooth comb. She described her situation this way: "My lawyer started in June of 1990. By January of 1991 I had not received a bill. We didn't seem to be getting anywhere. I had already paid him $2,500. I was assuming he was ethical." She remembers what he said when she asked him to send her a bill: "He said, 'I'm not set up to bill monthly. I keep it in my head.' "[13]

According to Carol's description, her lawyer's billing procedure was more than a little unorthodox. Can you imagine any person in business offering a service in exchange for a fee, saying, with a straight face, "I keep it in my head"? Imagine a response to the question "Doctor, how much will this medical test cost?" "Ms. Patient, don't ask. My head is a cash register, and I'm hearing bells ringing right now." Or "Mr. Architect, how much do you charge for the kind of apartment I want designed?" "I don't know, Ms. Contractor, but don't worry. I'll build up the charges in my head as we go along and believe me, you'll find out in the end. I'll let you know when I've reached the ceiling."

I presented Carol Murray's problems to legal ethics expert Burnele V. Powell, dean of the Kansas City School of Law at the

University of Missouri and former chairman of the standing committee on professional discipline at the American Bar Association. Dean Powell told me that the client has every right to expect prompt bills from his or her lawyer, as well as open communication regarding fees throughout the proceeding. "The expectation is that fees will be itemized early on and there will be a full explanation and your client will understand what they have to pay and why they have to pay," Powell said. "You've got to communicate with the client and you can't lie and cheat and lie to the court. When the client comes into the office you say to the client I'm willing to take your case. Here's what I charge and if you have any questions just ask. That's expected."[14]

Certainly that was what Carol expected, and when her lawyer was so evasive she sensed that something was wrong. She pushed more aggressively for an itemized bill, and finally it arrived at a court hearing. Carol says, "He almost threw this bill at me. He said, 'Here, read it and weep.' I said, 'read it and weep?'"

Carol had never before seen the hieroglyphics contained in a typical legal bill. Instead of clearly showing the amount owed in dollars and cents, the whole thing was computed in fractions of hours. "I said, 'What is this?' He said, 'All you have to do is add them up and figure it out.' I said, 'I'm not going to add anything up. I want a statement telling me what has been spent and what is left.' A week later I got a statement, and it was $5,000 over my retainer. And I had no idea it had gone over the retainer at all. That's when I really got nervous."

Carol knew that without proof of her lawyer's shenanigans, any complaint she made would come down to her word against her lawyer's. Her lawyer may have known right from wrong, but that didn't matter, because in the black hole of justice there are no clear regulations, laws, or enforcement mechanisms regarding lawyers' fees. This is not justice, but this is the system we presently have. (The exception is New York, which in 1993 started requiring divorce lawyers to submit their bills to the court administration for review.)

Carol was catching on fast. If she was going to avert further financial harm she decided she would have to start documenting all correspondence with her lawyer in writing in order to prove what was happening. As she said: "I started putting everything in writing to him. But when I began documenting everything that took place he didn't like it. That I think was the beginning of his discontent with me. I was putting him on notice and I had a record, so the more I challenged him to do the right thing, the more he seemed to refuse to want to do the right thing. He felt as if he didn't want to be accountable to me. I was trying to make him accountable now too—not just my husband and the court. I had to make my own lawyer be accountable too, now."

As the time drew near for the crucial court hearing to conclude her divorce, her lawyer began pressuring her to sign a promissory note and then a deed of trust to her home. When she refused, her lawyer quit and sued her—nine days before her court hearing. He was claiming $12,000 in unpaid fees, and additionally contended that Carol wasn't paying him.

At the jury trial, Carol was ready. She had uncovered numerous misstatements and erroneous charges in his bills. As she relates, "I went through his bill item by item and I pulled out everything he said and I tabbed it with that charge. I'm very detailed and analytical. Let's face it. I was being sued." By going through every item charged, she found that her lawyer had:

- Billed her $125 an hour for transportation to and from court, even though his out-of-court rate was $100
- Billed her $50 to read a *two-line letter* to the court
- Billed her $3 a page for incoming faxes
- Billed her $75 for a $50 consultation fee she'd already paid
- Billed her double rates of lawyer time for mimeographed copies of documents he produced
- Billed her $30 for a three-line message via telephone from her husband's attorney to her attorney (but probably received by his secretary). The entire contents of the message

read: "Needs to change date of the Cm'r [Commissioner] hearing.¹⁵ Got his tickets to the Dallas game. It's the same weekend. Sorry! Please call ASAP. Says he has a hot Mexican waiting."

According to the law, a lawyer may not collect legal fees if he quits a client's case without "just cause." By the second day of the trial, due to Carol's prepared defense, the judge had already determined that Carol's lawyer's fee demands were illegitimate and therefore he should not have abandoned her case. Carol Murray—a woman with smarts and a fine sense of ethics—had prevented her divorce lawyer from gouging her, thus averting unnecessary financial catastrophe. But lest readers conclude that her problems were thereby solved, note that Carol still had to find a new lawyer to finish procuring her divorce, thus creating more delay and expense in her case.

NONREFUNDABLE RETAINERS

Lawyers' practice of using nonrefundable retainer agreements is another problem for clients. Many divorce lawyers who take retainer fees feel entitled to keep the money, even if no work was performed on the case. In New York, this is precisely what happened when one of New York's foremost divorce attorneys, Joel Brandes, kept $15,000 and would not refund the amount to a couple who reconciled after only a few hours of legal work were performed. Was the lawyer entitled to keep the $15,000? To the layperson, the answer seems easy—of course not. But for lawyers, the answer depends on what state you are in and whom you ask.

When I posed this question to legal professionals in New York in 1991, I got three different answers. One divorce judge told me she was sure that the practice of keeping unearned money was illegal. She explained the law of *quantum meruit* (literally, as much as one deserves), a Latin term that means an attorney is only supposed to base fees on actual time spent working on the case. But her view contradicted the ethics opinion of the New York State Bar Association.[16] According to them, a lawyer could keep the full amount, as long as the nonrefundable provision was spelled out clearly in the retainer contract and the fee was not excessive—*even if no work was performed by the lawyer.* (The legal profession does not clearly define what *excessive* means.) Other lawyers I asked told me that they thought the practice was unethical but permissible because there was no clear-cut rule forbidding it.

When the New York couple sued Joel Brandes to get their refund, they eventually won. New York Justice M. Hallstead Christ ordered Brandes to return all but $1,305 of the $15,000 retainer, ruling that the $15,000 fee was "both grossly excessive and shocking to the Court's conscience." This rebuke was dramatic and ironic in light of the fact that Brandes was a leader in the matrimonial field, having written a six-volume treatise on matrimonial law.[17]

Two years later, in 1993, a similar case arose involving a lawyer named Edward M. Cooperman, who also wouldn't return a retainer to his former client. In this case, the higher court created a new precedent, outlawing nonrefundable retainers altogether. This was the first time in the country that a higher judicial court invalidated nonrefundable retainers as unethical.[18]

Around this same time in New York, public hearings were being held in which then–Consumer Affairs Commissioner Mark Green, I, myself, and other consumer advocates testified against the use of nonrefundable retainers. One of the rules Chief Judge Judith Kaye passed in 1993 barred nonrefundable retainers specifically in divorce cases.[19] If divorce lawyers violate this rule, they could be subject to admonishment or worse by their own tribunals. However, most other states do not have a court rule banning nonrefundable retainers, even though the practice is considered to be widespread. Therefore, the way things stand now in most states, to get a refund a client must challenge his or her lawyer with a lawsuit.

MOTION CHURNING

In addition to illegitimate billing, another way unscrupulous lawyers can illegitimately boost fees is to needlessly drag out a case. Such a lawyer will bring court motions when the legal task could be taken care of much more efficiently with a simple phone call. This is known as churning.

Professor Stephen Gillers, a legal ethics expert who teaches at New York University Law School, confirmed that the problem of churning in divorce cases is a very common practice; he told me a true story that he later repeated for the *New York Times*.[20] A friend of his, a state judge who had decided many divorce cases, was invited to speak at a meeting of divorce lawyers. She was looking for topics, and Professor Gillers asked her if two seasoned divorce lawyers could accurately predict the results of a divorce trial. The judge told him, virtually always. Gillers then suggested that she urge her audience to push for early settlements, thereby saving much money and avoiding acrimony for their clients. "If she did that," she told me, she would be chased off the stage. "They can't settle until they've earned a fee," he recalled her saying. Professor Gillers later expressed his repugnance at this practice: "The idea that a case's longevity is partly determined by the fee expectations of lawyers is as repulsive as the practice is unethical. It happens, though, and it is impossible for courts or disciplinary authorities to detect or prevent."

UNSCRUPULOUS DEBT COLLECTION METHODS

Clients are generally not aware that lawyers use many debt collection devices to wrangle improper fees out of their clients. One particularly insidious device is the use of *confessions of judgments*.

Confessions of Judgments

The confession of judgment is a form document that states the client has made a voluntary admission that a debt is owed. Once it is signed, the client does not have the right to dispute the bill in court. The lawyer, without informing the unsuspecting client, files the "confession" in court, where it then becomes an automatic lien on the client's property. A lien is a claim upon the property as security for a debt. If the lawyer is really greedy and he gets a woman to sign a confession of judgment, he could conceivably foreclose on the property to satisfy the alleged debt. (In 1993, foreclosure on marital property for lawyer fees was banned in New York.) In one type of scam, the lawyer deliberately doesn't bill the woman, and then after the fees have ballooned, he calls her into his office and tells her she is in deep debt. Knowing her financial condition and that she won't be able to pay, the lawyer would then pressure her into signing a confession of judgment.

Promissory Notes

Lawyers also use promissory notes, in which the client agrees to pay a certain amount, to lock women into paying potentially huge amounts. Because these notes are sometimes presented to the client on the eve of trial or a crucial court hearing, when the woman is at her most vulnerable and caught off guard, they can verge on extortion. In one case the appellate court in New York rejected a lawyer's claim for $404,000 in fees, basing the decision partially on the fact that the law firm made the woman sign a promissory note "nearing the end of the trial [which] cannot be viewed as anything other than coercive whether or not it was accompanied by threats of withdrawal from the case."[21]

The deception involved in using these collection devices is that lawyers don't have to present itemized bills in most states, so the woman may not even know how much she owes. The lawyer avoids having to account for the amount of time he or she has spent on the case, then puts the woman in a helpless position right before the court date when she will be more willing to comply with their inflated fee demands.

Lawyers have defended the use of confessions of judgment and other "security liens" on property, such as promissory notes and requesting mortgages on clients' property. They say it's the only way they can collect their fees. "It's naive to say to lawyers that [they're] not entitled to a security interest in fees. . . . It's the same as saying to a bank, you're not entitled to a security interest for your loan," Donn C. Fullenweider, a Houston divorce lawyer, told the *Wall Street Journal*.[22] Lawyers defended the use of mortgages, promissory notes, and confessions of judgment at a public hearing in New York after the practice was exposed in 1992.[23] At these public hearings, however, it was revealed that confessions of judgment and other similar security devices for collecting fees conflicted with the disciplinary rules for lawyers. There is a "significant conflict of interest which arises between attorney and client in a matrimonial case when the security interest [lien or mortgage] attaches to the marital home," wrote the Committee to Examine Lawyer Conduct in Matrimonial Actions.[24] The new court rules require the lawyer to get permission from the judge before taking a lien on the client's property, and this has caused considerable resentment among some attorneys, who feel entitled to the large fees that had heretofore been easy to collect without having to account to anyone. One commercial attorney from Long Island, New York, complained to me that his wife, a divorce attorney, was unable to collect $25,000 in legal fees because the judge refused to grant her a lien on the client's home. When asked why the $25,000 fee wasn't taken out of the wife's share of the settlement, the lawyer responded that the fee was more than the entire settlement. In the old days in New York, the woman would have had to sell her home to pay the debt.

In Maine, the bar association prohibits lawyers from taking mortgages on clients' marital residences: "A lawyer for a client in a divorce action may not secure his legal fee by taking a mortgage on the client's married residence. Such actions give the lawyer proprietary interest in the divorce action that may cloud his professional judgment in the case."[25] This is only an ethical prohibition, however, and does not carry the weight of law.

Marital Settlement Agreements

In Illinois, lawyers also try to wrangle money from clients by using the written marital settlement agreement itself as an instrument to collect excessive fees from their own clients. The settlement agreement is a legal contract between the husband and the wife in divorce that specifies the arrangement of terms involving the couple's property, assets, and custody of children. In such cases, the attorneys' fees are inserted into the marital agreement and although they are supposed to account by an itemized bill to the client some lawyers do not. The lawyer drafts the agreement and puts in a provision that awards himself a specific amount of fees against his own client. The settlement agreement is then incorporated into a final divorce decree, with the fees automatically included. This becomes a judgment when the judge signs it.

This practice was uncovered in Illinois by CBS television reporter Pam Zekman, who investigated several such cases. The practice of inserting fees into settlement agreements is perfectly legal yet arguably unfair, according to Professor John Elson.[26] In one Illinois case, the appellate court wrote that the wife "was not in a position to take on her attorney as an adversary to contest the amount of his fees while he was representing her in the prove-up [final hearing] of the settlement." In this case, the court ruled that the wife was entitled to a hearing, despite the terms outlined by the lawyer for his fee in the settlement agreement.[27]

The Lawyer Sues the Client to Collect

Some attorneys sue clients who refuse to meet their fee demands. The lawyer will ask the judge for a judgment against the client. Doris Noonan[28] (name has been changed) had paid her lawyer $10,000 to take her case, but the money ran out only after a few months, so the lawyer took her to court. With the approval of the judge he got a judgment against her. The lawyer got a sheriff who came to her apartment and seized Doris's personal possessions—two gold wristwatches—to collect his fees. Doris was in a panic, fearing her crystal glass collection would be the next to go because the value of the gold watches only partially covered the bill.[29]

Holding the Client's File Hostage

Lawyers in some states are legally allowed to hold onto the work in the client's file until the lawyer's fee demands are met; they obtain a lien on the documents called a retaining lien.[30] The use of the retaining lien has taken many unsuspecting women by surprise. Some attorneys hold the file hostage at a critical stage of the proceeding. This can be extremely damaging to the woman's case. A lawyer is not ethically permitted to hold the file if it is damaging to the case, such as when the client can't continue litigation without it, but the practice continues anyway. According to the New York Committee to Examine Lawyer Conduct in Matrimonial Actions:

> [I]nstances have been reported of an attorney's refusal to relinquish not only papers generated during the action, but also personal documents placed in his or her keeping, such as deeds, etc. Some attorneys have been known to retain a client's passport to ensure payment of their fees. Other lawyers, reportedly, even have refused to comply with a court order directing return of the file. The consequence of such conduct is to bring the action to a standstill as the client is unable to proceed without the file even if new counsel has been retained. The client may be irreparably harmed by the inability to continue the litigation where the attorney has other means to ensure eventual payment.

The Committee concluded: "[T]he attorney's right to be paid cannot take precedence over the client's right to the case file."

Charging Liens

A lawyer can also put a charging lien on the funds or property that the client obtains from her divorce settlement or judgment. This device gives unscrupulous lawyers the opportunity to run up astronomical bills on a case and then claim them in the form of the woman's share of the marital estate. One example is Mrs. Merzon from Queens, New York, whose attorney "coerced" her into signing a promissory note for more than $200,000 near the end of her trial, according to a judge who reviewed the case. The attorney then obtained a charging lien that gave his firm legal permission to collect approximately $396,000 from her share of the settlement for his fees. This amount represented 80 percent of her share of the marital property and was in addition to $21,000 he had already collected in fees from Mrs. Merzon and her husband. She was entitled to a fee hearing, and a subsequent review of the lawyer's charges showed that $13,000 was charged for telephone calls alone. A total of $8,000 more was billed for conferences between the lawyer and his associate, both of whom billed her for their time. The judge concluded: "It would not be an understatement that this court is appalled by the amount of these requests for fees and disbursements. . . . Clearly nothing in this case called for the time of two attorneys totaling some 2,800 hours at times with an overlapping combined fee of $310 per hour." The lawyer's fee was thus reduced from $396,000 to $25,000.

WHEN THE HUSBAND PAYS THE WIFE'S LEGAL FEES

As stated earlier, a provision in the law that is available throughout the country gives the "needy spouse"—usually the woman—the legal right to have the "moneyed spouse"—typically the husband—pay her legal fees in the divorce. But sometimes women are particularly vulnerable to being compromised by their own attorneys precisely because of the way legal fees are paid in divorce. When the wife's lawyer is to be paid by her husband, it puts both lawyers in the position of being employed, in effect, by the husband. Thus the woman's lawyer might become more interested, for financial reasons, in accommodating the husband. In this compromised position, the woman's attorney can pressure her into making concessions that aren't in her interest, or can fail to disclose her options to her.

Many women in this position feel as if their lawyers are working for the other side, but they have no substantial proof to back up their hunches. What appears on the surface as incompetence or aloofness can be readily explained in light of the lawyer's real motives. The task of uncovering the husband's assets may be hindered by the wife's attorney because the lawyer's bread is being buttered by the husband. Knowing that the unsuspecting woman doesn't know what she is entitled to under the law, the lawyer can easily induce her to settle. The lawyer then obtains a handsome fee after having deliberately neglected his client's rights.

Many times cases of lawyer neglect are interpreted as incompetence on the lawyer's part, rather than being questioned or perceived as deliberate deception. In any case, it is hard to tell if the lawyer was just sloppy or if the lawyer deliberately neglected the wife's rights because of the disincentive provided on the husband's part.

One woman recalled the divorce proceeding, and a crucial deposition session in which her lawyer was supposed to question her husband about the contents of the marital estate: "My lawyer, my husband, and his attorney were joking together, talking about the ball game before the deposition, leaving me out of their talks completely and then interrupting me whenever I tried to raise an important question during the deposition."[31]

In a similar case in 1977 in Wisconsin, Jeanette Helmbrecht's lawyer told her that the agreement he and her husband's lawyer had worked out was a fifty-fifty split of the assets. She later proved that her lawyer had negligently failed to investigate the extent and value of marital assets, beyond asking her husband about them at a deposition session.[32]

Many women complain that they feel like outsiders when their own lawyers are dealing with their husbands. They relate how their lawyers seem to avoid asking the really pertinent questions of their husbands during court hearings, questions that would lead to uncovering their husband's assets. One sixty-four-year-old woman from Chesapeake, Virginia, put it this way: "I don't know why my lawyer didn't question my husband more to the point. He didn't ask the right questions. So the commissioner [acting judge] didn't have anything to go on."[33] She recalled asking her lawyer to obtain past accountants' records so she could prove her independent financial worth, but she says her lawyer refused to comply with her request.

Of course, the deceptions described above are not supposed to happen. Lawyers are not supposed to be free to make their own rules and ignore the law when it affects their self-interest. But, as the cases cited show, the lack of strong protections against these abuses guarantees their perpetuation. While New York started an effort in 1993 to curb some of these abuses, they have not yet been eradicated. In December 1994, the *New York Law Journal* carried a front-page story reporting that the new protections were not being adequately enforced. Lawrence Pollack, on a committee to oversee the new rules, acknowledged the problem: "Nothing is going to change overnight. . . . It's very difficult to change lawyer behavior."[34]

✺ 6 ✺

THE BLACK HOLE
OF JUSTICE

ALL LAWYERS operate in the same universe, which has at its center a gaping black hole of justice. Once you understand how the black hole works, then the actions of individual lawyers become understandable. How does a lawyer get away with charging his or her client more in legal fees than the entire worth of the client's marital estate? How can divorce lawyers lie in court papers without getting caught? How can a lawyer hold a client's file hostage when the client doesn't agree to the lawyer's fees—even when there's no way to know the fees in advance? Looking at the ways unscrupulous divorce lawyers behave naturally raises the question: how can they act with such impunity?

Divorce lawyers (and judges) are governed by their own system of self-rule; they set their own professional ethical standards and regulations governing practice; and they wield the power to discipline or disbar lawyers who commit infractions. That is, lawyers are responsible for overseeing and regulating other lawyers' practices. Obviously as chief subjects of their own profession's proscriptions, lawyers have a powerful interest in protecting and sustaining their own self-interest. And for some—if not many—lawyers, given the choice between ethical practice and fewer profits or unscrupulous outright profiteering, there's no contest. The foxes are watching the hen house and unethical lawyer practices flourish. Three overlapping factors encourage unethical practices in divorce court: the profit motive, the absence of independent oversight, and the lack of strong rules by any monitoring agency that would expose and prosecute the abuses.

THE PROFIT MOTIVE

The one great principle of the English law is to make business for itself. There is no other principle distinctly, certainly, and consistently maintained through all its narrow turnings. Viewed by this light it becomes a coherent scheme, and not the monstrous maze the laity are apt to think it. Let them but once clearly perceive that its grand principle is to make business for itself at their expense and surely they will cease to grumble.

CHARLES DICKENS, *Bleak House*

The influence of money on lawyer practices is an old theme, as old as 1853 at least, when Dickens finished *Bleak House*. But never were so many people potentially affected by this pernicious influence as right now in the United States, because never were so many people in need of lawyers for their divorces. The sheer volume of divorces the courts handle each year is coupled with another phenomenon: the transformation of the profession of law into a market-driven business. Nowadays, law firms function just like any other commercial enterprise. This applies to divorce practice as well. Divorce lawyers advertise; their rates are gauged to the commercial marketplace; they exchange their professional services for a fee-for-profit. They use sales techniques, such as well-honed pitch lines, to attract business. They read articles on how to market their services. A few even hire publicists to boost their image in public. All the intense interest in the bottom line has created a freewheeling industry, one that remains entirely self-regulated. This market-driven climate makes the words of late Supreme Court Justice Benjamin N. Cardozo seem like a quaint anachronism: "The final cause of law is the welfare of society." Nowadays, the final cause of law can be welfare dependence. When I asked a prominent Wisconsin divorce attorney if women should have to choose between paying their divorce lawyers and putting food on the table for their children, he responded, "Nobody has to starve. That's what welfare is for." Apparently driving people into destitution is an acceptable outcome of divorce, and it isn't a lawyer's "business" to worry about the impact and cost of his or her fees.

The temptation for divorce lawyers to put profit first above all other considerations can be very strong. The divorce industry is a huge business. In 1992, domestic relations cases made up more than one third of all civil cases filed in state courts, and experts say that this figure is probably closer to half.[1] With the frequency of divorce—more than one million divorces take place a year—the industry annually generates several billion dollars. No one knows the exact number for sure because no one tracks divorce lawyers' collective profits, and lawyers are often reticent about their incomes. No definitive demographic studies exist, and this seems curious given the wide scope of the industry. A total of 846,036 lawyers practice in the United States and any one of them can call him or herself a divorce lawyer.[2]

It's clear that lawyers can accumulate vast sums in a very short amount of time. High fees are routine, even if the woman becomes impoverished by them. Consider the Duluth, Minnesota, woman whose entire net earnings averaged less than $5,000 a year as a grocery store cashier. She was charged $15,000 by her lawyers just to get child support orders enforced.[3] Or the switchboard operator in North Carolina earning $17,000 a year who was billed $71,000 for her divorce.[4] Indeed, the profit motive has become so strong that even the American Bar Association's own Commission on Professionalism has urged lawyers to "resist the temptation to make the acquisition of wealth a primary goal of law practice."[5] Despite the moral tenor of the ABA, however, the whole American capitalistic system stresses financial success above all. Divorce attorneys I have interviewed say they have absolutely no moral responsibility to preserve the family estate for the family.

The scope of the divorce industry is bigger than the profits grossed from lawyers in private practice. A growing number of lucrative sideline industries have sprung up to profit from families in divorce. Court reporting services rake in tremendous profits because they charge 200 to 300 percent more than the current commercial rates for Photostat copies. Ex-judges are getting into the act too, making a profit by performing auxiliary tasks. Some judges appoint ex-judges as "receivers" who take over management of large estates until the issues are resolved. These receivers obtain a hefty fee, usually a fixed percentage of the estate. Another lucrative field for ex-judges is divorce mediation—in which the couple is required by the court to negotiate an agreement with a third party appointed by the court. More and more state judiciaries are discussing the possible use of mandatory mediators as a way of keeping divorce clients out of the court altogether. This topic has generated much recent debate in law journals, but very little has been written specifically on the monetary benefits to lawyers and mental health professionals who are getting into the fast-growing business of mediation, although now there is attention focused on the potential pitfalls that face women in divorce mediation.

The Hidden Costs of the Commissioner System

Although our courts are free public institutions belonging to all citizens, a few states are now denying divorcing couples free access to court. These spouses, whose taxes pay for judges' salaries, must now in addition hire an extra divorce lawyer who functions as a quasi-judge to hear their divorce case before it goes to the real judge. This privatization system has created a new niche for lawyer profits. Under this system, each couple has the financial burden of paying fees to three lawyers, instead of two, to have the issues formally adjudicated. In Virginia, for example, lawyers called commissioners are appointed by the local courts to hear divorce proceedings, and charge couples an hourly rate, which can run into thousands of dollars. The hearing itself takes place in the law firm instead of the court-room. The commissioner then makes a report to the judge, who rubber-stamps the decision unless one of the parties objects.

Judges, of course, are government employees whose salaries are publicly funded. This follows the presumption that every American is entitled to free access to the court as a privilege of citizenship. If the couple can't afford the commissioner's hefty fees? "Then they don't get their divorce," according to William Oast III, a commissioner in Portsmouth, Virginia. Oast acknowl-edged that he had delayed proceedings in one case because the husband wouldn't pay his fees.[6] In Pennsylvania, which has a similar system, the lawyers who act as judges are called masters, and the couples must also pay them for their divorces to be com-pleted. Whether this trend will develop in other states is unknown.

Compounding Hidden Costs

Lawyers' profits are easily compounded by the multitude of fee-generating tasks that are typical in contested divorce proceed-ings.

Because the need for legal services in a divorce case can arise at any time, a constant supply of funds for legal help is needed. For example, if a mother and her children are physically and financially abandoned by the father and husband, she will have to hire a lawyer to take certain legal actions in court to compel her husband to pay at least temporary support. Appropriate legal forms will have to be submitted, a court hearing will have to be held, and a judge will have to make the determination in a written order. How many middle-class women in divorce can afford to pay $1,200 for half a day in court? Yet it is precisely when a woman is financially abandoned that she is most in need of court intervention.[7]

Ancillary services are also prohibitively expensive. For example, if a client needs a transcript of her court hearing for future court dates, each photocopied page will cost $2 to $3, and there's no other way for court consumers to make copies of the transcripts. Women in a lower- or middle-class income bracket can't easily afford these prices, and yet these are standard "legal" fees. If she can't meet these demands, she can't defend her rights in court on crucial issues. If, for example, a judge errs in a custody decision and she has unjustly lost custody of her child, the woman must appeal to a higher court to have the decision overturned. For her appeal she is required to obtain the transcripts of her case for documentation purposes—yet this paperwork alone could easily cost thousands of dollars, given the copying costs.

The Billing System

Divorce lawyers' billing procedures are designed to maximize profit and favor lawyers who cheat. Lawyers use an hourly billing system, and some proponents are now arguing for an even more consumer-unfriendly system called value billing, which would give lawyers the power to arbitrarily decide their fees without having to account for them. Both systems offer a major means to exploit clients because analysis reveals that there is no way of gauging how much time a legal task should take.

Charging by the hour, rather than by work that's actually performed, only provides an incentive to pad bills. Even the legal profession itself has acknowledged the corruptive power of this billing method. William Brewer and Jennifer Martin, from the Dallas firm of Bickel & Brewer, told their colleagues at the American Bar Association's annual convention in 1992: "Billing by the hour creates a conflict of interest between the client, who almost always wants the matter resolved quickly, and the lawyer, who knows that the more time he spends on the case, the more he can receive in fees."[8] At the same ABA conference, Zoë Baird, former general counsel for Aetna Life and Casualty Company, and President Bill Clinton's first choice for U.S. Attorney General, called hourly billing "a demon" that "pushes law firms to a near obsession with billable hours. And this in turn supports the great unwritten rule of all law practices: that those who want to get ahead must tally up the hours."[9] The vast majority of lawyers—including those who practice family law—use the bill-by-the-hour system to achieve their profits. In Middle America, hourly rates start at $150 and up. On both coasts and in wealthy suburbs, $250 and $300 an hour is commonplace among so-called top litigators and high-profile attorneys. Lawyer fees add up fast in a contested divorce, which is very much in the interest of the attorney.

But the popular alternative being proposed—value billing—would not be any safer for consumers and would seem to create the opportunity for even more abuses than hourly billing. With value billing, the client is billed according to the outcome of the case, depending on the results. Under value billing, if lawyers think they have done a terrific job, then they feel entitled to ask for a bigger fee—much bigger. The problem is that there is no objective standard to measure the value of the lawyer's performance other than the lawyer's own opinion. How can a client know if the lawyer is doing a good job? Or if the outcome was indeed good or fair for the client?

At least in hourly billing, the lawyer theoretically has to account for services claimed in time expended. Everyone knows, for example, that a two-line letter should not take an hour to produce. But in value billing, the lawyer's time expended in labor would no longer be a factor in determining the lawyer's fees. If a lawyer did minimal work and then said the value of the settlement agreement was $10,000 in legal fees, the client would have no way of knowing what the actual value was. Given the lack of an objective measure, the routine division of marital property could turn into an even bigger financial nightmare for couples under the value billing system than it already is under the present bill-by-the-hour system.

A third and infinitely fairer alternative to hourly and value billing is possible. Some corporations are now demanding that lawyers use flat rates.[10] Whether this trend will carry over into family law remains to be seen.

How Clients Get Hurt by the Profit Motive

When a lawyer is overly interested in profit maximization, there are two distinct disadvantages for the client. First, the client's needs come after the lawyer's, if they figure in at all. This can result in absolute disaster. As we have seen, if the woman runs out of money after paying huge fees to her lawyer, and then has no current funds left for the court hearing, the lawyer might abandon her. As a result, she cannot defend her rights in court. Abandoning a client who runs out of money before the proceeding is finished raises a serious question of ethics. After all, a lawyer can wait till the completion of the divorce to receive fees from the settlement proceeds. But some top earners in the industry advocate otherwise. Raoul Felder, whose rates were quoted at $450 an hour, advises his peers: "Often, when once retained, whether through lack of original ardor or finances on the client's part, the client falls behind in payments. The lawyer must decide if there is sufficient light at the end of the tunnel to continue unpaid. If not, it is advisable to leave the party before the party turns ugly."[11]

Second, when the drive to profit is so obsessive, the line between legitimate and illegitimate practices blurs. For example, the lawyer has a duty to keep his client informed of her rights. But a lawyer preoccupied with profit might "forget" to tell the woman she has the right to dispute the lawyer's fees in court if she disagrees with them. A lawyer also might ask a woman for $15,000 in a nonrefundable retainer without telling her that she has a right to a refund if no work is done on the case. These examples are drawn from actual cases. Legitimate fees quickly turn illegitimate when lawyers, under the spell of the profit motive, fail to inform clients of their rights or deliberately misrepresent the facts to boost their fees.

Divorce lawyers argue that their business practices are not

that different from other business practices that place profit ahead of people's social welfare. After all, insurance companies often discontinue covering people who have suffered major illnesses, leaving them unprotected from huge medical costs. If someone has to mortgage the family home to pay the hospital bill, and then can't pay it, foreclosure and homelessness can be waiting right around the corner. The insurance company is not thinking of the human life involved but of how much they will save by eliminating expensive coverage. In one example, the *New York Times* reported that managed health-care plans have policies against paying for visits to emergency rooms that aren't on an approved list, unless the patient gets prior approval for the visit from the company. When a person is bleeding or in labor—true emergencies—having to go through the process of getting approval is difficult, if not impossible. Recent history is filled with tragic examples of profit maximization guiding the interest of companies at the expense of people's lives. This is one of the unfortunate by-products of capitalism, unregulated by democratic governmental restraints.

In today's world, it is commonplace for businesses to use devious means to further their financial interests. The newspapers are filled with daily horror stories of the profit motive gone haywire. When major prestigious companies are involved in life insurance fraud, Medicaid fraud, security industries fraud, it barely raises a collective eyebrow. Divorce lawyers are no different from any other commercial business in this regard. That some lawyers, even prestigious lawyers, engage in a variety of deceptive practices to further their own financial interests is not therefore surprising. By virtue of their role as officers of the court and fiduciaries, lawyers are supposed to put their clients' interests first, but virtue doesn't increase profits and earnings. Some observers, however, don't see the excesses of capitalism as the problem, but rather that lawyers possess certain inherent advantages over their clients that create the specific risk of clients being manipulated. In Northwestern University Law Professor

John Elson's view, "There's an economic term called 'bilateral monopoly' often used in commercial cases, but that applies to divorce cases. . . . A monopoly limits competition. Here it's the monopoly of one party over the other. You have to go along with the lawyer, because you've already paid so much [in fees] that you can't afford another one."

THE ABSENCE OF INDEPENDENT OVERSIGHT

Generally, lawyers are not held accountable to the state consumer statutes that regulate business practices. If they were, such abusive practices would not be tolerated. But lawyers have special privileges. They don't have to live up to strong standards of accountability as do people in other professions—just one of the many unique advantages that separate lawyers from other businesspeople. For instance, plumbers and architects require licenses issued by the state, but lawyers are licensed by their own private trade group, the bar association. This is a little like putting the safety approval of a new drug into the hands of the pharmaceutical industry. Would you feel secure taking such a drug?

The national, state, and local bars function as lobbies for lawyers' interests. But these lobbies have all the authority and weight of government. The bar holds much decision-making authority, and when the bar tells the government what to do, the government goes along. Why? Because *the legal profession has rule-writing power that has the force of law*. As Philip Stern, who discusses this point in his book *Lawyers on Trial*, writes: ". . . the power of the state is used to give teeth to the rules written by private bar associations."[12] In other words, even though the bar is a private organization with private interests, the judicial branch of our state governments OK's the bar's rules as public law. For example, about half of the publicly funded lawyer disciplinary agencies that claim to regulate lawyer conduct are operated by the private bar associations.[13] And the lawyers' ethics rules that have been adopted by the states were modeled by the American Bar Association, which is a voluntary, private organization.

Quoting from a former Justice Department official, Stern writes that "[r]ules of the [legal] profession are typically initiated, debated and approved by the bar association, and then ratified (many times without separate hearings or discussion) by a state supreme court . . . made up of lawyers. So automatic is court rubber-stamping of bar rules . . . that when the American Bar Association changes its regulations and a state bar group follows suit, the rules of the [state] court are [modified] automatically."[14]

The legal profession's influence over legislation runs extremely deep. In fact, for all practical purposes, the legal profession controls the practice of law. The legal profession has granted itself the power to police itself through the bar association, which has its own disciplinary system for regulating the conduct of lawyers. Every state has a disciplinary or grievance agency, and more than half are run by the bar associations. The other half are supposed to be independent, but the state bars wield heavy influence over the grievance agencies' policies and procedures.[15] These agencies are taxpayer-funded, but the lay public is not allowed to intervene in public policy concerning lawyer discipline. The regulatory structure of the grievance committees is exclusively the domain of lawyers.

The one exception is California, where the lawyers' disciplinary system was notorious for its backlog of cases and poor administration. The system got a major overhaul in 1987 after the state legislature intervened in response to consumer complaints.[16] The bar established an independent monitor, Robert Fellmeth, a law professor and director of the Center for Public Interest Law at the University of San Diego. Fellmeth called for numerous reforms, including a review board with citizens on it. The citizen-dominated panel (called the Complainants' Grievance Panel) was given the power to review those complaints against lawyers that had been dismissed by the state bar's attorney grievance committee, and to conduct audits of the disciplinary system. "People who complained about lawyers and had their complaints dismissed could appeal to the citizen-dominated panel. The panel could review those complaints and then recommend that the complaints be investigated further. But that aspect was eliminated by recent legislation," said Theresa Meehan Rudy, a spokesperson for HALT (Help Abolish Lawyer Tyranny), a national legal reform organization. Rudy explained that the panel was reconfigured under a new name (now called the Discipline Audit Panel) and is now only able to conduct audits of the disciplinary system. "HALT's position is that they should have kept the Complainants' Grievance Panel intact," she said.[17]

Critics charge that the lawyers' disciplinary system has woefully inadequate enforcement procedures. The legal establishment has acknowledged this problem for twenty-five years, but still it remains just as severe.

In 1970 the first nationwide evaluation of lawyers' disciplinary procedures, known as the Clark Report,[18] released its findings. Among the revelations were:

- There is inadequate financing of the disciplinary agencies for investigations.
- The local and fragmented nature of the disciplinary structure makes the system ineffective; local jurisdictions are often so small that all the lawyers know each other personally.
- The disciplinary structure is cumbersome, causing delays. Case processing can take from several months to five years.
- Disciplinary agencies have inadequate, undertrained professional staff.
- There is an absence of training programs for disciplinary agency staff.
- Disciplinary agencies rarely investigate unless there are specific complaints.
- Disciplinary agencies insist on unnecessary formalities, such as verifying complaints.
- There is no provision for suspending lawyers convicted of serious crimes (pending disciplinary proceedings).

- Disbarred attorneys are too readily readmitted to practice.
- Lawyers and judges are reluctant to report instances of professional misconduct.
- Judges are not trained in ethical standards and disciplinary enforcement responsible for lawyer discipline.

The Clark Report identified the problems that make disciplinary systems ineffective but it had little real impact on lawyer practices. As Stanford law professor Deborah Rhode noted, "A quarter century after the Clark Committee issued its report, some of the most significant problems that it had identified remained pervasive. Although most disciplinary agencies revised their procedures, increased their budgets and imposed sanctions with greater frequency, almost every major study found serious inadequacies in the regulatory process."[19] As a result, less than 2 percent of all complaints nationwide result in public discipline (meaning discipline resulting in censure, suspension, or disbarment).

The problems for legal consumers in California (with the second-highest number of lawyers after New York)[20] still continue. After an extensive four-year effort at reforming the lawyers' disciplinary system, bar monitor Robert Fellmeth issued this statement in his final report in 1991: "What is needed are some bounds, some clear and defined limits. . . [to restore] a measure of honor to a profession which is in a current state of well-deserved dishonor."[21]

When we go to buy a car at a used-car lot, we know we have to be careful because used-car dealers have a reputation for taking advantage of unwary consumers. But currently there is more protection against a shady car dealer than an unscrupulous lawyer. Used-car lots, unlike law firms, are governed by any number of state and local consumer protection laws and caveat emptor disclosures to protect consumers against fraudulent and deceptive business practices. But divorce lawyers are generally exempt from the consumer laws that regulate business practices. Nevertheless, some of the very same types of consumer deceptions are occurring in legal suites throughout the country. Many of the unethical practices I have described in these chapters—such as lawyers making false claims or misrepresenting facts in order to attract customers—fall into the category of deceptive consumer trade practices.

For example, many lawyers use a version of the old game of Bait and Switch, which is a common scam among disreputable retail stores. In this practice, the store offers an item on sale but when the customer goes to buy it, the store is "suddenly" out of the item and offers a similar item at a higher price. In the lawyer's version of this game, a prominent member of the law firm meets with a client and offers to handle her case. The client then assumes that this lawyer will represent her, but after plunking down the hefty retainer fee, the client finds her case has been turned over to an inexperienced associate instead. The senior lawyer may not even bother to show up at the hearing.

Another consumer deception is to make false claims. If a business makes a promise it can't keep, it is in violation of consumer laws against false claims. For example, rapid weight loss programs in the late 1980s often claimed in their ads that their clients could lose weight and keep it off, but in response to consumer complaints, Congress and the Federal Trade Commission stepped in and found that 95 percent of people who follow these programs regain their weight within a couple of years. The companies were found to be engaging in a deceptive trade practice and had to withdraw their ads. Yet when lawyers make false claims to lure business—such as "I'm an expert in this, you'll win hands down, don't worry about it"—they do not have to answer to any regulatory authorities.

Lawyers typically balk at these conclusions, asserting that clients who complain about lawyers' fees and practices don't want to pay their bills or are transferring their anger at their spouse onto their attorneys. But client-bashing doesn't account for lawyers' deceptive bills and dishonest behavior, according to Northwestern University Law Professor John Elson, who has represented many suburban Chicago women in claims against their attorneys. Elson writes: "What these advocates fail to explain is how this demonization of divorce clients, even if it has some basis in reality, could possibly justify attorneys making false and partial disclosures, padding fees and exerting extortionate pressures to pay."[22]

States could easily adapt their consumer laws governing business practices to crack down on deceptive fee practices and misrepresentation of claims in law practices. Not to do so keeps lawyers above the laws that citizens and consumers depend on to protect them. As Professor Lisa Lerman wrote, "The absence of specific rules concerning deception of clients amounts to tacit permission for lawyers to continue to use deception."[23]

It seems obvious that even though law firms aren't commercial businesses they should still have to obey consumer law. Yet this proposal was fiercely debated after the report I wrote for New York's Department of Consumer Affairs, *Women in Divorce: Lawyers, Ethics, Fees, and Fairness,* was released in 1992. After public hearings were held, the report's suggestions for reforms were turned into new court rules for lawyers but not without a vicious fight from lawyers who did not believe consumer rules should apply to them. In fact, the Nassau County Bar Association voted to file a lawsuit if major provisions in the new rules were not changed.[24] Nassau County, New York, by the way, represents the seventh wealthiest suburb in the nation (as of 1992), where divorcing spouses bring massive windfalls to lawyers.[25]

Why should lawyers be exempt? The self-regulation of the legal profession has proved itself to be a dismal failure. The resulting lack of consumer safeguards has made divorce court a bonanza for lawyers, and arguably the latest frontier for white-collar crime. The techniques the unscrupulous lawyer uses to deceive the client are, after all, the techniques of white-collar criminals, according to the following textbook definition of white-collar crime:

I. Intent to commit a wrongful act or to achieve a purpose inconsistent with law or public policy

II. Disguise of purpose or intent

III. Reliance by perpetrator on ignorance or carelessness of victim

IV. Acquiescence by victim in what he believes to be the true nature and content of the transaction

V. Concealment of crime by:

   A. Preventing the victim from realizing that he has been victimized, or

   B. Relying on the fact that only a small percentage of victims will react to what has happened, and making provisions for restitution to or other handling of the disgruntled victim, or

   C. Creation of a deceptive paper, organizational, or transactional facade to disguise the true nature of what has occurred.

(Source: Criminology: Crime and Criminality[26])

To repeat, much of what passes unnoticed by our law enforcement agencies in fee abuse practices by lawyers is a form of white-collar crime—that is, criminal behavior. Yet criminal statutes aren't readily enforced except in the very worst cases of criminal behavior, usually when lawyers steal large amounts from escrow accounts or resort to corporate embezzlement. Much white-collar crime goes uninvestigated in the United States, and this extends to economic fraud by divorce lawyers.

LAWYERS' LACK OF STRONG RULES

Given the absence of independent oversight, lawyers' self-regulation policies are extremely weak. The serious and glaring deficiencies in the lawyer's ethics code and disciplinary system are described below to help provide an understanding of how lawyers can commit serious abuses with impunity.

The Vague Language of the Lawyer's Model Code

The Model Code of Professional Responsibility and the Model Rules of Professional Conduct were written under the auspices of the American Bar Association as models to guide lawyers' behavior. But the way the present code is written and enforced ensures that deception can flourish. One of the main reasons for this is the extremely vague and unspecific language of the ethics code. For example, if you believe your lawyer overcharged you, your lawyer could argue back that the fees were "reasonable." The lawyers' Code of Professional Responsibility doesn't exactly say what *reasonable* means. Instead it gives judges a wide range of possible interpretations, based on a set of guidelines. According to New York's Code of Professional Responsibility, Section DR 2–106, for example, several factors are weighed to interpret the reasonableness of a fee. Some of them include: "1) The time and labor required, the novelty and difficulty of the questions involved, and the skill requisite to perform the legal service properly. . . . 3) The fee customarily charged in the locality for similar legal services. 4) The amount involved and the results obtained. . . . 5) The experience, reputation and ability of the lawyer or lawyers performing the services. . . ." Under this standard, it might seem "reasonable" for a lawyer to collect $50,000 from a divorce where the settlement is only $25,000.

Reasonable is a vague concept conveniently open to broad interpretation. So who gets to finally decide how to interpret *reasonable,* to determine how much the lawyer should collect? Judges do. Asking if judges, themselves ex-lawyers, favor lawyers over clients is like asking if the Pentagon favors an arms buildup over conversion to a peacetime budget. Because of judges' natural allegiance to the legal profession, a judge's interpretation of *reasonable* may be far different from yours or mine.

The rules about how lawyers should communicate to their clients about their fees are also extremely loose. As Catholic University Professor Lisa Lerman notes, "The Model Code similarly encourages, but does not require, a written fee agreement." As a result, only a few states require contracts between lawyers and clients to be in writing. Lerman adds that although both codes list factors that lawyers may consider in setting fees, "the requirement is so vague that it arguably would be satisfied by an extremely general disclosure. . . . The Rules require no particular methods of tabulating hours worked and require no particular disclosure in bills sent to clients."[27]

The rules regarding deception are equally murky. Professor Lerman wrote: "The ethical rules governing the profession, however, do not make it clear under what, if any circumstances it is permissible for lawyers to deceive their clients."[28] Without strong, specific rules to ground the profession, ethics are sucked out of the legal universe, like light that is sucked out of our galaxy and into a black hole, never to be found.

Lawyers accused of serious crimes who pose a danger to unsuspecting clients can keep doing business because of the skewed technical language in the Code. For example, under the Code, a lawyer in some states can't be temporarily suspended if there is good reason to believe he or she is stealing money. Why? Because the aim of suspension is ostensibly to prevent a lawyer from engaging in dangerous future conduct, and under the disciplinary committee language the lawyer must be shown to have caused the client "irreparable harm."[29]

As used in civil cases, *irreparable harm* means the lawyer has gone beyond causing *substantial harm* and has actually financially ruined the individual. For example, if Company A claimed that Company B had stolen so much money from Company A that it should be temporarily restrained from doing business, according to the meaning of "irreparable harm," Company B's actions would have to be shown to threaten the very existence of Company A's business. The loss of money by theft, in and of itself, would not be considered a good enough reason for the court to require Company B's business to be temporarily shut down, according to the precedent set by civil law. According to the precedent, Company A could ostensibly sue to get its money back, so irreparable harm would not have taken place and therefore Company B should not be closed down.

While this reasoning makes sense in civil cases, it is a very dangerous leap to apply this same rationale to lawyers who keep practicing after allegedly stealing from their clients. The ABA's McKay Commission, which examined lawyer discipline, found that the term should be dropped on the grounds that it is not applicable to lawyers and is harmful to clients because it "seriously limits the ability of the court to temporarily suspend respondents who pose a serious threat of harm to clients and the public."[30] The Commission recommended changing the words *irreparable harm* to *substantial threat of serious harm.*[31]

Because the rules are presented as confusing abstractions, with little attention paid to the possibility or practice of lawyer deception, the clear distinctions between right and wrong, fair and unfair, and ethical and unethical behavior are hopelessly blurred. What is the effect of not having strong rules regulating lawyers' professional conduct? Lawyers can remain legally unaccountable for their unethical and sometimes criminal actions.

Enforcement of the Code

Instead of relying on strong rules, the legal establishment maintains faith in the honor system, which is essentially faith in the lawyer's word that he or she is acting in good faith and with integrity. The honor system might have worked when there were only a few thousand lawyers practicing and maybe competition wasn't so fierce, but today the United States is glutted with lawyers. Each year, more than 30,000 graduates of law school flood the already crowded legal marketplace, intensifying competition. This, combined with the industry's strong profit motive, renders the honor system a total failure. There is no way for the bar or for consumers to personally judge the honesty of a lawyer who is entrusted with a client's finances. It is a logistical and legal impossibility.

Still, the bar maintains its obsolete honor system. Faith in the honor system remains so strong that the drafters of the Code do not even formally acknowledge the issues of fee deception and fraudulent billing practices. According to Lerman: "the drafters appear to assume that lawyers are always honest with their clients and that regulation is not needed in this area."[32]

In Stanford law professor Deborah Rhode's words: "[State disciplinary] agency review is limited because of resource constraints and/or convictions that other remedial alternatives are available through malpractice actions and breach of contract suits."[33]

As Rhode explains, the disciplinary agencies do not have adequate regulatory mechanisms for dealing with deception. Instead, many disciplinary agencies throughout the country do not define fee complaints as within their review process. Some agencies, for example, classify lawyer conduct involving overcharging and fee padding as Fee Disputes. Once the complaint is classified as a Fee Dispute, the agency will send the complaint to the lawyer who has been accused, asking the lawyer to respond. The lawyer will write back, defending against the accusations, and in turn, the lawyer's response will be sent from the agency back to the client. After this letter exchange, a few or several months will elapse. (Many disciplinary agencies are notoriously backlogged and there's no telling how long consumers must wait.) The day will finally arrive when the consumer will receive a typed form letter in the mail from the disciplinary agency, telling her there is no further reason to investigate. In fact, no investigation has ever taken place, because the complaint has been summarily dismissed "for lack of jurisdiction." How common is this paper-pushing routine? According to the ABA's McKay Commission: "*It is clear that tens of thousands of dissatisfied clients are being turned away. The disciplinary system was not designed to address complaints about the quality of lawyers' services or fee disputes* [italics mine]." "Despite such improvements, the percentage of complaints resulting in public discipline is still extremely low. Ninety percent of those who file charges never see their attorneys prosecuted," Rhode wrote.[34] The McKay Commission's findings are supported by figures provided by the National Organization of Bar Counsel (representing disciplinary agencies nationwide), which reported that fee disputes were the second largest category of complaints dismissed, on the grounds that the disciplinary agencies don't handle fee disputes.[35]

Clearly, disciplinary agencies often automatically consider lawyer misconduct a simple disagreement between the lawyer and the client, ignoring the fact that, as the McKay Commission acknowledged, "Fee disputes may arise because a lawyer fails to provide services in the manner promised, delays performance, fails to clarify the computation of the fee, gives an unrealistic initial estimate of the fee or behaves in other ways that are unfair to the client and unprofessional."[36]

In California, where there have been significant attempts to reform the disciplinary system, described earlier in this chapter, the legislature-appointed bar monitor urged: "The Bar must search for ways to deter attorney deceit, particularly in the practice of civil law. The level of attorney dishonesty in representations to the court, in promises to clients, in dealings with adverse counsel, and perhaps especially in points and authorities and legal briefs, is embarrassing."[37]

As Professor Lisa Lerman pointed out: "The bar associations mirror the general unconcern about lawyer honesty with clients that is reflected in the ethical rules. The bar counsels who receive and respond to complaints of ethical violations by lawyers tend to undervalue client complaints and to be biased in favor of the lawyers."[38]

The failure of the lawyers' disciplinary system to deal with lawyer deception, misrepresentation, and substandard service within the profession is not news to the bar. In 1991, the McKay Commission urged the American Bar Association to improve the disciplinary system for the sake of the public and the reputation of the profession. But the ABA's members ignored the Commission's advice and today remain blasé about lawyer deception and fraud. The legal establishment, meaning the echelon of lawyers that command and influence public policy within the bars, wants to maintain the status quo.

Very recently (in February of 1995), in a major policy shift, the ABA passed a voluntary rule urging states to adopt mandatory arbitration of fee disputes. While reformers say this measure is commendable, it is too early to know when and if the states will actually adopt the requirement for lawyers to submit to arbitration. Mandatory arbitration is considered very good in one respect, because it lessens lawyer litigation against clients, but weak in that it still does not deal with fee deception as a form of misconduct. Also, arbitration panels that are composed of lawyers are subject to peer influence and bias against non-lawyers, which may result in skewed findings against consumers.

The overall weak ethics code and the system's lax enforcement methods described above combine to form a black hole of morality in the legal system, where right and wrong cease to exist. If it isn't illegal, it's OK. And if it's illegal but there's no enforcement, then it's OK too. Here one finds an ethical nether world of the abstract where right and wrong are replaced by the narrow interpretations of the ethics code and lawyers' self-interested definitions of what constitutes misconduct.

Secrecy

Another privilege lawyers have is the secrecy they are able to maintain when they are accused of misconduct. As a result, lawyers can commit horrendous deceptions without any fear of detection or the embarrassment of public scandal.[39] Other licensed professionals are not shielded by confidentiality rules to the degree that lawyers are in many states.[40] Why do lawyers have this privilege and no one else? The answer is that they write their own rules, which then carry the weight and effect of law.

In the settling of marital estates, enormous amounts of money may be at stake. The temptations for lawyers to cheat are strong when there is so much profit to be made, with nobody watching. Yet most states open attorney records to the public only after formal misconduct charges have been brought by the lawyers' disciplinary agency against an attorney. Since most complaints are dismissed before they ever reach the formal stage, records remain secret in the vast majority of cases.

Until recently in many states, even a lawyer accused of the worst misconduct could keep it in the closet until he or she was disbarred or suspended. The authors of the McKay Report had warned their peers that the confidentiality rules were damaging public perception of the system, so most states now make public the records of those attorneys accused of serious crimes, such as embezzlement. Secrecy is no longer an exclusive privilege of the legal profession in New Jersey after a commission appointed by the New Jersey Supreme Court concluded: "To continue to bestow such a benefit upon the legal profession, which earns its living in an open system, is anomalous and unfair. The self-serving nature of such an action invites public criticism and further undermines public confidence in the system and the profession as a whole."[41]

Despite lawyers' fears of being sabotaged by disgruntled ex-clients who bring false complaints, Ray Trombadore, chairman of the McKay Commission, said that in the six months following the new law in New Jersey, lawyers he has spoken with have not experienced any harm from this new policy of openness. In New Jersey, the records become public after the agency decides to pursue an investigation. However, as I mentioned earlier, since these types of complaints represent a tiny fraction of all complaints against lawyers, the public is still being kept in the dark about the majority of allegations involving fee deception and misrepresentation.[42]

Many lawyers oppose eliminating the secrecy—"opening the system"—in the majority of cases on the grounds that vindictive clients will file false complaints to ruin lawyers' reputations, but there is no evidence that this has happened thus far, according to the ABA's own Commission's findings. "The arguments against open disciplinary systems are based on conjecture and emotion, not experience," authors of the McKay Report wrote in 1991, after examining Oregon's open system.[43]

Three states have gone further than the rest, and make information available to the public in all phases of misconduct proceedings, not just in the worst cases. To their credit, Oregon, Florida, and West Virginia have made all lawyer punishment public—from admonitions to suspensions to disbarment. Florida's new policy has had the effect of improving the performance of the disciplinary agency staff, according to one official.[44] Oregon has gone even further, allowing full disclosure to the public from the time the initial complaint is made.

"KILL ALL THE LAWYERS"

It is safe to say that most Americans are tired of having lawyers rob them and would prefer harsher consequences for lawyers' crimes. The amount of public resentment over lawyers' stealing, in all its deceptive forms, seems to be reaching a new high. A glance at the polls shows that public opinion of lawyers has sunk to an all-time low. "The findings support the widely held perception that resentment of lawyers ranging from lawyer-bashing jokes to outright vilification is running at a fever pitch," reported in the *National Law Journal*, August 9, 1993,[45] after a national survey was taken. The negative feeling is fueled by the perception that lawyers are avaricious and dishonest. In another national survey in 1993, the American Bar Association found that 59 percent of the people believe lawyers "are greedy."[46]

But we don't need more studies in order to understand what the public is feeling. Look at the casual vilification of lawyers in a mail-order gift catalog routinely sent out to middle-class consumers at Christmas time. There, in a sign of the times, a few pages past the Mickey Mouse Waddle Book and Peter Rabbit Videos, is a picture of a jigsaw puzzle with the title "To Kill A Lawyer." On the same page: *The Lawyer and Other Reptiles Book*. A sampling: "It was so cold that a lawyer had his hands in his own pockets." On the next page were more jokes: "How do you tell when a lawyer is lying? His lips are moving." Part of the reason these disparaging jokes are so popular is that the profit motive has such a prominent place. They clearly indicate the lack of effective oversight in dictating lawyers' professional behavior.

We have seen how the profit motive, the absence of independent oversight, and the lack of strong rules all contribute to the black hole of justice, leaving consumers unprotected from unethical, illegal practices by attorneys. Underlying these influences is a fundamental problem, and that's the corruption of our society's basic values and morality. Lawyers who find creative and clever ways of circumventing the law to avoid the appearance of wrongdoing are functioning in a moral vacuum, creating the black hole where right and wrong doesn't matter. Rather than thinking "I'm not going to do this because it will hurt the other person," they rationalize "If it's legal it must be OK." Lawyers must live up to their obligation to the general good, on which the foundation of law rests.

Unfortunately, lawyers who learn how to protect themselves and their friends from the consequences of their unethical practices too often move up the ladder to become judges. In that capacity, they continue to be sheltered by the protective embrace of their colleagues.

ᴥ 7 ᴥ

PROTECTING YOURSELF FROM JUDICIAL MISCHIEF AND MISCONDUCT

ALL THE CRUCIAL issues a woman brings to court in a divorce case are ultimately decided by the stranger in black robes who is known as "Your Honor." She and her lawyer must respect the judge's authority, and in return she expects the judge to respect her (and her children's) rights and needs. Unfortunately, judges often don't hold up their end of the bargain. The legal system is set up to protect judges who make decisions by whim, who don't take the time to properly consider all the factors in the case, who are ignorant about the ramifications of custody decisions, who are biased for personal reasons, and who are careless in their interpretation of the law.

Granted, judging family law proceedings is not easy. Judges can be uncomfortable dealing with the spouses' often charged emotions, so it's not surprising that some judges see having to preside over family law cases as a punishment, "an assignment to Siberia."[1] Then too, some judges think of domestic relations as a "women's issue" that is beneath them. This negative attitude toward the proceedings can affect the judge's ability to listen impartially to the evidence presented by each side and to render a fair decision based on his or her knowledge of the law and the probable economic and psychological outcomes of his or her rulings.

When a woman in the throes of a divorce proceeding comes to divorce court, she usually needs a judge to help her in some vital way. If she has been financially abandoned and has children, she will need the judge to order her husband to pay child support. If she is an older homemaker without the means to pay the mortgage on the house, she will need the judge to order her husband to continue to pay it. If her husband threatens to remove her personal property from their home, she will need the judge to stop him. If she has been beaten or harassed by her husband and is trying to leave him, she might need an order of protection. When the dissolution of the marriage threatens a woman with harm, whether it is losing her children, home, or money or being in danger of physical harm from an abusive, battering husband, a wife especially relies on the judge in divorce court to remain faithful to his obligations and live up to the oath he takes to honor the laws and to engage in ethical practice.

We assume that the man or woman in the black robes is ethical and competent at presiding over the cases he or she is assigned. After all, it is not easy to become a judge, so of course bad judges have been weeded out along the way. But is this really the case?

HOW JUDGES ARE SELECTED

Judges are lawyers who are elevated to the bench by appointment or election, neither of which, as we shall see, guarantees that they are ethical or even competent. Both the appointment and election systems put lawyers' interests first and consumers' interests second, and both are subject to the influence of politics in different ways.

In states where judges are elected, they are subject to the same corruptive political pressures as other elected officials. The

American Bar Association's Commission on Professionalism noted in 1986: "The elective system has given us some very good judges, but also some bad ones. . . . On the road to the bench, judicial candidates often become embroiled in reciprocal obligations to political sponsors, as well as to campaign contributors, many of whom are likely to be lawyers who will appear before the judge. Judges may feel under pressure to return these favors."[2]

In addition to encouraging political patronage, the elective system is also seriously flawed because the voters generally know little about the judges they are electing. There is no public scrutiny of the candidates, and citizens learn nothing about judicial candidates other than what they advertise about themselves in their campaign literature.

Many states have attempted to depoliticize the judicial selection process by instituting a nomination system for electing lawyers to the bench. In what is known as the "merit selection system" a committee of judges, lawyers, and laypeople submits names to the governor, who then makes a selection. The judge is appointed for a period of time and then periodically must run against himself or herself on an unopposed ballet. No one is permitted to run against the judge, and the voters are supposed to decide if the judge should be retained for another term.

As the name of the system suggests, the nominee is supposed to be selected on the basis of qualifications rather than partisan connections. But critics of this system have found that the merit selection plan just replaces one kind of politics with another. Charles R. Ashman commented in his book *The Finest Judges Money Can Buy:* "[All] that has happened is that the politics of the governor and the bar association have replaced the politics of the county party chairman and the electorate. . . . A judge is no more nor less obligated to an organization that elected him than are governor and nominating commissions to those same political groups."[3]

In his book *With Justice for None*, maverick lawyer Gerry Spence notes: "The governor, a political being, still appoints judges and creates political obligations thereby. Moreover, the committee that presents the governor with the lists of names from which his appointment of the judge can be made is often dominated by special interest groups, who attempt to make the appointment themselves. . . . In Wyoming, where the governor is presented with three names, I have known the committee to include the name of two candidates wholly unacceptable to the governor, leaving as his only practical choice the candidate the committee itself had chosen. Once the judge takes the bench, unless he gets involved in his own Chappaquiddick, he will probably remain in office for the rest of his life."[4]

In the area of family law, the current selection systems have led to a decidedly low caliber of divorce court judges based on findings documented by task forces commissioned by the states' own highest courts. Judges are "apathetic," "uninterested," and "untrained," according to a report issued by California's Administrative Office Judicial Council of the Courts of California.[5] Florida found that divorce court judges were "uninformed" and "insensitive," with the majority disliking the work they do![6]

One problem is that the nominating commissions are known to give short shrift to those areas of law, such as domestic relations, that aren't perceived as "male," and they don't necessarily screen applicants for their own family histories. The task force commissioned by the Florida Supreme Court found: "Commissions do not sufficiently emphasize an applicant's family history with regard to divorce and support matters, areas with which a trial judge may deal if selected."[7] In Vermont, lawyers with domestic relations experience who apply to be judges report that they are bypassed in favor of lawyers with jury trial experience but no domestic relations experience—even though domestic relations has accounted for half of the civil court cases in Vermont.[8] Even lawyers who send their names to the commission to apply for judgeship positions report that they don't know what qualifications the commissions are looking for in candidates. The selection process is cited as a possible factor in the low caliber of California's judges. The task force commissioned by the California Supreme Court found that "the selection process for family law judges may be one factor that contributes to the lack of interest and training [in family law]. . . ."[9]

It is not so easy to keep off the bench those family law judges who cannot put aside their bias against the kind of work they do, or who lack experience and knowledge about family law, which prevents them from making fair decisions. In fact, it is extremely difficult to force even outright incompetent and unethical judges off the bench because of the weakness of judicial ethics commissions.

WHY JUDICIAL COMMISSIONS DON'T WORK

Judicial ethics commissions are supposed to make sure that judges abide by the Model Code of Judicial Conduct, to which they swear. This code identifies three particular standards for ethical judicial practice, which are identical in all fifty states, of which three are cited in part below:

- A judge shall be faithful to the law and maintain professional competence in it.
- A judge shall accord to every person who is legally interested in a matter, or his or her lawyer, full right to be heard according to law. . . .
- A judge shall respect and comply with the law and shall conduct himself or herself at all times in a manner that promotes public confidence in the integrity and impartiality of the Judiciary.[10]

Unfortunately, under the present judicial system a woman seeking divorce may be sadly disappointed in her expectation and hope that the judge will adhere to these ethical standards and preside fairly in her case. A large part of the problem is that like lawyers, judges suffer no restraint from acting above the law, because our society has granted the judicial branch the power to police itself through judicial ethics commissions. This self-policing policy has resulted in extreme leniency toward corrupt, incompetent, and biased judges. The findings that follow may come as a shock to the average reader, but it is crucial to understand that there is little to check and balance the wide inherent latitude of judicial powers. Self-serving regulatory policies do not work, and oversight committees are ineffectual.

The government has left the discipline of judges up to the states' own judicial branches. Most of these state judicial review commissions are set up to recommend or to impose discipline. In cases where the commissions recommend discipline, the state supreme courts have to decide whether discipline should be imposed. In some states, the judge can appeal the decision. Also, the state legislatures can impeach a judge and in some states, the governor can remove a judge, with approval or at the request of the state legislatures. But the executive or legislative branches of state government rarely take these measures against judges. Supposedly set up to protect the public from dangerous judges, the judicial commissions aren't doing even a minimally adequate job, for several reasons.

First, although the commissions claim to protect the public from dangerous judges, the lawyer- and judge-run commissions rarely impose public discipline (public censure, suspension, or removal from the bench) on one of their own. For example, one of the state's top judges in Connecticut was suspended for six weeks in 1994, after hearing a murder case argued by a lawyer with whom he had a close personal relationship; his suspension was notable because it was the most severe punishment meted out to a judge in Connecticut in twenty years.[11]

Follow-through rates of the state judicial ethics commissions are dismal nationwide. The state commissions reject as invalid the overwhelming majority of complaints citizens make against judges. The 1993–94 record for Florida, for example, shows that citizens made a total of 474 complaints against judges (455 in the year 1994 and 19 pending from the previous year). Out of this total, 99 percent were dismissed. During the same years in California, out of 1005 complaints, 94 percent were dismissed.[12] Between 1991 and 1993, with a total of 14,887 complaints made against judges nationwide, only twenty judges were removed from the bench and another fifteen suspended for improper conduct.[13] Of course, not all complaints against judges have merit. A person on the losing end of a lawsuit has the incentive to strike back at the judge who made the decision. But without public scrutiny there is no possible way to assess the fairness of the Judicial Commissions' decisions.

Second, since the government has left discipline up to the individual states, uniform operating standards are lacking and some states' standards are very low. "Judicial conduct organizations differ in structure, authorized sanctions, and record-keeping and reporting methods," according to the *Judicial Conduct Reporter,* a newsletter for commissions.[14] In some states in which the commissions receive complaints severe enough to warrant suspension of a judge, they can't suspend the judge because the state legislatures have not passed the laws authorizing such a suspension.

Third, some complaints against judges are dismissed without being adequately investigated because the commissions lack adequate resources. In some states, for example, the lack of funding is so severe that the commissions operate with only one part-time staff person.[15] According to Gerald Stern, administrator for the New York Commission on Judicial Ethics, "Determining whether legal error constitutes misconduct often depends on the procedures and resources made available for investigations."[16] In other words, if the commissions don't possess the resources (staffing), the investigations don't get done, thereby allowing corrupt, incompetent judges to remain on the bench.

Finally, some commissions, which need to appear as if they are doing a proper job, are known to single out small-town judges for minor misconduct, such as fixing traffic tickets, rather than investigate more serious allegations that involve powerful, politically connected judges. This may be because these judges are judicial associates of the commission's own members. The commissions thus give the appearance of legitimacy while directing public attention away from major potential scandals. New York is one of the states that has been criticized for this pattern.

WHY IT'S SO HARD TO GET RID OF BAD JUDGES

Since women can't expect to be protected from dangerous, law-violating judges due to weak judicial ethics commissions and the ineffective judicial selection process, when faced with judicial wrongdoing can women (who are disproportionately affected by judicial bias) bring a lawsuit against a bad judge? The answer is generally, no. Judges who commit wrongdoing can't usually be sued for their actions. Judges are usually protected from lawsuits by what is known as the judicial immunity doctrine, embodied in traditional common law. Even if the judge acted in outright maliciousness, the judge in some states can claim judicial immunity, according to Jeremiah McKenna, former counsel to the Crime and Correction Committee of the New York State Senate (in an interview). In some other states, the law has been reinterpreted and legislation reformed so that it is now technically possible to sue in cases where the judge has shown that he or she did not act in good faith.[17] When a judge is sued for violating his or her responsibilities, the little guy or gal has little chance of prevailing. It's like fighting City Hall. In most states when it comes to a lawsuit against a judge, the Attorney General, the highest law enforcement official of the state, defends the judge in the litigation.[18]

Given the lack of adequate standards in the selection of judges, the largely ineffectual judicial ethics commissions, and the lack of independent oversight, the woman's or the man's chances of getting a bad judge are pretty good. With no one outside their profession watching, judges need not adhere to the legal standards and laws that all other citizens must abide by, nor do they need to adhere to their ethics code.

HOW THE ETHICS RULES ARE BROKEN

A judge shall be faithful to the law and maintain professional competence in it. . . a judge shall respect and comply with the law. . . (when he or she feels like it).

Nationwide, judicial commissions go out of their way to give the benefit of the doubt to incompetent, cruel judges who make arbitrary or illegal rulings. They do this through their two universal policies of (1) referring to the judge's breaking of the law as a mistake, or "legal error," and (2) not investigating judicial rulings. Thus, large-scale injustices can be routinely dismissed as error and incompetence (i.e., couched in benign terms). This policy has become a source of outrage to some domestic relations litigants in Pennsylvania, whose newsletter *Legal Focus*[19] states:

> When attorneys and judges fail to follow the practices and procedures set forth in the Pennsylvania Rules of Court a complaint can be filed with the Pennsylvania Judicial Conduct Board or with the disciplinary board of the Supreme Court. These agencies were established supposedly to review the wrongful conduct committed by judges, lawyers and officers of the court. . . . These Boards routinely process valid complaints of wrongdoing, and continually inform litigants that complaints brought by them have been "investigated" and have been dismissed as "legal error," which does not constitute ethical misconduct. The notion of legal error is an ethical and moral violation, an injustice of the worst kind. . . . This notion serves to empower and to enrich corrupt men and to work gross injustice. It is clear then that the notion of legal error is at the root of our problems with the court system in Pennsylvania.

Since illegal judicial rulings fall under the category of legal error, they are not evaluated as wrongdoing. The *Judicial Conduct Reporter*, the official organ of the American Judicature Society, states plainly: "The role of a judicial conduct organization is not to review judicial decisions but to discipline judicial misconduct."[20]

WHEN LEGAL ERROR IS THE NORM

Under the commissions' policy, the judge can violate the law occasionally, frequently, or extensively before the authorities act. According to De Paul University law professor Jeffrey Shaman, the pattern of misruling has to be "so extensive that it demonstrates that a judge does not possess adequate competence in the law."[21]

Says Shaman: "When the judge's ruling results in legal error and these 'errors' occur repeatedly, it demonstrates that a person does not have the proper temperament to be a judge or is unfit for a judicial office. So there are a number of different provisions in the code of conduct which may be violated when a judge renders an incorrect legal decision."[22] But these provisions are rarely taken, as the judicial organizations' enforcement figures, cited earlier, show.

LEGAL ERROR, OR LEGAL FOLLY?

Couching judicial misrulings as legal error and then refusing to investigate the rulings unless scores of litigants have complained leads to a very grave situation for consumers, and for women in particular, who are disproportionately subject to misruling from prejudiced judges. If rulings aren't generally investigated, what kinds of judicial abuses do the judicial commissions typically investigate? In 1993 when the American Bar Association held its annual meeting, one of the morning seminars was a poorly attended panel headed by law professor Jeffrey Shaman. He described several such cases that appear absurd and outrageous:

"In one case a judge had a dartboard and would sentence by throwing a dart at a dartboard—I don't know what would have happened if the judge missed the board completely," Shaman said, smiling. "There was another case in which a judge took a vote of spectators in the courtroom to determine guilt or innocence. . . ." Shaman's remarks at this point caused laughter to erupt among the lawyers in the audience. A judge appearing on the panel with Shaman gave the thumbs up and thumbs down sign in a mock gesture of arbitrary power. "Yes, very similar to that," he said. "Unbelievable as these cases may seem, there actually are a number of them."[23] It was difficult to ascertain whether Professor Shaman, who purports to advocate for judicial ethics, was not taking the issue seriously or whether he was just amused by the outrageousness of the judges' aberrational behavior being described.

Rulings can be bizarre, too. When an Ohio woman filed a claim of domestic abuse, after her boyfriend punched her in the mouth, Cincinnati Judge Albert Mestamaker ordered the man to marry her. In July 1995, the CBS television show *Hard Copy* exposed Judge Mestamaker, and asked the audience whether the judge went too far. A National Organization for Women spokesperson commented: "Remove this Neanderthal from the bench."[24]

The problem then for women is that the judge will either have to "dance a jig naked on top of a table," as one angry activist put it, in order for the woman's complaint to be addressed, or commit so many abuses that large numbers of women have to unjustly lose their children or their property before any action is taken by authorities. Couching judicial misconduct as legal error and then refusing to investigate the rulings unless the number of complaints threatens to embarrass the judicial establishment provides a huge smoke screen for the commission to hid misconduct. This policy presents a very grave situation for consumers.

What if the judge claims the error was made in "good faith"?

"Good faith" justifies mayhem. The states' judicial ethics commissions do not punish judges who "overlook" the law or misrule, as long as the commission believes the judge didn't do it on purpose.

Family law judges are granted especially wide power to make abusive decisions because of vague legal standards. If judges don't understand the law, it is deemed acceptable because they were acting in good faith. If they are biased and interpret the law in unintended ways according to their bias, that's considered acceptable too. Judges don't have to prove their good faith. Their prejudice is not recognized as misconduct, and their rulings are acceptable if they fall into the category of ignorance or error.

The law, written by lawyers, is deliberately vague to give judges the choice to decide cases as they see fit. The legal establishment's term for judicial decision-making power is *judicial discretion*. It means that the judge has a wide range of choice as to what he or she decides. The 1914 definition given in *Bouvier's Law Dictionary* supplies the most definitive definition, according to the National Judicial College's 1991 book, *Judicial Discretion:* "*The power exercised by courts to determine questions to which no strict rule of law is applicable but which, from their nature, and the circumstances of the case, are controlled by the personal judgment of the court.*"[25] (Italics are theirs.)

As Gerald Stern, director of the New York State Commission on Judicial Conduct, wrote: "The universal view is that judges should not be disciplined for acting in good faith within a wide range of discretion."[26] The judicial ethics commissions will take it for granted that the judge was acting in good faith, given the judge's wide discretionary power. As a result of this policy, perverse rulings become acceptable and "business as usual." Thus cruel judges are provided with a major protection and defense. There are few concrete rules to limit their power; judges can plead ignorance and good faith.

When judges freely abuse their position of power by making

decisions that violate the spirit or the letter of the law, this is called abuse of discretion. But the lines between legal and illegal can only be blurry, given that judicial discretion is so wide.

The danger with the legal system's giving judges so much power in general is well known. More than twenty years ago, writer Kenneth Culp Davis noted: "Where law ends, discretion begins, and the exercise of discretion may mean either beneficence or tyranny, either justice or injustice, either reasonableness or arbitrariness."[27] In other words, judicial discretion can be used wisely or poorly—for good or evil—depending on the individual judge.

In the area of family law, the judge's latitude in deciding issues on a case by case basis has come into serious question because of documented systemwide judicial biases. The impact of judicial discretion in deciding divorce and custody issues is extremely far-reaching. Bias can intrude on the decision-making process like an axe coming down on the head of an innocent. For example, in arriving at custody decisions, judges are supposed to weigh those factors that are in the child's best interest. But the judge has the freedom to interpret the "best interest of the child" standard any way he or she sees fit. Using the latitude of judicial powers provided by open-ended legal standards, the biased judge can weight his or her decision against the mother, without regard to the child's welfare at all. This problem was severe enough for California officials to conclude: "When judges are asked to make custody decisions, they do so within a relatively uncharted zone of discretion, and biases about the proper roles of women and men inherently affect those decisions." The committee urged: "Research on the nature of custody arrangements that will truly be in the best interests of our children is urgently needed."[28]

GENDER BIAS

Gender bias can infiltrate judicial decisions given the latitude inherent not only in the judges' powers but also in the law itself.

For example, in a new, perverse trend, wife beaters are being granted custody of the children after the women complain of the beatings to their judges. Nechama Masliansky, who oversees direction of the National Center on Women and Family Law, a legal rights organization based in New York, explains: "This agency gets a lot of letters from individuals with very compelling stories to tell. There is a whole pattern of letters from women who were victims of domestic violence and lost custody to the abusers. This is happening all over the country."[29] How can turning a child over to a violent parent be in the best interest of the child? Experts cite many studies that show the severe emotional problems that develop for children who are forced to witness violence against their mothers. Why would judges side with wife beaters? In the article "A Judicial Guide to Understanding Wife Abuse," author Laura Crites explains: "Gender bias can affect a judge in spouse abuse cases in the following three ways: (1) blaming the victim for not meeting her husband's needs and for provoking the violence; (2) tending to accept the husband's testimony over his wife's, and (3) identifying with the husband as a victimized male."[30]

Thus, a judge may believe the woman deserved to be beaten or that she fabricated the abuse to get back at her husband and therefore she deserves to be punished by severing her parental right to physical and legal custody of her children.

Judicial bias can also be strong in child sexual abuse cases, with potentially devastating consequences for mothers and children.

In a widely documented phenomenon that has also been the subject of federal and New York state hearings, mothers who make allegations of sexual or physical abuse against their ex-husbands are often punished by biased judges who conclude that the mothers have fabricated the abuse and then order the children to live with the alleged abusing father. This can happen even when the evidence of abuse is clear-cut and the law is on the mother's side.

One of the most tragic and highly publicized cases on record involved the Brooklyn mother Dr. Amy Neustein, a sociolinguist who lost custody of her six-year-old daughter, Sherry, in 1986 to her ex-husband after she was branded "overemotional" by the Brooklyn Family Court system for making sex abuse charges. Court records show that over a three-year period, various individuals, including Sherry's grandmother, a foster mother, a nurse, and the child herself made and backed up complaints of the father's sexual abuse, according to a story in *U.S.A. Today* (Nov. 3, 1995) by columnist Barbara Reynolds. Amy Neustein was charged with "emotional neglect" for "brainwashing" her daughter and prosecuted *by the state*. The charges against Amy Neustein were later dropped. The father, meanwhile, refused to discuss the complaint of abuse with the investigators handling the case, and under the law they could not legally compel him to, according to Brooklyn Society for the Prevention of Cruelty to Children (BSPCC), which handled the case. The BSPCC testified that Sherry displayed the behavior symptoms of child sexual abuse.

In 1989, on a visit to her daughter, Amy Neustein broke a judge's ruling and sought emergency medical treatment for her daughter, who looked severely emaciated, without first getting permission from her ex-husband. Doctors at Kings County Hospital diagnosed the child as suffering from anorexia nervosa, in which the victims refuse food to the point of starvation and death. This disease is often associated with child sexual abuse, especially in victims who are very young. Sherry was hospitalized for six weeks on intravenous feeding, and doctors credit Amy Neustein with saving her daughter's life. But because Amy didn't first get permission from her ex-husband—a doctor named Ozzie Orbach—to take the child to the hospital, the Brooklyn judge, Leon Deutch, indefinitely cut off all her visitation rights. Amy hasn't seen her daughter for seven years. She appealed, but Justice William C. Thompson and his colleagues in Brooklyn rejected her plea to resume visitation.

Thompson, who sits on one of the busiest courts in the country, said he does not believe any allegations of child sexual abuse that come to his court. Said Thompson: "You know what happens in every matrimonial case now? They go to the lawyer and the lawyer says, 'You know we're going to holler sexual abuse.' Everything stops.... That's become the password now.... Holler sexual abuse and every goddamn thing slows down. It's getting to be a disaster now because that's the password now."[31]

In 1995, New York State Senator David Paterson asked federal investigators to look into the Neustein case. In a memo Paterson wrote to Robert Flores, Deputy Acting Chief of the Child Exploitation and Obscenity Division of the U.S. Justice Department, Paterson said he was being blocked from investigating the Neustein case due to political interference from certain elected officials.

Needless to say, any woman in a custody battle who genuinely believes her child might be being abused is at automatic risk of being disbelieved in Thompson's court. The ABA's own study, among others, shows that most sex abuse allegations in custody cases are made in good faith, and are not the result of vindictiveness.

Biased and cruel judges are given a green light to act as they please. Such abusive judicial discretion is dangerous because the latitude inherent in judicial discretion is used to tyrannize, punish, and oppress women and keep them in their place. Under the guise of judicial discretion, if judges ignore the law because they don't like its intended meaning, their prejudiced ruling is not deemed misconduct and is dismissed as ignorance or error.

A judge shall conduct himself or herself at all times in a manner that promotes public confidence (but only with those who count—lawyers, judges, and with men in positions of prestige or with financial clout).

The same judges who charm and schmooze with their peers from the bench can turn into ugly bullies, tyrants, or preachers depending on the social status, class, gender, or race of the litigant before them. Individuals who are perceived as weak in the judge's mind, such as women, children, or minorities accused of crimes, may be subjected to cruel, tyrannical treatment as the judge hurls insults or acts in a demeaning and intimidating way. These judges use harsh language, subject litigants and their lawyers to derogatory comments, and in general act rudely, refusing to acknowledge the litigants' rights.[32]

Such a judge will use the bench as a pulpit from which to thrash those in need of punishment in the judge's eyes. For example, one judge in Utah told a woman in a divorce case to "get down on [her] hands and knees and pray about what [she was] doing." The judge awarded custody of the children to the husband because he disapproved of the wife's lifestyle—her wanting to work full-time—telling her she would now be free to "go to the big city, work full-time, and see what it's like." When the case was concluded and the husband received custody, the court bailiff reportedly applauded.[33]

These instances of tyranny are not unique. Out of all the possible forms of misconduct, authorities say the single largest category of complaint from citizens in many states concerns judges who are abusive in their courtroom demeanor.

THE JUDGE AS GOD

Unfortunately, judges freely violate procedures, laws, rules, and women's Constitutional rights. This has been reported in study after study across the United States. One California lawyer trying to help her client enforce her rights recalled to investigators for the Bias Task Force what the judge told her: "When I would question him, and say, 'But Your Honor, I understand that she has a right to do this by law,' he [the judge] turned around to me and said, 'I do not care what the law says. When you are in my courtroom, I am God, and what I say goes.' "[34] Of course, no one gets to haul "God" into court for an appeal. Not only is the judge putting himself above the law, he's also putting the litigant in the position of being outside the law. In "God's" courtroom, a litigant has to act "in good faith" with this particular judge, and acting in good faith under the law is rendered irrelevant. In Utah, for example, the task force of lawyers and judges who investigated judicial practices and gender bias in the state found that: "some judges and commissioners will not conduct full evidentiary hearings in domestic relations cases. . . . Some refuse to hear parties not represented by counsel."[35] Such a judge deprives the woman of the chance to present evidence for her side of the case to be heard. It is illegal under our Constitution for a judge not to allow a woman to represent herself in court.

Judges can arbitrarily refuse to hold hearings, hear evidence, or enforce their own court orders. Oddly, however, these are not considered obstructions of justice and are therefore not criminal acts, because of the judge's wide discretion, so there are few if any ramifications for the judge.

A child rights coalition, the American Coalition for Abuse Awareness, documented scores of family law cases over the past decade involving allegations of incest against fathers that were rife with civil rights violations, obstruction of justice, and mail fraud committed by child protection agencies and the court. These allegations were presented in 1993 in a memorandum to U.S. Attorney General Janet Reno. The authors of the memo alleged that court and child welfare officials were "effectively obstructing criminal investigations into these [child sexual abuse] matters."[36] The FBI was known to be gathering information on one of these documented cases in 1994. That same year, U.S. Congressman Jerrold Nadler introduced the Children's Equal Protection Act that would allow parents and child welfare activists into federal court, specifically in child sexual abuse cases, because state courts are violating the Constitutional rights of children in these cases.

Some judges have been known to alter or delete transcripts of proceedings, or have refused to allow any documentation of proceedings. In Alabama, Judge Charles M. Nice Jr. was found by the judicial commission to have ordered a court reporter to delete portions of a court transcript in a family court case.[37] He got a slap on the wrist—a six-month suspension.

Altered transcripts are not generally discussed with the public, but judges do communicate about this problem with each other. The American Judges Association, in its newsletter "Benchmark," published a revealing article in 1990. In a laundry list of judicial no-no's that included "using judicial powers to assist a personal friend or political associate" and judges who "accept favors (cabins, trips, dinners) from attorneys" was judicial tampering with transcripts.[38]

Alabama isn't the only place where altering of transcripts has come to public light. A case in Pennsylvania has attracted much local press. It involves the alleged tampering with judicial files in the divorce case of Carolee Medico, wife of a wealthy businessman in Luzerne County. In a federal civil rights lawsuit, Mrs. Medico accused several court officials of tampering with court records. In one instance, Medico claims an audio tape of the proceedings was made, which differed from two transcripts produced by the court reporter. Although the court found the defendant's conduct troubling, Medico's case was dismissed because of the defendant's judicial immunity.

Other judges have been known to keep proceedings secret, which is illegal. They refuse to provide court stenographers or keep records, as required by law, or they deny the litigant the right to see the information. This has serious consequences for the woman who cannot get a wrongful decision overturned without proof of what transpired in the proceeding. Katheryn Fahnestock runs the Rural Justice Center, a nationwide organization located in Vermont that researches problems litigants have with judges. She said that lack of record-keeping is a widespread problem, particularly in courts of limited jurisdiction. Fahnestock went on to describe one town court in upstate New York that hadn't made an entry in the docket books for fifteen months, even though in some cases people who were before the court were in the position of being fined and going to prison. Alabama has mandated that records of proceedings in juvenile court (where domestic relations and domestic violence issues are heard) are to be kept, but no money was budgeted for tapes and recorders. The problem is that when there is no record, no one is accountable. As Fahnestock says, "In a court in which no record is kept, judges are more likely to shoot from the hip. . . at the expense of parties before them."[39]

Mary Sue Johnston, sixty-three, knows this all too well. She attended a conference in Armstrong County, Pennsylvania, on September 17, 1985, with her husband to determine the amount of temporary support he would be required to pay pending the conclusion of their divorce. Soon afterward, Mary called the Domestic Relations office to obtain a copy of the report of the conference. But the administrator told her they had no record of it in their files. Failure to keep records of conferences is a legal violation of Pennsylvania's rules. Rule 1910.11—effective in 1981—specifically states in part (e): "At the conclusion of the conference or promptly thereafter, the officer shall prepare a conference summary and furnish copies to the court, and, upon request, to both parties."

Since no record of the conference was made, Mary had no way of verifying what transpired at the conference. She couldn't get a judge to review her case or issue a support order without the hearing report, in apparent violation of her rights. Two sources verbally confirmed that notes weren't taken during conferences. One source said, "Apparently back then, they didn't keep conference records. They didn't do it for anybody." Court records show that a judge testified under oath that "She's [Mrs. Johnston] also correct that conference reports were not routinely prepared during the time period of 1985."[40] Furthermore, the litigants in the Armstrong County Court are barred from viewing their own files at the Domestic Relations Support Office.

As a result of the office's systematic failure to keep notes, in apparent violation of Pennsylvania law, Mary Sue was forced into the position of waiting for a formal hearing to be scheduled—several months down the road. Her financial circumstances were dire, she said, and she had no choice but to concede to her husband's original offer, giving up her rightful share of what she was entitled to under the law.

Judges aren't supposed to commit misconduct or fail in their duties to uphold the laws, but without a better judicial selection process and stronger disciplinary enforcement structures, judges will continue to break the laws they require others to uphold. The commissions' policies provide the means by which corrupt judges hide misconduct: not to investigate judicial decisions as misconduct, to summarily dismiss complaints as legal error without a proper evaluation, and to assume that judges are acting in good faith are policies that protect the guilty and hurt the innocent. The violation of women's rights takes many forms, from the judge's refusing to hear evidence, to altering transcripts, to proclaiming His Honor as "God." The standard-bearers of justice must be held to higher standards. The glaring lack of effective oversight and paper tiger ethics commissions remain the perfect breeding ground for judicial corruption.

∽ 8 ∽

COURTHOUSE
OR CLUBHOUSE?

Aʟʟ ᴏꜰ ᴛʜᴇ written rules and official procedures that lawyers and judges use to formalize the proceedings in divorce court are often superseded by unwritten rules that guide lawyers' and judges' business etiquette with each other and shape the outcomes of litigants' cases in unseen ways. Women are disproportionately hurt by these unwritten rules because they usually favor the spouse with the most power and clout—most often men. Many of these unwritten rules are carried out in informal ways, beyond the scope of public scrutiny. And although they aren't often openly discussed, these rules function to protect, preserve, and reward the interests of lawyers and judges. All of these unwritten rules have another thing in common: they subordinate the client's interest to the private interest and will of the lawyers and judges and those they favor. Seen in this light, all the seeming inconsistencies, irregularities, and casual or brazen inattention to facts and laws and ethics codes are not isolated or accidental incidents, but the symptoms of a thriving subculture in our justice system. This subculture is a world apart from the interest, concerns, and welfare of good faith consumers of our country's justice system.

INTERTWINED INTERESTS

The intertwining of interests—professional, personal, and political—produces the secret courthouse subculture. What the woman sees of the interactions between her lawyer, her husband's lawyer, and the judge amounts to a mere fraction of the time judges, lawyers, and possibly her spouse spend together. Much networking and deal-making takes place outside of the court. Lawyers and judges form strong social and political allegiances as members of the same political clubs, country clubs, and bar associations. In any particular case, the litigant's judge and lawyer may be planning a vacation together or may even be business associates. The litigant has no way of knowing or even suspecting that these associations are subtly or not so subtly influencing the decisions being made in the case. What the client doesn't know can hurt her. Friendships and associations between judges and lawyers naturally make them much more open to each other's opinions and biases than to the client's. She is, after all, a stranger in this club.[1]

But there's another problem as well. Close business and personal associations give lawyers and judges every opportunity to privately discuss cases "off the record." Private communication between a lawyer and judge concerning a current case, that excludes the other side's lawyer, is called *ex parte communication* and is a serious violation of the legal and judicial ethics codes.[2] Ex parte communication can be exceedingly dangerous because the judge can make decisions based on one-sided communication without hearing evidence from the other side.

Inside the legal system, lawyers and judges are also institutionally wed. If, for example, the legal consumer complains about a judge to the judicial review board that is supposed to discipline judges, the person that hears the complaint could very well be the judge's close friend or colleague at the same courthouse. Perhaps they sit on the same committee at their local bar association, or maybe they belong to the same political club. These personal and professional associations create for lawyers and judges a potential conflict of interest in which their allegiances may supersede all other considerations. Sometimes lawyers and judges are more than institutionally wed.

What would you think the chance for justice is for a woman whose husband's lawyer is married to a powerful judge who sits on divorce cases in the same courthouse? Would the husband's lawyer's formidable power and influence be a fair match against the wife's attorneys who must deal routinely with her husband the judge on other cases? Could the wife's lawyer, or any lawyer for that matter, adequately defend the wife's interests under such circumstances? This was exactly Peggy Hammond's situation.

One summer day in 1991, Peggy Hammond, age fifty-two, learned that New York State Supreme Court Justice Kristen Booth Glen, who was presiding over her divorce case, had denied Peggy's lawyers' request to gather more financial information from her husband, despite the fact that information was still missing. With all the respect she felt for her law firm, Peggy said that she was perplexed by what she perceived was her lawyers' passivity in court that day.

Not too long after this disappointing court date, Peggy decided to take a look at her file at her lawyer's office. There, buried in the papers, she found something her lawyers had not told her about, according to testimony she gave in 1993 before the New York State Assembly Standing Committee on the Judiciary. It was a copy of a deed for a house and land in North Carolina that her husband, blues musician John Hammond, purchased, in which he described himself as "unmarried." The deed was dated and signed six months before John left Peggy. The deed was affixed with her husband's first lawyer's name and office address. Peggy testified: "[W]hen I asked my lawyers why didn't you show me this deed, they said, look, we have other cases in front of Judge Wilk and we can't go up against Betty Levinson [her husband's lawyer] because we will lose all the cases for the rest of our clients. . . . They said that to me."

Peggy was referring to the fact that her husband's lawyer was Betty Levinson and Betty Levinson's husband was Justice Elliot Wilk, one of four judges in 1991 who were assigned to handle the bulk of thousands of matrimonial cases that pour through Manhattan's State Supreme Court. According to the law of averages, if Peggy Hammond's lawyers were handling only twenty matrimonial cases, they would have at least five divorce cases pending before Judge Wilk.

Peggy further testified: ". . . I believe there is a conflict of interest here when a matrimonial lawyer is married to a matrimonial judge, and even if she doesn't practice right in front of her husband, obviously there is a very chilling effect going on."

Under the judiciary's conflict of interest rules, Justice Wilk was permitted to sit as a judge in the same court house where his wife, Betty Levinson, practiced matrimonial law (so long as she did not appear before him), according to Gerald Stern, the administrator of the New York State Commission on Judicial Conduct. Peggy was in a tough spot.

After the deed incident, Peggy fired her lawyers and sought out another lawyer. She selected Rosalind Berlow, a newcomer to the field with a practice in Manhattan. Peggy liked the mild-mannered ex-history professor. She had integrity, and didn't seem overly impressed by Levinson's influence, according to Peggy. Berlow dug into the task by asking Levinson for more financial documents from John. She also made a settlement offer that his lawyer rejected.

Then unexpectedly one day, everything changed for Peggy. It happened when she received a phone message from an anonymous court employee that Wilk had been reassigned from the matrimonial bench. A few days later, official word went out that Justice Wilk was tired of handling matrimonials, and had decided not to handle them anymore. For reasons that remain unknown to this day, Peggy's case was subsequently reassigned to another judge and shortly thereafter, a decent settlement was finally offered, which she accepted.

POLITICAL TIES

Another way lawyers and judges can be wed is through political ties that create conflict of interest. Lawyers and judges depend on mutual cooperation and reciprocity to further their political careers. These often combine to compromise a client's interests. For example, in many states, judges are dependent on their bar association's nomination to become judicial candidates to the bench. If judges report lawyers for misconduct—especially established lawyers with connections and credentials in the bar—judges face reprisals from the bars, which can eliminate their chances of being nominated to the bench.

Just like the political action committees that buy the influence of U.S. Senators and Congressmen through campaign contributions, lawyers, who are some of the biggest campaign contributors to judges' campaigns, can buy influence. The lawyer representing your spouse may have just plunked down $250 to the judge on the case for his or her election campaign. It's not illegal; it's not considered an ethical violation; nor is it even considered to give "the appearance of impropriety." In fact, New York lawyers frequently give to both Democratic and Republican parties to grease both sides of the wheel that may spin them forward in their careers. There are laws forbidding judges from knowing the identity of the campaign contributors, but in New York state the contributions are made to a committee rather than directly to the judges, and there is no oversight in place to keep the committee members from telling the judge the identities of his or her benefactors.

A judge's ruling in Kentucky that banished a mother as the custodian of her young son in 1992 was based on a questionable hearing because of the judge's one-sided communications with a lawyer and the apparent influence of campaign contributions, according to Kentucky Court of Appeals Judge Michael O. McDonald in a dissenting opinion. Saying the case was awash in illegalities and irregularities, Judge McDonald strongly dissented from two other judges in the Commonwealth of Kentucky

Court of Appeals who upheld the decision of Kentucky Circuit Court Judge Larry Raikes.

In 1992, Judge Raikes reversed a custody award and placed the child into permanent custody with the father—who is a lawyer—whom the child claimed was sexually abusing him during visits. Judge McDonald later noted, "In the prior trial over custody, Judge Raikes expressed his outward bias against Mrs. Halloran [the Mother], yet with this settled aversion toward her he remained on the case to pass judgement on her in the second trial."

In his dissent, Judge McDonald (who is now retired) criticized Judge Raikes for reversing the custody award on behalf of the ex-husband, saying the change was disruptive to the child. Judge McDonald also criticized Judge Raikes for ignoring the physical evidence showing convincing *anal scarring*, according to a pediatrician's report. Child protective services and a psychiatrist had also backed up the child's claims of sex abuse. Despite this evidence, Raikes ruled that Halloran was a "vindictive and manipulative" woman, who had brainwashed her child into fabricating the allegations. Judge McDonald, however, questioned not the mother's actions but Judge Raikes's actions. McDonald wrote: "He appointed a campaign contributor as guardian ad litem [a lawyer] for [the child] who had a professional relationship with [the father's] good friend and the godfather of [the child]. . . . Mr. Hubbard [the child's appointed lawyer] began advocating for a position on behalf of [the child] prior to having any opportunity to review the record or discuss the case with the experts involved. This is evident from comparing the date of his court appearance to those on his itemized bill. That he had personal knowledge of the case and was lined up with the appellee [the father] from the time of this appointment should have been apparent to the trial court. . . . The court, upon Mr. Hubbard's ex parte urgings, ordered that [the child] be released from Ten Broeck Hospital where he had been placed by his treating physician and further ordered that the child's physician be restrained from having any contact with the child . . . "

Judge McDonald concluded: "We have not only failed the appellant and [the child], but every other custodial parent who may not be able to convince the trial court that his or her child is the victim of abuse."[3] The entire text of Judge McDonald's dissenting opinion appears in Appendix VI.

The American Bar Association's own Commission on Professionalism warned: "On the road to the bench, judicial candidates often become embroiled in reciprocal obligations to political sponsors, as well as to campaign contributors, many of whom are likely to be lawyers who will appear before the judge. Judges may fall under pressure to return these favors. No matter how hard a judge may try to be fair to contributors and non-contributors alike, the necessity and the practicalities of campaign fundraising can only create the public expectation that judges will not be impartial."[4]

The Committee's remark contrasts with the abundant literature on judicial ethics, which is loaded with high-minded rhetoric on the need for judges who are free of influence from special interests. This literature calls again and again for impartiality in judicial decision-making. Yet something is wrong with this picture. As long as the whole nature of a judge's career is political, formed on political allegiances to the right clubs and to power-players who can move their careers forward, how can there be true freedom or independence of the judiciary?

The symbiotic relationship between the lawyer and judge bears directly on how the lawyer acts in court. The lawyer who doesn't accommodate the judge risks alienating the judge not only in this case but in future cases, and the risk is real. Lawyers know that a judge's decisions can make or break a lawyer's career. The blending of political, social, and career interests of lawyers and judges creates a very tight cohesiveness that maintains their power and their support of each other's interests—at the expense of litigants.[5]

THE FIVE UNWRITTEN RULES
#1 *Lawyers and Judges Don't Snitch on Each Other*

Lawyers and judges generally do not report each other for misconduct, even serious misconduct. Like the police officers who embrace a "blue wall of silence," lawyers and judges consider snitching on each other disloyal. The problem is not the lack of written rules about reporting misconduct of lawyers and judges—there are plenty. If a lawyer, say, commits perjury on behalf of his or her client, these rules provide a judge with many options. Depending on the seriousness of the offense, the judge has the authority to (a) impose financial sanctions against a lawyer; (b) report the lawyer to the disciplinary agency that regulates lawyer conduct; or (c) report the lawyer to the District Attorney's office. Likewise, a lawyer can report a judge for an alleged crime or judicial ethics violation. But these options are rarely taken.

In Illinois, a major FBI sting called Operation Greylord led to convictions in 1985 of thirty-one lawyers and eight judges. Professor Deborah Rhode observed: "Not a single member of the bar volunteered evidence of pervasive and systematic corruption. . . ."[6]

Former New York Mayor Ed Koch (a lawyer) and New York State Supreme Court Justice Myriam Altman acknowledged unwritten rule #1. Participating in a lengthy panel discussion entitled "Courts Under Attack" at the 1993 annual meeting of the American Bar Association in New York City, Altman and Koch openly spoke to the political liabilities for judges in reporting lawyer misconduct. Said Altman, "You become an adversary to lawyers, and that's all well and good when you're elected to state's highest court for a fourteen-year term, but what if you're sitting on that court on an acting basis and you have to go before screening panels where you want to be on the good side of the lawyers? Therefore you don't impose sanctions. . . ." Koch added: "In real life when your job is at stake and you know you're coming before a panel of politicians. . . and you know they are going to decide your fate. . . [judges] are going to be very careful not to make enemies."

Besides winking at unethical conduct of lawyers, judges also maintain silence when it comes to economic fraud by wealthy, self-employed men. Often in these cases, judges do not punish lawyers who help men defraud their wives of assets, even in cases where clear evidence of misrepresentation is presented.

#2 Lawyers and Judges Keep Clients from Learning Too Much about Their Own Cases

Divorce court lawyers and judges often insist on secrecy and routinely forbid clients from attending discussions about their cases. They do this by holding conferences in the judge's chambers. The litigant is prohibited from attending the secret proceeding even as a spectator. These chambers conferences are held "off the record" without witnesses and without court stenographers, so the client must rely on her lawyer for any information about what went on.

Laura Preston (name has been changed), whom we met in Chapter 2, learned the hard way that closed-door conferences can result in an enormous sense of helplessness. Her divorce trial had been under way for several days when the judge invited the lawyers into his chambers to try and force a settlement. The conference in the judge's chamber was held "off the record." No court reporter was there to record the conversation. There was no way to prove what really went on.

Laura's attorney claimed in court papers later that Laura's husband's attorney had dictated all of the terms, which were horrible. Under the proposed agreement, Laura lost her right to possession of the house (which, you will recall, she had risked when she moved out to get away from her husband's harassment). She got no alimony even though Jim earned $64,000 a year and Laura had become unemployed after she returned from maternity leave and the office was reorganized. The terms also called for joint custody, with the child to reside with Laura. Under the agreement, Jim would pay child support, but only $600 per month for three months and $550 per month after that, which amounted to 8.59 percent of Jim's income. This departed from federal guidelines, which say a parent should pay about 20 percent of his or her income toward child support.[7]

Laura's attorney protested the terms of the proposed settlement, but, she claimed, the judge and her husband's attorney refused to listen to her. In fact, she wrote in court papers that the judge threatened that if Laura did not go along, Laura would have to pay $30,000 to her husband in addition to his attorney fees. When Laura's attorney emerged from the judge's chambers and told Laura the terms and the threat, Laura still demanded a trial. After several days of trial, however, Laura said her own attorney refused to go on and demanded more money. At that point Laura capitulated and agreed to the one-sided terms first presented at the secret settlement conference.

There is no way to substantiate what was said in the secret conference. Judges don't allow any proof of what they say behind closed doors. After the secret court conference in the judge's chamber, back in the courtroom the judge made sure to say boldly—on the record—that the settlement terms were not coerced and that Laura voluntarily agreed to everything.

Laura appealed the judge's decision to a higher court but lost. The appellate court found no evidence in the judge's stated remarks that indicated any pressure was used on Laura's attorney to settle. But here is the flaw. The higher court judges based their conclusion on a review of the testimony that was recorded in the courtroom. Laura's attorney couldn't prove that the judge threatened her privately in his chambers, since all remarks in the chamber were "off the record" and not recorded, so the appellate judges denied that anything improper had happened. The one-sided agreement stood. Was Laura Preston's lawyer telling the truth? If so, how could Laura prove it, much less do anything about it? Under Rule #2, she had no recourse.[8]

Why the secrecy? Most judges argue that clients are too emotional, so allowing them into these proceedings would inhibit discussions between the judge and attorneys. Then again, conceivably the backroom dealing cuts legal and ethical corners that would give the appearance of impropriety if witnessed by the clients. One lawyer said that if the client were present, the lawyers would have to do "too much pretending." By that he explained that if clients saw signs of friendship between opposing attorneys they might (understandably) suspect that personal camaraderie would get in the way of allegiance to the client.

The problem with not permitting clients into their own conferences is that the lack of scrutiny invites abuse. The client has no way of knowing whether the lawyer's performance was tailored to the case or to the personal or political priorities of the husband's attorney or the judge.

Secrecy in the court is extremely dangerous because information kept from litigants lessens the possibility of their controlling what happens to them. Keeping someone in a confused, uninformed state is an effective way of maintaining power. When a lawyer does not tell his client about significant developments in her case, she cannot know what her options are. The culture of secrecy can understandably make clients feel like outsiders in their own cases, alienated from lawyers and judges.

A SECRET CONFERENCE AT THE JUDGE'S HOME

Heather Saville-Hyde from California was outraged by the secrecy involved between the lawyers and judge on her case. She had just received news from one of her attorneys that she was not permitted to attend a judicial hearing concerning her. The hearing was planned as a strictly private conference between the lawyers and the judge. No one—not her own lawyer, or her adversary's lawyer, or the judge presiding over her case—would disclose the proposed location of the hearing to Heather. She didn't know why it was such a closely guarded secret. She knew no legal reason why she should be barred from the hearing.

Heather was involved with costly spin-off litigation from her divorce. Her ex-husband had sold his share of one of their homes to a stranger, leaving their grown children, who owned the other shares, to deal with the buyer. According to Heather, the day after the sale was made the new part-owner started renovating the property without consulting her children and then charged them for the cost of the construction. To stop this buyer, Heather had to sue. She hired a lawyer on behalf of her children, and the costs of the renovation would be sorted out at a court hearing, as well as lawyer fees. The lawyers were supposed to argue down the costs of the renovation, each on behalf of their clients. Heather felt she had a right to be present.

A few days before the hearing was scheduled, Heather saw the judge at the courthouse and decided to confront him. In a complaint to California's Judicial Council, the ethics arm of the state judiciary that disciplines judges, she recalled what happened: "Judge Brunn said the parties were prohibited from attending," she wrote. "I said that I had heard that, too, but as a litigant I had the right to attend a hearing on my own case and wished to exercise it. . . . Judge Brunn ignored the question and sailed through the doorway."

Heather still believed her rights would be enforced, so she complained to the head judge of the court. He met her complaint with stone-cold indifference. "He informed me he had no control over other judges, his title notwithstanding," she wrote in her complaint to the Judicial Council. After both judges rebuffed her request to attend the hearing, Heather had no choice but to accept what was happening.

The hearing went off as scheduled on July 20, 1987. But the lawyers and Heather's judge could not be found at the courthouse that day. They were meeting in the Berkeley hills—at the judge's private residence. This unusual location for the hearing was at the suggestion of Heather's adversary's lawyer, who had wanted to make the hearing as "convenient" as possible for the judge. The day after the hearing, Heather's lawyer informed Heather that the meeting had taken place.

A judge on public duty using his private home to conduct state business presents a questionable appearance of impropriety. Heather Saville-Hyde hoped that the Judicial Council would not endorse her lawyer's and judge's behavior. She wrote in her complaint: "Do judges have the authority to arbitrarily exclude litigants from hearings on their own case? Should they? What of the fundamental right of litigants to KNOW?" Heather's complaint was dismissed by the Judicial Council on November 24, 1987.

Imagine if all public business were conducted at private homes. What if police officers felt the same way as this judge? "I think I'll just handcuff this prisoner to my bedpost at home and hold him there because I don't really feel like going all the way to the precinct."

Heather didn't know of the other unwritten rule for lawyers and judges that was guiding events at court, Rule #1, that lawyers and judges will protect each other. This secret agreement can take precedence over the written ethics rules, which seem to exist for appearances' sake only.

#3 Judges Blame the Clients for Their Lawyers' Mistakes

Another unwritten rule is that when a litigant's lawyer misadvises her or presents misinformation (deliberately or not), the client is held responsible by the judge for her lawyer's mistakes. If a lawyer, say, misses a deadline, the woman—not the lawyer—will be blamed. If the woman is told to do something illegal on her lawyer's advice, she can get into serious trouble because judges do not consider ignorance an excuse. Clients are held responsible for knowing the law, but lawyers are not held responsible for educating their clients. Why doesn't the judge hold the lawyer accountable for his role in what happened? Because in the civil court system, unless the client sues the attorney for malpractice, lawyers do not have to answer for their own mistakes.

Financially dependent women tend to be particularly affected because they are heavily dependent on their lawyers' advice. For example, in Chadds Ford, Pennsylvania, a woman's attorney advised her to earn money by leaving her home temporarily and renting it out until her divorce trial. She said the attorney then refused to continue with the trial unless she gave him the rent to pay his legal fees. The lawyer then allowed the husband's attorney to persuade the judge to forbid the woman from moving back to the marital residence. They planned for her to keep renting out the home so the husband wouldn't have to pay as much alimony to her. Once she had agreed to the move, it appeared as if she had consented to the situation.

What can a client do? Appeal? Hire a second attorney to take on a malpractice case against the first? It is widely acknowledged in the legal profession that malpractice attorneys won't take a case for under $50,000. Even if the client is affluent, he or she still has to find a lawyer who is willing to sue a colleague. In small towns, where lawyers know each other, this is nearly impossible. Then, if the client manages to secure a new lawyer, she will have to devote the next two, three, or four years of her life to litigation.

#4 Force the Woman to Settle

Some divorce lawyers are known to mislead their female clients into believing they will go to trial and then, at the last minute, force the women into settlements. This manipulative pressuring to settle is sometimes sprung on the woman in the hallway of the court, after the lawyer schedules the court appearance and gets the woman there on the premise that she is going to her own divorce trial. Then, before the trial, the wife's and husband's lawyers and the judge meet for a secret conference in the judge's chamber. The woman and her husband are not allowed to be present. A deal is struck in chamber. The woman's lawyer then presents the proposed settlement to her, saying it's the best he or she can do. If she doesn't agree, the lawyer might well apply psychological pressure, threatening to quit or making new on-the-spot financial demands in order to continue—knowing she has run out of resources. The woman wants a trial precisely so that the judge can weigh the evidence presented and then make a decision based on the facts. But these threats by the attorney usually work and the woman surrenders her better judgment to the lawyer's demand to settle.

One housewife from Rockland County, New York, remembers how her divorce was finalized the day she thought she was going to trial. She was prepared for the trial, but when she got to the courthouse her lawyer pressured her into a settlement that was unfair. Her accountant had confirmed that her husband had undervalued his income by $100,000 and she wanted the evidence to be presented to the judge. She didn't get the chance because her own lawyer pulled her aside and said, according to the woman, that he wanted another $35,000 "right now" to proceed. "There was no way I could instantly produce that much money. I had already given him my last bank account."[9]

She went on to say that she didn't even understand the settlement she was signing because parts of the agreement were handwritten in at the last moment, so hastily that they were illegible.

#5 Judges Do Not Enforce Court Orders

As thousands and thousands of women looking for child support enforcement have sadly learned, judicial orders are often nothing more than worthless pieces of paper because judges deliberately won't enforce court-ordered awards. The reluctance to enforce awards is a pervasive problem in divorce court, with extremely undermining consequences to women and children. Judges have the power to enforce awards but are typically reluctant to force men to honor their support obligations to their families because, under the law, men who don't comply would have to be jailed, and judges are often highly reluctant to jail deadbeat dads.

The federal government mandates that a person's wages can be attached to automatically deduct child support payments, but this system has met with very limited success for three major reasons. First, parents can manipulate the system by moving or by being self-employed and staying off a payroll. Colorado found: "The parents who most need help are dependent on self-employed or transient ex-partners, who are more or less invulnerable to wage assignment."[10] The chief of Florida's child support enforcement program testified that one father looked him straight in the eye and said with a smile, "You can't touch me," because the father was unemployed and living off his girlfriend, who had even provided him with his own car, even though her earnings were only $6 an hour.[11]

Second, delays and bureaucratic roadblocks plague the system. Nevada reports: "Delays have been reported of up to four months merely to get an appointment to file a complaint."[12] It is also particularly tough for agencies to enforce collection when the parent is out of state. Even though there is a tool for interstate enforcement called the Uniform Reciprocal Enforcement of Support Act (URESA), "all states have their own URESA laws. . . [and] many of these laws are out of date and incompatible, which makes interstate child support enforcement relatively ineffective," according to Congress's 1992 Green Book, which looks at federal entitlement programs.[13] One third of the nation's 18 million active child support cases are interstate cases.

A few states have tried other, innovative means for collecting child support within their states, with much success. Maine revokes drivers' licenses of parents who don't pay child support but can afford to. The good news for women and children is that Maine's program is about to be adopted nationwide, as part of bold new legislation initiated by President Bill Clinton. Title Four of the new Work and Responsibility Act, which is expected to be signed into law in early 1996, will create simplified administrative procedures and deliberately remove judges from the process of enforcement and collection, according to David Gray Ross, Deputy Director of the Office of Child Support Enforcement at the U.S. Department of Health and Human Services. "The courts are the most ill-defined people to work on these issues. I can say this as a judge," Ross said. As a former Family Court judge in Prince George's County, Maryland, Ross achieved the nation's second-highest collection rates in any county by making child support enforcement a priority. Nowadays in his new position, he says he spends a lot of his time on the phone trying to get judges to give up their jurisdiction over child support because, as he explains, they don't make child support a priority and have overcrowded calendars.[14]

The failure of judges to order wage assignment (taking the payment out of the man's paycheck) before the federal government mandated it, and the forgiving of arrears were pervasive problems documented all the way back in 1985 in *The Divorce Revolution* by Lenore Weitzman. The Clinton administration's new initiative comes not a moment too soon for women who find that in the current divorce court system, they must become like Sisyphus. The mythical Sisyphus rolled a boulder up a hill, only to have it fall down again once it reached the top, whereupon he had to roll it up the hill again. Women have to return over and over to court, spending more money on more lawyers to collect what they are already owed.

Artelia Court (her real name), a fifty-six-year-old writer/artist in New York, found herself in this dilemma. She was owed more than $100,000 in child support and medical expenses after her husband, Alen MacWeeney, a fashion photographer, refused to honor their separation agreement, violating it periodically over the course of ten years. Artelia unsuccessfully hired a succession of lawyers to collect her child support. Her lawyers' fees accumulated to $65,000 and still she couldn't collect what was due her. She had no more money to pay for legal fees when Justice Walter Schackman, instead of ordering her husband to pay the amounts owed, ordered Artelia to go back to mediation to haggle over the actual amounts owed. Schackman also refused to enforce collection of an earlier judgment he himself had made.

Artelia decided to appeal the judge's decision, but more lawyers' fees were out of the question, so she had to represent herself. She won in the appellate court in 1993. The appellate judges ruled that the original judge had erred in directing Artelia back to mediation, so they sent the case back to lower court and Artelia had to begin all over again to try and collect the ever-increasing debt her husband owed. The court delayed further, bypassing many procedural laws in her case. Then, in December 1995, it appeared as if events were finally turning in her favor after a dozen years of trying, when a judge determined that MacWeeney's "failure to obey this court's order . . . to pay child support arrears and other expenses and post a security with this court, was willful, deliberate, contemptuous and calculated to and actually did impair, impede, and prejudice the rights of remedies of plaintiff (Artelia Court). . . . "

Justice David Saxe ordered MacWeeney to pay his ex-wife $25,000 initially, to be followed by another $25,000, and then in $10,000 installments. However, MacWeeney appealed the decision, which put the bulk of his payment to his ex-wife again on hold.

PART THREE

THE
SOLUTIONS

✒ 9 ✒

FIGHTING BACK

A SMALL NUMBER of divorcing women battered down by the legal system, have declared: "No more." Like Scarlett O'Hara, who raised her fist to the heavens and vowed to God that she would survive, these women found a similar determination that surfaced within themselves during their plights. These women started out like the others. They looked up to their lawyers. They dutifully obeyed the court rules. All the while they waited, waited for justice, as if it were some mystic force that would magically restore them to their rightful property, return their children to them. Many of these women stayed "good girls" and remained passive to the people in charge of their cases, believing that if they were obedient, the system would treat them fairly. Once they accepted this belief they became trapped in the system with no way out. Drawing off the women's estates, the lawyers enriched themselves until nothing was left for the women to claim. Backed into unfair settlements, these women retreated to the margins of poverty. When Peggy Hammond and Joanne Pitulla saw this fate approaching, they were not about to accept it. They fought back—and won.

NO GAG ORDER: PEGGY HAMMOND'S STORY

Peggy Hammond, age fifty-three, is a soft-spoken woman with a statuesque Gibson Girl presence. She appears demure, but underneath she has the quiet, understated power of a Kung Fu master. She had been trapped in limbo by the legal system for three years when she decided to fight back. She bolted to economic safety, defying the lawyers and judges involved in her case, and came out on top.

These days Peggy is known in Manhattan as a preservationist of historic buildings,[1] but her own history includes a fourteen-year marriage to blues musician John Hammond. Being in love with a successful musician may seem romantic and glamorous to fans, but Peggy's life with John was not easy. He was on the road touring 200 to 300 days out of the year, while Peggy stayed home to raise their daughter, which made life lonely for both of them. The couple saw little of each other, and John's life on the road as a musician proved stressful to the marriage. A gradual process of disillusionment set in, Peggy recalled. She would no longer be a "good girl" and began her first extramarital affair. The couple had been married for thirteen years at the time.

By the winter of 1988 John and Peggy were barely talking and the marriage seemed over. So when John asked her to join him on a Caribbean vacation over the Christmas holidays, Peggy was surprised. John was presenting the possibility of reconciling, so she eagerly agreed and even called her mother with the good news. Peggy's mother was so hopeful that she offered to pay for the hotel and to care for Peggy and John's daughter so the couple could be alone together. According to Peggy's mother, John asked her not to buy a return ticket for him, because he might have to return home early to perform on New Year's Eve.

Peggy, John, her mother, their daughter, Amy, and Peggy's brother and his family arrived on St. John's on December 22, 1988. But the next morning, John abruptly announced to Peggy that he was leaving her, and he flew back to New York immediately, using a return ticket he bought on his own. Peggy tried to get the next plane back, but all the airlines were booked until after the holidays. She finally returned to New York on January 5th. When she returned to their Manhattan apartment alone, she was surprised to discover that John had removed from the apartment some of the couple's possessions. "The whole downstairs was empty, and a lot of other things were gone—like our bed, and some paintings that were wedding presents," she recalled. Among the missing items were significant financial records. Additionally, all the bank accounts had been emptied and the utilities turned off, and the insurance was canceled, according to Peggy's testimony before the Judiciary Committee of the New York State Assembly.

Peggy dialed Gustin Reichbach, the family's attorney, to tell him what had happened. For some reason, he didn't return her calls. She needed legal help. Peggy's uncle was Haliburton Fales, one of the lawyers in charge of the disciplinary committee that oversees complaints against lawyers in Manhattan and the Bronx. Fales recommended the pricy, prestigious Manhattan law firm of Milbank, Tweed, Hadley & McCloy. Peggy hired the firm, who found out that John Hammond's divorce lawyer was none other than the family lawyer, Gustin Reichbach.

Peggy was shocked when she found out. "I said how can that be? He was our family lawyer for fifteen years. He's a friend of mine. He wouldn't do that." At first she didn't comprehend why Reichbach was suddenly taking her husband's side. Then she realized why he had not taken her calls. "It began to dawn on me," she said. "Was the abandonment preplanned?" It would take Peggy three years of struggling to locate missing documents to prove that the abandonment was indeed preplanned. She also thought that the family attorney helped to plan it.

Peggy filed for divorce, charging her husband with abandonment, and John countersued with charges of adultery. John's lawyer insisted to Peggy's lawyers that John was "not going to pay support to Peggy" so she could live a "new life with another man."[2] To claim her rightful share of the marital estate, Peggy began to search for the documents that had disappeared from the couple's apartment. In the meantime, the Milbank firm was charging her fees that seemed way out of proportion to what little they were accomplishing. Between January and March 8,

1989, Peggy was billed $6,101.65. The bills show that six people at the firm had charged Peggy for working on the case. They made telephone calls and held conferences with each other, totaling nearly forty hours. There was no indication that anyone at the firm gave Peggy any information on John's financial worth, other than the rudimentary tax returns.

Peggy's mother complained to the firm's attorneys Squire N. Bozorth and Alexander Forger in a letter dated April 19, 1989: "Finally, when you urged her to accept his totally inadequate offer, *before* you had obtained his income tax deductions she realized that she had better change counsel."

Still, Squire Bozorth thought he was giving Peggy a financial break. "As you can see, I have set the bill at an amount substantially below our time charges," he wrote, in a letter dated March 8, 1989. "This is simply in recognition of the fact that the representation did not continue beyond the early stages of our relationship."

Peggy replaced the Milbank firm with another Westchester lawyer whom she discharged after he made sexual advances toward her. Lawyer number three only lasted a couple of months also. "He was negligent but he gave me my retainer back," she said. Next she hired another Manhattan team of lawyers, but her paper-chase to track down assets was mired in delay for the next three years. By 1991, when I met Peggy, she owed $60,000 in legal fees. In the meantime, John's lawyer, Gustin Reichbach, had withdrawn from the case and John hired as his new divorce lawyer Betty Levinson. As you'll recall from Chapter 8, she was very influential as the wife of a powerful judge, Elliot Wilk, one of four judges who handled the bulk of the divorce cases heard in Manhattan's State Supreme Court.

Perhaps it was her sixties idealism or her family's Quaker roots of principled rebellion, or maybe she was just fed up with staying in limbo for so long, but at some point, Peggy Hammond became an emboldened rebel in her divorce. Her rebellion began spontaneously without a plan, springing forth suddenly as true rebellions do, from prolonged pain and pent-up frustration. The triggering incident was a meeting of lawyers and judges at the local bar association that included Justice Glen and Betty Levinson. As Peggy recalls, the judge was telling the audience (and her?) that men often don't have as much in assets as their wives claim. Peggy stood up and blurted out to the room full of lawyers: "I have been excluded from two [court] conferences, my character has been slandered and I couldn't even hear what the character assassination was, and I felt that way of handling a matrimonial case was a travesty of justice." She got even madder when she saw Levinson and Glen climb into a cab together after the event ended.

Her revolt was only beginning. On July 14, 1992, Peggy and a group of divorced-women-turned-activists headed to 60 Centre Street, to complain to Judge Wilk's supervisor. They were there to see the administrator of divorce court, Judge Stanley Ostrau. A large man with a nervous air, Ostrau's behavior at the meeting suggested that he was inviting potential trouble makers in only to size them up. His suspicion of the women boiled up in comments like: "What lawyer sent you here?" and "The judge you are complaining about has a fine reputation." It seemed like a scene from the Wizard of Oz, as if at any moment Ostrau were going to send Peggy out to bring back Betty Levinson's broomstick.

After the meeting ended, Peggy kept waiting for justice. She was developing a new career as a representative in the decorative ironworks business, and her earnings were inconsistent and low. She knew she was going against all the odds in the court system. Sometimes she would get discouraged. "What am I going to do?" she despaired. "Become a cashier at the age of fifty and work for $4.60 an hour?" That would be just fine with the court, she thought.

Luckily, Peggy found a new, more aggressive lawyer and got assigned a new judge who was willing to look into her husband's assets after all this time. But when a decent settlement was finally offered, there was a catch.

Betty Levinson said John would only go along on the condition that Peggy Hammond sign a gag order not to discuss the case in public. Peggy refused. At the next court date, Levinson passed a yellow legal pad to Peggy's lawyer, Rosalind Berlow. It was the handwritten text of the gag order. Roz handed it over to Peggy with a note that said to sign the gag order. On impulse, Peggy ripped the note in half and threw it on the floor. As the pieces floated to the courthouse floor, Roz asked her to pick it up. "I will not pick it up," Peggy insisted. Roz gathered up the torn note. Today, Peggy still has the pieces of that note as a remembrance of the day she won her rights in court. She was divorced a week after the incident, and a gag order was not included in the agreement.

For Peggy Hammond, there was only one thing to do—fight back. This type of revolt requires a tremendous inner courage and a lot of raw nerve. Challenging the system is not without serious risks. Few people know what power judges wield. Any abusive judge can easily retaliate by taking away a woman's home, children, credit, all with the stroke of a pen. Sometimes, though, there is no choice but to take the risk. Peggy also complained to the First Judicial Department Disciplinary Committee that Gustin Reichbach had violated the ethics code by representing her husband as a divorce client after Reichbach had obtained prior confidential knowledge about Peggy, as the family attorney. Reichbach maintained that he was trying to facilitate the divorce, and he withdrew as John Hammond's attorney as soon as it became clear that acrimonious litigation was inevitable. The complaint was dismissed without explanation by the Disciplinary Committee. Subsequently Peggy sued Reichbach for malpractice and fraud. She lost after a judge decided that Peggy failed to show that she had an attorney-client relationshp with Reichbach. Peggy remains undaunted and was appealing the decision as of December 1995.

PAY ME $10,000 AND DON'T ASK WHY

One of the risks of fighting back is having to face strong-arm tactics by lawyers and judges who have at their disposal legal machinery that can be used as a weapon. Joanne Pitulla's prominent lawyer used many of the devices and more when all she wanted was an itemized bill, but after a courageous thirteen-year court battle she proved he had misstated his fees and got restitution.

Joanne Pitulla, a pretty, forty-five-year-old housewife and mother of three, went to her divorce lawyer's office in May 1981, unbeknownst to her husband. She felt guilty but that didn't stop her. She rushed nervously past the crowds toward LaSalle Street, her heart pounding with every step. She was trying to summon courage—more than anything else, she would need courage.

Joanne's twenty-three-year marriage had been dying for some time and there was nothing she could do about it. Her husband, a self-employed horticultural broker, controlled all the money. He would dole out a weekly allowance to her. During the early years of the marriage when she worked as an English teacher, she had to turn over her paychecks to him. But his need to control all the financial decision-making was only one example of the ways he made her feel like a child. What she wanted was to feel like an equal partner in the marriage. When she tried to tell him how she felt about his need to dominate and control, he said to her, "Take it or leave it. That's the way I am." So, she decided to leave it. Now what she needed most was a strong, expert lawyer to defend her financial rights. Her uncle, a lawyer, recommended a firm that specialized in matrimonial law.

She took a deep breath, entered One North LaSalle Street, and ascended to the sixth floor. A trim, well-dressed lawyer named Richard Rinella beckoned her into his office. His confident manner announced success. Less than one hour later, she emerged feeling as if she had made the right decision in choosing Rinella to represent her.

Richard Rinella's family history and credentials were impressive. His father, Samuel, and his mother, Katherine, had established the firm in 1940, making it one of the oldest in the nation concentrating in domestic relations law. Among lawyers, Richard

Rinella, then forty-one, and his older brother, Bernard, then forty-four, were part of Chicago's elite inner circle. Their father had helped found the American Academy of Matrimonial Lawyers, an exclusive membership group of 1,200 divorce lawyers throughout the country. Richard was on the Illinois Chapter Academy's board of governors. Their mother's history was equally impressive: she was the daughter of the first Italian-American judge in Chicago. The Rinella sons had contacts, prestige, and influence—which counts heavily with judges. Joanne needed a competent lawyer, and Richard came across with a lot of confidence. She felt she was in good hands.

Joanne didn't ask Richard why, when he took her case, she didn't have to sign any written agreement, or why he didn't disclose his hourly rates. Joanne was under the impression that the relationship between a lawyer and client was a matter of trust. The next day she mailed him the $1,500 retainer he had asked for to get started on the case.

Rinella filed dissolution papers for the Pitulla marriage, Joanne's husband got a lawyer, and then the waiting began. Three months passed, while tensions increased. Joanne was unemployed and had decided to go to law school to become a lawyer and support herself. During this time Joanne and her husband were living under the same roof. She asked him to leave, so she could remain at home with their fifteen-year-old daughter, but he refused. She couldn't stay in the house much longer due to the pressure of their strained relationship, and she had no funds to live elsewhere since he controlled all the money.

In late August Joanne received a copy of the settlement agreement in the mail. Joanne was shocked when she saw an $8,500 fee for Rinella's legal services inserted into the terms of the settlement agreement. This $8,500 fee was on top of the $1,500 she had already paid him as a retainer. She asked him to send her an itemized bill; in response he told her he'd explain everything later at the court hearing, and no bill was sent.

Joanne was desperate for her divorce and extremely upset.

She needed money to pay for law school tuition and to live, so she agreed to the terms, not knowing if they were in her best interests. She said she tried several times to find out details, but Rinella always had a vague response to her questions.

The day of the "prove-up" (where husband and wife are asked if they agree to the terms of the settlement) came in September 1981. Before the proceeding began, Rinella told her to agree to everything in the settlement and she did. This included the $10,000 provision for his fees. Then, in the hall outside the courtroom, he told her that he would not enter divorce decree until she paid him the $8,500. Joanne Pitulla felt as if she'd been mugged in the hallway of the court by her own lawyer. She was desperate to get on with her life. What could she do?

On September 30th, as soon as she received the funds from the settlement, Joanne sent Rinella a check for his fees. On October 14th, after the check cleared, Rinella recorded her divorce decree in court. Afterward, Joanne again asked him for an itemized bill, but he did not send one. Lawyers are only supposed to charge for the time they actually work on a case, but without any detailed account of the work he had performed, Joanne didn't know if Rinella had earned his fees or not.

When she realized the bill would never arrive, she filed a complaint with the Chicago Bar Association Committee on Professional Fees, but after debating the case for eight months they told her they were powerless to act since Mr. Rinella refused to arbitrate. The voluntary organization didn't have the authority to pursue an investigation. With those doors closed, she was forced to take her own former lawyer to court. Fast-forward to three years later, June 1984. Joanne was still trying to get an itemized bill from Richard Rinella, but Rinella's lawyer and the judge twisted it into a harassment proceeding against her.

Judge John Reynolds, who would later be convicted in the FBI Greylord sting, presided over the hearing and decided to fine Joanne $3,500 as a sanction for filing the suit, agreeing with

Rinella and his lawyer, Leonard Timpone, that Joanne's petition was fake and without reasonable cause.

Another person might have thrown in the towel at this point, but Joanne refused to accept it. She appealed, and the higher court said she was right—she was entitled to an itemized bill. Their decision stated: "We believe that in every contract for hire between an attorney and his client, there is implied in the contract the client's right to always know what the attorney did or does, and how much time he took to do it." The appellate court also reversed the $3,500 sanction against her, saying "the trial court abused its discretion in imposing sanctions against Pitulla, and. . . erred in entering the judgment against her for $3,500."[3] The appellate court sent her back to the lower court to determine the fairness of the fee.

As the Pitulla case wound its way through the courts, Richard Rinella and his brother presented themselves wonderfully to the press. "Rinellas Upholding a Family Tradition" said a glowing feature article that appeared in the *Chicago Daily Law Bulletin* in 1986. Richard and his brother, Bernard, in a front-page photo, were the picture of integrity and polish.

"People come to us because we're recognized as one of the leaders in the field," Bernard was quoted as saying. "If the people you've represented over the years are satisfied with the results you've got, they're going to toot your horn and be good publicity for you. The vast majority of our business comes from satisfied clients who have talked to their friends."[4]

A very different picture of Richard emerged, however, in the ensuing hearings over the reasonableness of his fee demands in the Pitulla divorce.

Fast-forward to February 23, 1988.

At the rehearing ordered by the appellate court, Circuit Judge Donna L. Cervini called for a recess in the proceedings, and Joanne Pitulla was about to leave the courtroom to go to the bathroom, when Richard Rinella stepped in front of her, blocking her exit. According to Joanne, he growled, "I'm going to get you—you bitch." Joanne backed up, crying out, "He threatened me." At that point her lawyer moved forward to help her. Rinella pushed past her and then allegedly said to her lawyer, Andrew Maxwell, "I'm going to get your license, Maxwell." Rinella looked furious and a court deputy intervened. When the judge returned to the bench, Pitulla and her lawyer told her how they had been abused by Rinella, but the judge commented that she had not been present to witness it.

"I cannot erase the image of Richard Rinella stepping swiftly in front of me, stopping me in my tracks, with contorted face only inches from mine, baring his teeth and telling me he was going to 'get' me," Joanne Pitulla wrote in a complaint to the Attorney Registration and Disciplinary Commission.

When Joanne got home the night of the hearing, she played back a message on her answering machine. A guttural masculine voice, filled with venom, snarled, "You bitch!" but Joanne couldn't identify the voice, and she turned off the machine in fear. "All I wanted to do was to put it out of my mind because I had to return to court the next day," Joanne wrote in a letter to the lawyer for the commission that regulates lawyer conduct.[5]

Joanne stayed strong.

As for Pitulla's case, on June 30, 1988, Circuit Judge Donna L. Cervini ruled that Rinella's $10,000 fee was unreasonable and ordered him to immediately refund $6,270 to her.

The legal action wasn't over, though. Joanne had also taken the legal step of seeking financial sanctions against her former attorney, contending that he presented false facts by stating higher rates to the court than the rates he actually charged when he represented her in 1981.

On January 31, 1989, another incident occurred in Judge Cervini's court. This time Rinella allegedly called Pitulla a bitch in front of the judge.

"Your Honor, on the record I would like to ask you to tell Mr. Rinella to show a little courtesy to Ms. Pitulla and counsel," Joanne's attorney, Andrew Maxwell, protested to the judge. "I don't think I need to hear the kind of profanity I hear on a daily basis. The type of things I have heard this morning, I wouldn't want my mother to hear."

> Judge Cervini: Mr. Rinella, I believe I heard you swear. I am not exactly sure what you said, but I don't appreciate it in this courtroom.
> Mr. Rinella: No, I will swear to him outside the courtroom.
> Judge Cervini: No, you won't!
> Mr. Maxwell: It has been inside and outside.
> Ms. Pitulla: On the record, I heard Mr. Rinella call me a bitch right now and I believe everyone else in the courtroom heard him also, including Your Honor.

Despite this abuse, Joanne still did not wither. At the hearing, evidence was shown determining that Richard had indeed misstated his hourly rates. He stated his hourly rates at $175 to $200 but Joanne Pitulla and her lawyer, in court papers, had shown that in 1981 when he represented her, the rates were really $100 to $125. Still, the judge denied Joanne's motion for sanctions against Richard and court costs. But Joanne appealed and won again. The appellate court upheld the lower courts' decision on the refund to Joanne, but it reversed Judge Cervini on the sanctions issue, saying the judge should have imposed financial sanctions against Richard Rinella for what it cost Pitulla to refute his false fee claim.[6] The appellate court sent the case back to Judge Cervini's court again and the judge made the sanctions ruling, awarding Joanne $19,496 plus interest on the $6,270 that Joanne had overpaid. Rinella appealed. In 1993, the Illinois State Supreme Court, the state's highest court, denied his appeal, in effect saying the lower court was right.

Joanne's case set a new precedent in Illinois, and strengthened existing laws by stating explicitly that lawyers are required to present itemized bills to their clients.

By the time it was over, the battle had cost Joanne more than $45,000 in legal fees, but the financial strain was not the only toll she had to pay. In 1989 at the Illinois Gender Bias conference, Joanne testified: "I did not expect and do not deserve to be cursed and threatened in court. I did not expect to have my present attorney also abused and threatened. I did not expect to be attacked as a woman and a mother. . . . I do not believe that I have to endure such conduct in silence."[7, 8]

Joanne Pitulla could have let her personal experience with her divorce lawyer destroy her, but instead she developed an intense interest in improving the legal system. After she obtained her law degree, Joanne became an ethics lawyer. She now gives talks and writes articles about improving lawyer ethics. She says she is glad to finally put her ordeal with Richard Rinella behind her. She now fights to improve the system that hurt her and speaks out for the rights of consumers in divorce.

As for her adversaries, Judge John F. Reynolds's career came to an abrupt halt in 1985 when he was charged with racketeering and extortion, convicted, and sent to prison, in Chicago's famous Greylord indictments.

Richard Rinella's lawyer, Leonard Timpone, was suspended from practicing law for three years after the Illinois Attorney Registration and Disciplinary Commission (ARDC) found him guilty of mishandling his client's funds.[9]

And in the end, Richard Rinella finally got himself into serious trouble with the disciplinary authorities, the ARDC, for having made false statements to the ARDC about having sex with a client. He was eventually charged and found guilty of sexual misconduct involving three clients at the Rinella firm. According to the Report and Recommendation of the ARDC Hearing Board, Rinella lied under oath and was charged with deceit, dishonesty, and misrepresentation. He was also charged with failure to represent a client with undivided fidelity and conduct which tends to defeat the administration of justice or bring the courts and legal profession into disrepute (involving two more allegations of sexual misconduct).

The ARDC recommended that his license be suspended for three years and his reinstatement to the bar be conditioned on the grounds that he rehabilitate himself before he be allowed to practice divorce law again. The ARDC recommendation must be submitted to the Illinois Supreme Court, which will make the final determination on whether Rinella should be suspended. Rinella is currently appealing the ARDC decision, and meanwhile is continuing to practice law.

Peggy Hammond and Joanne Pitulla both possessed a strong sense of inner determination and had the perseverance to fight for their rights, despite the opposition of authority figures who told them they were wrong. More women will be learning these lessons of self-empowerment the hard way, if the divorce industry continues to resist fundamental reform.

✦ 10 ✦

THE FUTURE
OF DIVORCE

As the stories in the earlier chapters demonstrate, the lack of accountability on the part of judges and lawyers can and does deeply and adversely affect women's and children's lives. So does the glaring imbalance of power between consumers and lawyers; the lack of judicial training and low performance standards; the absence of a unified, standardized approach to deciphering complex cases; and the obsolete, arcane procedures that encourage delay and obstruction. All of these dangerous conditions have created a potential minefield for the woman, and in some cases the man, who embarks on divorce. But what to do about it? How can this leviathan be challenged? Who is fighting back?

There are many examples of courageous women who have individually managed to change case law, changes that have made the system respond more fairly to others. As a result of Joanne Pitulla's court battle with her lawyer (described in the last chapter) a new law in Illinois now requires lawyers to itemize their billing. And remember Jeanette Helmbrecht, the Wisconsin mother of five, from Chapter 4? Jeanette represented herself in court after she charged her former divorce attorney with malpractice for negligence in the way he handled her divorce. The jury awarded Jeanette $250,000 in damages against her former attorney. On appeal, the case went all the way to the Wisconsin Supreme Court, which ruled that her attorney was negligent for not adequately defending her financial interests under the law. The court awarded Jeanette additional recompense in the form of interest on her award from the date of the original jury decision, bringing her total award to $331,000.[1] But the ultimate success in this case should not obscure the fact that tackling the law through an individual appeal is a hard, lonely, uphill road, financially and emotionally.

Lone lawyers and legislators working hard for reform face the same obstacles the individual woman does. Special interests put up stone walls in their path, causing stalemates and inertia. After several women in Pennsylvania made allegations of corruption in their cases, some courageous legislators tried to help, without success. On August 28, 1990, Pennsylvania State Representative Timothy L. Pesci wrote to State Senator Roxanne H. Jones asking for her support on a bill he wanted to introduce to investigate the injustices. His letter stated in part: "I am sure you are aware of the extensive documentation of the injustices of domestic relations judicial proceedings. People are being victimized by the entity which is intended to help them seek justice." Two years later, when the problems remained pervasive, Representative George Saurman wrote to a top judge in Pennsylvania: "I am repeatedly amazed and dismayed by the domestic relations horror stories that I hear all over the commonwealth. . . . One can overlook an occasional report of inaction and financial rape by the system, but when it repeats itself over and over again, there must be some explanation."[2] A proposal for reform was made in the Pennsylvania state legislature, but the sponsors couldn't get the legislation out of committee for a vote on the floor.

These reformers face ostracism or worse by the profession and have their own horror stories to tell. Ask Raymond Trombadore, a distinguished lawyer with a long list of credentials as past president of the New Jersey State Bar Association and chairman of the Disciplinary Review Board for the Supreme Court of New Jersey. Perhaps he is best known for chairing the famous McKay Commission investigation into improving methods of lawyer discipline, which was presented to the American Bar Association in 1991. But when Mr. Trombadore tried to advance reforms for divorce lawyers, he said he was heckled by the matrimonial section of the bar. He recalled the disastrous meeting: "They pilloried me. They said, 'Who sent you here?'" On another occasion, his peers refused to renominate him as a member of the House of Delegates of the American Bar Association—in retaliation for his desire to improve the profession, he said.[3]

Trombadore continues to fight for what he believes is right, but the system he is up against retains much power and tight control over policies that affect the public. To reiterate, lawyers and judges who engage in illegal or morally indefensible practices do not function in a vacuum. They are part of a tightly cohesive group, bonded together by their trade organizations, the local, state, and federal bar associations. While there are a few strong individuals within the profession, like Trombadore, the rank and file membership has a self-serving interest in maintaining the status quo. It is clear to activists and some experts within the legal system that change cannot come from within. When well-meaning critics within the bar try to improve safeguards for consumers, they too are disassociated from the club.

In 1984, the American Bar Association established a Commission on Professionalism, at the recommendation of Supreme Court Chief Justice Warren E. Burger, who was concerned that the bar might be moving away from principles of professionalism. In 1986, the Commission on Professionalism released its findings, noting: "We have attempted to be both honest and forthright, even when conclusions reached reflect poorly on the profession."[4] In that spirit they made the following recommendations:

1. Preserve and develop within the profession integrity, competence, fairness, independence, courage and a devotion to the public interest.
2. Resolve to abide by higher standards of conduct than the minimum required by the Code of Professional Responsibility and the Model Rules of Professional Conduct.
3. Resist the temptation to make the acquisition of wealth a primary goal of law practice.
4. Encourage innovative methods which simplify and make less expensive the rendering of legal services.

What were the results of the report? The ABA refused to officially adopt it. The cover of the report bears a written disclaimer: "The views expressed are those of the Commission on Professionalism. They have not been approved by the House of Delegates or the Board of Governors, and, accordingly, should not be construed as representing the policy of the Association."

Organizations outside of the legal/judicial system have a better chance at achieving reform, and yet, strangely enough, the most obvious sources of help have looked the other way. Woman's advocacy groups, the most likely lobbyists, have not taken a concerted interest in challenging the legal system on behalf of divorcing women. Part of the reason, I am told by academics, is that many professional women don't identify with or sympathize with dependent women. Most feminists advocate that women break free of financial dependency on men. Feminists and professional women therefore have been less than zealous in supporting mothers' rights and can't relate to what they perceive as women fighting for their share of their husbands' earnings. There may even be an unconscious resentment on the part of some feminists who may think that full-time homemakers and mothers deserve what they get for putting themselves in a dependent position.

What these professionally successful women fail to realize, however, is that no matter how strong their belief in independence, they can wind up in the same boat as their "dependent" counterparts. For example, a professional woman working in an elite career like medicine or law can lose custody of her children simply because the judge doesn't believe the woman should work so many hours to hold down a career. If a man works long hours to earn more money, the judge may consider him "economically superior" to his wife, a decided advantage if he decides to battle his wife for custody of the children. As we have seen in previous chapters, the double standard operates on many levels, crossing socioeconomic boundaries. If a woman is financially successful, her lawyer or the mediator may pressure her to give her husband a disproportionately large share of her earnings, in order to settle quickly. Her husband may go after custody not because he genuinely desires the children but to make her pay child support. Professional career women are just as likely to experience injustice as are full-time mothers and homemakers.

One would think the American Civil Liberties Union would be active in defending women's rights to due process. Yet reformers I have interviewed who have tried to contract the ACLU say they have met with indifference. Elizabeth Bennett, a family law attorney in Pennsylvania, who served on the board of the ACLU in her state for fifteen years, said she resigned in despair over the organization's lack of commitment to civil liberties issues affecting women and children. According to Bennett and others, the ACLU has not offered solutions for mothers and their children. Divorcing women are apparently so marginalized in our society that they do not receive the status of "underdog" that would prompt help from civil rights lawyers who take an interest in cutting-edge issues. The inequitable treatment of women in court and abuses at the hands of their divorce lawyers and judges have not even been recognized, in many cases, let alone prioritized along political lines. Without the momentum of civic groups advocating for reform, and given the power structure that gives rise to abuse, the job is left to the victims, themselves, to lobby on their own behalf. Yet women who have been victimized are obviously in the worst position to lobby for themselves.

The most vulnerable groups in our society stay disenfranchised precisely because they are the least likely to have the time or resources to help themselves. Women under siege in the court system are usually too overwhelmed by their cases to think of organizing themselves into an effective lobby. Organizing a march or starting a letter-writing campaign is not practical for the woman who is worried that she is going to lose custody of her children because her lawyer walked out on her for nonpayment of an inflated bill. As Professor Geoffrey Hazard, Jr., co-author of *The Law and Ethics of Lawyering*, points out, it's not that lawyers have so much power, but that women have none: "They [lawyers] have some power and influence in a situation in which there is no concerted and sustainable political pressure to make the situation change. You don't have to have very much power if nobody else has very much power. Divorcées are not an organized interest group."[5]

This situation, in which victims have absolutely no power base, has resulted in some very desperate actions by individuals. For example, public attention to judicial corruption was heightened when a woman in Harris County, Texas, chained herself to a pillar in front of the Harris County Law Center to protest corruption in the Harris Family Court. She was urging then Texas Governor Ann Richards to investigate cases in which judges have ordered children to live with their alleged rapists. Law officers broke the chain on the evening of December 7, 1992, but the woman maintained her vigil and went on a hunger strike. Thirty-four days later, when the protester was taken to the hospital on the verge of collapse, another woman took her place on the courthouse steps.[6] A Virginia woman who lost custody of her child due to intimidation and "dirty tricks" tactics by the child's father, tattooed the docket number of the case and the judge's name into her forearm. She will die with the memory of her case and consequent loss of her child engraved on her body.

History teaches that civil protest, not the legal or judicial institutions, pushes reform—from the bloody labor strikes of the thirties to the civil rights marches of the sixties. As lawyer Elizabeth Bennett sees it, "Courthouses can be picketed; court policies can be challenged, as can the policies of corporations like General Motors or Exxon. Citizen oversight and involvement in the system is crucial to the successful enforcement of legislative reforms in the courts."[7] Therefore, as Bennett and many other activists see the situation, it is incumbent on women to take the fight up themselves.

Sometimes it does not even take that many to achieve major reform, or miracles, for that matter. Historically speaking, it seems as if change results from a few strong individuals agitating and protesting to get things done. Consider this: In the 1840s, it took three women in New York actively agitating over an eight-year period to get the state legislature to consider a law that would allow married women to own property.

According to author Norma Basch, "Between 1840 and 1848 a number of bills introduced by highly competent legislators failed to emerge from judiciary committees to the voting stage. Occasional reports from those committees intimated that there was little point in wasting the Legislature's time on a bill that had no chance of passage." Basch credits three New York women—Ernestine Rose, Paulina Wright Davis, and Elizabeth Cady Stanton—with persisting in lobbying efforts until the bill finally succeeded.[8] It would take eighty years more, however, for women to get the right to vote.

In looking at reforms, there are really two movements to track: the drive to improve the accountability of lawyers and judges in the divorce court system and the struggle to improve domestic relations laws for women and children. Unfortunately, both are splintered without a national focus.

REFORMING THE LEGAL SYSTEM

As for the first reform, the action groups working to stop unethical, illegal practices by lawyers and judges consist of dozens of tiny, shoestring-budgeted organizations across the country. Some of these organizations are run by women, others by men. In many instances, gender differences are being put aside in a call to unify against abusive lawyers and judges. In Pennsylvania, reformers recently began publishing a little newsletter called *Legal Focus*. It boldly states: "We intend to have law enacted to hold judges and lawyers fully accountable for their actions and to make them personally responsible for their *legal errors* in the same way that litigants have paid for them time and time again. . . ."[9] In Chicago, the grassroots organization Citizens for Legal Responsibility informs its readers: "Election time is coming. Remember, VOTE NO FOR LAWYERS."

In Texas, the aggressive little newsletter *Anti-Shyster* is published by Alfred Adask, who suffered enormously both financially and emotionally in his divorce. *Anti-Shyster* takes a militant approach, proclaiming: "Lawyers know what's happening in our courts. They know of the corruption, crime and injustice in the legal system. They know the deeds, they know the names. But they just watch, saying nothing. Most argue they're 'good' because they 'didn't (personally) do anything bad.' But they're wrong. . . . Within the judicial arena, lawyers are more than spectators, more than individuals merely privileged to act on issues of right and wrong—lawyers are legally obligated, by law, to 'act' to uphold the law, and the 'good' that presumably underlies the law."[10]

Since the late 1980s, Monica Getz has been waging a war against divorce court injustice with her self-help organization the National Coalition for Family Justice, Inc., located in Irvington-on-Hudson, New York. She formed the organization following the extended litigation involved in her divorce from her late husband, musician Stan Getz. The Coalition provides support and information to women and men who have been hurt by the divorce court system. Coalition volunteers man phone lines, informing citizens in divorce nationwide of their legal rights. Among the issues Monica Getz has lobbied for is a citizen group to monitor the selection of judges and the lawyer disciplinary system.

Monica Getz, a dedicated reformer, offers a shining example of how to work both with the system and outside of the system to achieve real reform. For example, in the late 1980s when New York judicial officials wouldn't respond to women's complaints of being financially abused by their lawyers, Monica Getz did not give up but tried another, more unusual approach, which worked and ultimately led to serious reforms. She and a group of women took their complaints to the New York City Department of Consumer Affairs, headed by then-Commissioner Mark Green, who rightfully perceived the financial relationship between consumers and their attorneys as a consumer issue. If Monica Getz had not asked for help, there would have been no Consumer Affairs *Women in Divorce* report, no public hearings, and no reforms.

Another example of how Getz helps women and simultaneously makes an impact on the judicial system occurred when she intervened on behalf of one of the Coalition members and two of her children, who were in an emergency because of a judge who was out of touch with the severe problems women and children face in divorce proceedings. The woman and her children had been forced out of their New York home in the middle of winter, 1995, because they were without heat. The woman's husband—a multimillionaire businessman—refused to honor a judge's court order to hire a plumber to fix the heating system in the couple's townhouse. To make matters worse, the pipes had burst and flooded the home, making it entirely uninhabitable. Not knowing what else to do, the woman and her two children went to a hotel. There, the woman's young daughter came down with a bad fever and the flu, and they were all stranded together in the hotel room.

The judge sitting on this case knew about the woman's emergency, but he refused to take any action to force her husband to comply with the order to restore the heat and fix the pipes. Monica Getz heard what had happened, got in her car, and made the forty-mile trip to the Manhattan courthouse where the judge presides. She didn't have an appointment, but she asked for a meeting with the judge. The judge agreed to meet with her, and without discussing any other aspects of the case except the immediate plight of the children, Getz described the situation. A few hours afterward, the emergency was over. After hearing from the judge, both sides' lawyers showed up at the woman's flooded house and made arrangements for the necessary repairs. The woman and her children were able to move back to their home the following day.

Getz says she sees the same problems in other cases: "The judges are just out of touch with the women's and children's reality. They know at the end of the case there will be a decision. That's all they are concerned about. What happens to the family in the meantime?"

Most of these organizations encourage the use of court watching, open disciplinary proceedings for lawyers and judges, and more separation of powers between the legislatures and judiciaries, to counteract the pressures of lawyer influence. The organizations' addresses and phone numbers are included in Appendix II.

These organizations know that citizen involvement is the only way to shift the power from the few to the many. Still, new obstacles to improving the situation for divorcing women appear on the horizon.

MEDIATION

The mediation movement is a growing trend that threatens to further erode women's power in divorce court. Mediation—the use of a neutral third party to negotiate a resolution between the spouses—is touted as a way of circumventing expensive and painful litigation. But many researchers say it can be used as a political tool to keep women from exercising their legal rights in court. The problem with mediation is that the less financially powerful spouse—usually the woman—is without benefit of information or access to the protections of the court. University of California at Davis law professor Carol S. Bruch told investigators in the California Supreme Court Gender Bias Task Force: "The [mediation] process occurs in private, without the presence of attorneys or court reporters, and without access to appellate reviews. Even a skilled mediator cannot compensate for the sharp disparities in power and sophistication that often exist between divorcing spouses."[11]

While most experts agree that mediation can be a wonderful tool when both spouses are cooperative, cooperation is utterly meaningless if the woman is ill-informed of her legal rights and does not know to what she is agreeing. "The goal of mediation is to get an agreement. That doesn't necessarily mean a fair agreement," explained Lillian Kozak, former chair of the New York NOW Domestic Relations Law Task force.[12] The problem in all forms of mediation is that the financially weaker party, usually the women in divorce, gives up rights more easily because the weaker spouse is pressured to arrive at a settlement to resolve the dispute. Moreover, mediation is unregulated in some states, with no training or standards required. There are no requirements that the mediator understand the law and no minimum qualifications. In New York, for example, a paperhanger can hang out a shingle as a mediator. No one is required to inform the weaker party, usually the woman, of her rights. Another problem in mediation, according to the way the system is being set up in the courts, is that a woman also loses rights to confidentiality, another dangerous invitation to discrimination. What does this mean exactly? It means that if she does not go along, because she believes the agreement is unfair, she will be seen as "uncooperative" by the judge, who will punish her by wrenching custody or property rights. The harm of mandatory mediation was voiced by New York State Supreme Court Justice Phyllis Gangel-Jacob, who was quoted as saying: "Are we really suggesting that this important area of law and the family be reduced to a make-do disorganized, unregulated, improvised mediation without lawyers, without judges, without examinations or licensing, without standards, without protection, without codes of ethics, without disciplinary forums, without responsibility, without confidentiality, all in the name of settlement?"[13]

The effects of mandatory mediation reach far beyond the implications for women. To remove certain areas of law from court has much deeper political implications than is readily apparent on the surface of the issue. Mediated agreements, which block access to the courts, curtail the rights of citizens on several fronts. As anthropologist Laura Nader of the University of Berkeley warned: "Mandatory ADR [alternative dispute resolution] is an attempt to destroy the civil-rights, women's consumer, and environmental movements."[14] For divorcing women, the challenge remains to improve the judicial system, not to be removed from it altogether.

THE MEN'S RIGHTS MOVEMENT

The influence of men's rights groups as a lobby on the elite factions of lawyer associations (male dominated) and legislatures (also heavily composed of male lawyers) is having a direct effect on public policy and divorcing women's rights. The result is that any gains for divorcing women's rights are likely to be met with a growing backlash from the men's rights movement. Observers note that the men's rights movement is becoming stronger and more organized and is influencing legislation that is destructive to the interests of divorcing mothers and their children. The issues they are concerned with involve money, control, and power, according to some people who have dealt with them. For example, Tom Mato, counsel for Maine's Child Support Enforcement Division of the Department of Human Services, said his agency experienced intense lobbying by men's rights groups to block Maine's program, established in 1993, of revoking driving licenses of people who do not comply with child support orders. "They're [the men's rights movement] organized as a group, and they are trying to advance their agenda. We think most of them [men] have the ability to pay," Mato said.[15]

As the government takes more aggressive means to collect child support, women are likely to experience an increase in opposition from men's rights organizations, just as Mr. Mato described. But women can also expect to see an increase in custody battles brought on by men who are instructed by their lawyers to obtain custody in order to avoid child support payments. In Louisiana, a law was introduced in 1995, reportedly by a legislator representing a male constituent, that would have forced divorced women to account for every penny they spend on child support. If they were found to spend child support payments on themselves, the women would be punished by losing custody. Luckily, this bill didn't pass. A divorced-woman-turned-women's-rights-activist, Lynn Gillin, and Katherine Spaht, a law professor at the Louisiana State University, did ad hoc lobbying to prevent another bill from passing that would have amounted to mandatory mediation for divorcing couples.

But the few activists combating these proposals, each in his or her hometown, can't maintain constant vigilance. The job is just too big. Since there is no corollary organized movement among divorcing women, they will have no power in maintaining their advances or offsetting setbacks. A case in point is the law passed in the State Assembly of New Jersey that would allow affluent divorced fathers to stop paying for their children's college education. According to this new proposed law, noncustodial fathers would no longer be responsible for higher education costs. The bill still needed to come to a vote in the State Senate in April 1995. The *New York Times* reported that the law was considered after strong lobbying by a men's rights group.[16] The effects can be devastating. In Pennsylvania, for example, after the 1993 court decision in *Blue* v. *Blue,* children lost their right to receive funds for higher education past the age of eighteen. Following this decision, practically overnight 101 petitions were brought to court by fathers to stop higher education payments for their children. Consequently, the children were faced with the prospect of having to drop out of college.

Given these trends that are encroaching on women's and children's rights, and the legal system's seeming intransigence toward real reform, the need for divorcing women to organize themselves seems imperative. As New York University Law Professor Stephen Gillers told Peggy Hammond: "Frankly I do not think you should expect much protection from the bar or state agencies, including the courts. I would not put my energies there." Where then? The answers are a page away.

WHAT THE
GOVERNMENT CAN DO

Aꜱ Brooklyn mother keeps close to her heart a quote from poet and former Czechoslovakian President Václav Havel: "I simply take the side of truth against any lie, of sense against nonsense, justice against injustice." The working-class mom was under duress—fighting for custody of her young son—when her lawyer threatened to abandon her right there on the court-house steps on the way to her court hearing, unless she signed a promissory note for money he claimed she owed. She signed the note and was instantly plunged into deep debt without even knowing if the attorney's claim was legitimate. He did not have to account to her, because lawyers were not legally required to provide itemized billing.

When this woman's story and others like it came to the attention of judicial officials in New York, they created new rules to curb this abuse from ever happening again. Citizens elsewhere can contact their state chief judges to get these rules adopted in their states too. But even with these commendable reforms, a more fundamental change is needed to better protect women and children in divorce. Judges, for example, can still knowingly, willingly violate the laws with impunity. Most of the following suggestions are meant to attack the root of the problem, creating a new power balance between consumers and lawyers.

1. LIMIT THE DISCRETION OF JUDGES

The widespread discrimination patterns of judges against women and, by extension, their children, in divorce have been verified in research by more than half of the states' highest courts. The opportunity for judges to discriminate is due to one factor: judges' increased power over issues involving custody and property in divorce proceedings since the advent of no-fault legislation and new custody rules. This judicial power is embodied in one simple word: *may*. When a statute says a judge *may* do something, that means the judge is not required to do it. But when a statute says a judge *shall* do something, like order a child support award or legal fees in sufficient amounts, that means the judge must do it. Replacing the word *may* with *shall* in the divorce laws would limit the judges' powers to hurt women and children in divorce.

For example, in the New York legislature, Assemblyman Anthony J. Genovesi sponsored a bill in 1993 to amend the domestic relations law, changing the language from *may* to *shall* to require judges to award counsel fees to financially dependent spouses in divorce. Genovesi recognized that financially needy spouses are barred from access to the court because judges deprive them of their right to legal fee awards, when the financial circumstances of the spouses justify such an award. This proposed legislation was confined to the Assembly for consideration and was not adopted into law because it did not find any backers in the state Senate.[1]

The need to limit judicial discretion is especially crucial in the area of custody, as University of Chicago law professor Mary Becker writes: "It is time that we, whether judges, lawyers, legislators, or members of the general public, begin to think about how, in the best interest of children, to limit judicial discretion over the fate of children and their parents both at divorce and when parental rights are being challenged in other situations, such as when foster parents or a grandmother think that they would be better caretakers."[2]

As Professor Becker and other legal reformers point out, this discretion can be limited by adopting the "primary caretaker standard" already adopted by the Supreme Court of West Virginia. The primary caretaker standard ends custody disputes by providing a presumption of custody in favor of the parent who was the primary caregiver to the child during the marriage.

Richard Neely, the now-retired Chief Justice of West Virginia, defines what is meant by the primary caretaker: It is the parent who: "(1) prepares the meals; (2) changes the diapers and dresses and bathes the child; (3) chauffeurs the child to school, church, friends' homes, and the like; (4) provides medical attention, monitors the child's health, and is responsible for taking the child to the doctor; and (5) interacts with the child's friends, school authorities, and other parents engaged in activities that involve the child."[3]

As Neely and other legal experts point out, the primary caretaker standard would not only eliminate false custody suits but also reduce the backlog of unnecessary litigation clogging up the court system. Adopting the standard would also be fairer to women, who give up their economic rights on the threat of losing children in a custody battle. As Neely states: "Experience teaches that, if there is any possibility that the average mother will lose her children in divorce, she will either stay married under oppressive conditions or trade away valuable rights to ensure that she will be given custody of the children."[4] Applying the primary caretaker standard, particularly when the divorce involves young children, would ensure that destructive marriages could end, and that women would not become destitute in order to retain custody.

2. REQUIRE JUDICIAL ENFORCEMENT OF ORDERS

Another area that should not be subject to judicial discretion is the enforcement of maintenance and property awards. A woman who exhausts her resources in legal fees in order to secure a judgment for what already belongs to her from the marriage should not be driven into poverty because the judge won't enforce the order. The Clinton administration has a new plan to take enforcement out of the hands of judges, who typically do not readily enforce orders against affluent ex-husbands. One of the most naive beliefs is that once a judge orders a judgment, it will be automatically enforced. Under existing law, judges have the absolute authority to swiftly apply enforcement mechanisms, but they don't, as the states' own gender bias committees have found. Under Title 4 of the federal government's new Work and Responsibility Act, automatic enforcement mechanisms for child support will be established and the enforcement process will be simplified, thereby eliminating the horrible unpredictability in the enforcement of judges' own rulings. (Maintenance awards, however, will remain under the jurisdiction of judges.)

One of the provisions of the new law is modeled on a program in Maine, which now enforces collection by revoking the professional and drivers' licenses of spouses who deliberately refuse to pay child support. Even in the first week after passage of the bill, results were stunning, according to news reports. This law is going to be adopted nationwide as part of the new federal legislation, and not only for the benefit of children but also to lessen the taxpayers' burden of having to put poor women and children on the welfare roll when ex-spouses can afford to pay . As Tom Mato, counsel with Maine's Department of Human Services, who is monitoring Maine's program, notes: "For too long people [have been] just alibying and making excuses—they do have the ability to pay."[5]

Finally, judges should be required by law to comply with a provision to consider the disparity in incomes of parents in awarding child support. Some women who earn far less than their ex-husbands are forced to pay despite major discrepancies in earnings. In one instance a New York woman earning $40,000 as a teacher lost custody and was expected to pay 25 percent of her salary for child support while her husband earned $100,000 more annually than she did.

3. ESTABLISH INDEPENDENT CITIZENS' REVIEW BOARDS TO OVERSEE LAWYER/JUDGE DISCIPLINE

Let the light shine on the lawyer and judicial disciplinary systems. Make all records of lawyers' and judges' discipline public, from the beginning of the complaint to the final disposition.

To their credit, Florida, West Virginia, and Oregon now disclose complaints against attorneys to the public. In Florida, once the grievance committee makes a decision to either hold a hearing against the attorney or dismiss the complaint, it becomes a public record. In West Virginia, if anyone wants to see how many complaints were filed against a particular attorney, they have access to the records, once the grievance committee's investigation has been completed. Oregon is still the most progressive state on this issue. Oregon law allows full disclosure to the public from the time the complaint is made. As stated earlier, many lawyers oppose making the records public on the grounds that vindictive clients will file false complaints to ruin their reputations, but there is no evidence that this has happened thus far, according to the American Bar Association's own commission's findings. "The arguments against open disciplinary systems are based on conjecture and emotion, not experience," authors of the McKay Report wrote in 1991, after examining Oregon's open system.[6]

Independently appointed civilian review panels should be established, replacing the current disciplinary agencies, which are tribunals of the lawyers' peers and subject to too much lawyer influence. The panels should be composed of consumers and citizens, functioning much like a jury in weighing the facts and evaluating the claims against the attorney. An independent panel of consumers would balance the power between lawyers and clients and eliminate the influence of lawyers that prevents effective oversight of their disciplinary system.

A consumer-driven agency would also take a more proactive approach to the investigation of lawyer fraud and deception, rather than reacting to complaints by merely dismissing the bulk of them. This approach might incorporate:

- A centralized 800-number complaint hot line in every state, providing to consumers information on where and how to complain.
- Signs in courthouses listing the grievance committee's addresses and phone numbers.
- A public computer listing available at libraries and on the Internet of attorney complaint records, such as the New York City Department of Consumer Affairs provides for consumers about businesses. This information would give consumers a way of protecting themselves, at little cost to the system.
- Swifter punishment, particularly where multiple complaints are involved.

When New York attorney Roy Cohn (who earned notoriety in the 1950s as Senator Joseph McCarthy's aide) took Lillian Goldman as a client in 1984, a case involving one of the biggest marital estates ever—around $1 billion—she didn't know that Cohn had scores of complaints from other clients against him. In this case, Goldman's husband, who held a vast amount of real estate in New York, did not want to split up his empire when his wife asked for a divorce. So his attorney, Raoul Felder, and her attorney, Roy Cohn, asked her to agree to a reconciliation with her husband, on the condition that the estate would be fairly divided and that she could continue to live separately. She agreed. A few weeks afterward she discovered a letter to Felder, her husband's attorney, from her attorney, Roy Cohn, complaining that Cohn hadn't gotten enough money for saving her husband from equitable distribution. Seeking to overturn the agreement, she appealed the case, and based on the evidence she had found, the higher court ordered the issue back into the lower court so that the reconciliation settlement could be reconsidered. Raoul Felder said that Mrs. Goldman misinterpreted the letter and that Roy Cohn was asked about the wording of the letter in later depositions. According to Felder: "What he [Cohn] says he meant by this—but it might have been written in one of his cocaine hazes—was that he meant that we helped reconcile the couple together, which was, there was an element of truth to that. When they walked out of there they were reconciled. He wanted more money and he said Sol was chinsy because he got him his wife back and the lawyers usually break up marriages and here two lawyers worked to put them together. That was his perception: it was actually not true, by the way. Please, they were fighting like cats and dogs." In this controversial decision, lower court judge Kristen Booth Glen ruled against Lillian Goldman, saying that the letter was not consequential. But perhaps if Lillian Goldman had known to begin with that her attorney had been under investigation by the authorities for twelve years, she would have made a decision not to hire him.[7]

4. ADOPT NEW YORK'S REFORMS

After my report for the New York City Department of Consumer Affairs was released in 1992, public hearings were held and new statewide reforms were adopted on November 30, 1993. Some of the legal abuses documented in these pages could be eliminated if other states adopted the New York reforms. They include:

- Mandatory fee arbitration. This is a way of resolving fee disputes that eliminates the need to hire a second lawyer to challenge the first lawyer's legal bill in court. Arbitration has been in effect in California and New Jersey, among a few other states. But consumers need to be aware: According to reports from New York advocates, consumers are not receiving fair decisions from arbitrators. The selection of arbitrators remains problematic, too. One of the lawyer-arbitrators in New York was reportedly under indictment for theft. In 1995, the American Bar Association issued a report recommending that all the states adopt fee arbitration. The appointed panel of arbitrators should include two nonlawyers for every lawyer to avoid bias or influence over the proceedings.

- Restriction (or a ban) on the use of security liens on property. In New York, divorce lawyers can now only obtain security liens on clients' property as a last resort—by getting special permission from the judge, and under no circumstances can the lawyer foreclose on the property.

- Measures to certify the truth of net worth statements: this measure was taken to curb economic fraud against spouses in the division of marital estates.

- A requirement that lawyers distribute a statement of rights to clients (see next chapter).

- Ethical rule banning divorce lawyer/client sex.

- Elimination of nonrefundable retainer agreements, so that lawyers won't be able to keep unearned money, in the event that the client reconciles with her spouse or decides to discharge her lawyer.

- Requirement that lawyers provide itemized bills every sixty days.

- Requirement that written retainer agreements be provided to set forth the terms of the agreement with a full explanation of the expectations of the client and the attorney.

The original reforms also called for a ban on retaining liens, the lawyer's practice of holding the client's file hostage until the lawyer's fee demand is met. The proposed ban on retaining liens was rescinded in New York after intense lobbying by lawyers just three days before the reforms were due to go into effect. Without having access to the documents in these files, it is nearly impossible for clients to continue divorce proceedings. New York's need for a ban on retaining liens remains.

5. IMPROVE DISCLOSURE OF LAWYER FEES

As indicated above, divorce lawyers in New York are now required to submit retainer agreements to the judge at the judicial conference, and this rule is having a positive effect for consumers. Another way of improving disclosure is to require lawyers to file billing statements with the court administration at the end of the case, and making this information available to the public and press, upon request.

6. PROVIDE ASSISTANCE TO PEOPLE WHO REPRESENT THEMSELVES

The idea of providing legal help to people who represent themselves in court is considered heretical to most lawyers, who have fiercely guarded their role in the legal process. Bars have undertaken aggressive suits against paralegals and other nonlawyers who offer legal advice. Despite the attempt by lawyers to maintain monopolistic control, however, nonlawyer assistance in family law is a burgeoning field—all the better for consumers, in many advocates' opinion.

A 1994 ABA report found that "Legal technicians are increasingly providing help to self-representing persons in family law matters." Toward that end, some states are helping people by establishing formal programs to assist this process. The Florida bar, for example, at the direction of the Florida Supreme Court, has published an extensive set of forms for use in filing for divorce, support, visitation, and protective orders, that make it easy for people to represent themselves.[8]

Arizona has gone even further. Its state court has installed user-friendly computer kiosks in courthouses to provide court-approved forms for plaintiffs and defendants in domestic relations cases. Known as QuickCourt, this system supplies free via computer all the forms needed to institute or defend divorce proceedings, including detailed forms that calculate standard child support figures for up to six children. The litigant gets clear information on such issues as the correct number of copies to file, which forms to use, how and when to file motions, waiting periods, and setting a hearing date. The software was developed under the direction of the court, after a study by the

Arizona Supreme Court concluded that "information regarding divorce, family matters and landlord/tenant issues were matters in which the public had the greatest need."[9] State courts in California and Utah are now looking into this technology.

Another way to help people represent themselves is to employ legal advocates to monitor cases from a consumer's perspective. These advocates would not have to be trained as lawyers but would need to have a basic familiarity with the law, such as paralegals have, with a special emphasis on family dynamics, legal ethics, and consumer and civil rights. The legal advocates would retain independent authority and be independently hired through social service channels and consumer organizations to ensure their own impartiality and would deal with such issues as: Is the proceeding advancing effectively, in accordance with the law? What is the wife and child's financial position thirty days after the proceeding starts? Ninety days after the proceeding starts? Is the judge using his or her administrative power in accordance with the laws? Are the necessary steps being taken to ensure quick judicial intervention in custody cases? Is the lawyer billing the client in accordance with the law? Does the client understand the information being provided by his or her attorney? Is the lawyer neglecting to inform the client of information necessary to decide how to proceed?

The use of legal advocates could extend to an ombudsman role as well. If the client, for example, complains that the judge is not acting in an impartial manner, the advocate would have the authority to monitor the case and make a recommendation for corrective action.

7. IMPROVE THE METHOD OF SELECTING JUDGES

We need to select judicial candidates on the basis of their motivation, scholarship, and genuine interest in the people they are supposed to serve. Too often politics and cronyism dominate the current methods of selecting candidates—by appointment or election, as I mentioned earlier.

It is incredible to think that as a society we do not require higher qualification standards in our selection of judges for family law cases. As long as judges wield so much power over individual lives, we must put into place training and qualification standards in order to avoid egregious outcomes for families in distress. We need to establish uniform qualifications for those judges who handle domestic relations cases. Only those lawyers who are truly interested in these types of cases and who have an expertise in the areas of domestic violence, economic violence, and child sexual abuse should be chosen for the bench.

Furthermore, law schools need to establish separate tracks of training for those lawyers who aspire to judgeships, that extend beyond teaching the mechanics of law. No U.S. law schools provide separate tracks for judicial training. The National Judicial Education College in Arizona offers classes to judges on a voluntary basis, but a look at the curriculum shows that the college does not cover issues of judicial discrimination or judicial temperament in family law cases. The lessons should include civic responsibility and principles of leadership in governing individual courtrooms. The teachers in these classes should also be specially licensed by the university in order to prevent bias from infiltrating the lessons. This same training should also be required of legal guardians, on whom children depend to promote their welfare.

8. ADOPT CONSUMER LAWS THAT APPLY TO LAWYERS

We need to apply the same regulatory standards to the legal profession that apply to many other professional groups, such as certified public accountants. Law firms engage in business just like any other commercial enterprise, and there is no reason that they should not be subject to the same oversight and legislation. States with consumer protection laws already have the mechanisms in place to take action against attorneys who are engaging in deception. Without specific rules, however, deceptive fee practices are, in effect, condoned.[10] In September 1995, Northwestern University law professor John Elson made a recommendation to the Illinois state legislature, to amend the state's consumer fraud and deceptive business practices act to read: "The terms 'trade' and 'commerce' mean the advertising, offering for sale, or distribution of any services and any property, tangible or intangible, real, personal or mixed, and any other article, commodity, or thing of value wherever situated, and shall include any trade or commerce *including the practice of law*, directly or indirectly affecting the people of this State."

In the few places where consumer laws apply to lawyers, clients are experiencing very positive results. In Massachusetts, a jury found in 1991 that a well-known law firm handling a divorce case had violated the state's consumer protection statute by committing an "unfair and deceptive business practice" and that it did so "willingly and knowingly." The law firm sued the woman over a $17,668.97 bill they claimed she owed, but the jury found instead that the law firm was deceiving the woman and owed her $4,200. Among other allegations, the woman claimed that her lawyers did not tell the judge that her divorce trial was only a few months away and that they failed to give her file to her new divorce lawyers. The woman additionally alleged that the firm failed to provide her with documentation to substantiate their billing. It is interesting to note the outcome of the case: although the jury's verdict was only advisory, the law firm decided to settle the case out of court, before the judge rendered a decision.[11]

In 1988, a judge ruled that the New York City Department of Consumer Affairs had a right to forbid a lawyer from placing newspaper advertisements that were deceptive and misleading to the public. Lawyer Leo Raychuk had advertised that he could obtain divorces and immigration green cards for clients within ten days. State Supreme Court Justice Karla Moskowitz wrote in her decision that "although the State has a comprehensive scheme to regulate attorneys' conduct, it does not appear to preempt the city's attempt to protect its consumers. Rather than being inconsistent with the scheme, the City's law supplements it, providing additional protection to the consuming public." The decision was later upheld by the state's highest court.[12]

9. POST IN EVERY COURTHOUSE A STATEMENT OF LITIGANT RIGHTS

In addition to the Consumer Bill of Rights, citizens should require courthouses to post an easy-to-read Statement of Litigant Rights. Just as hospitals are required to post a statement of client rights, so too should courthouses be required, so clients would know what is expected of judges. Lillian Kozak, the former chairwoman of New York NOW's Domestic Relations Law Task Force, presented the following list of rights to the New York legislature:

STATEMENT OF LITIGANT'S RIGHTS

I. You have the right to have a judge who avoids impropriety and the appearance of impropriety.
    A. A judge shall respect and comply with the law and conduct himself/herself at all times in a manner that promotes public confidence in the integrity and impartiality of the judiciary.
    B. A judge shall not allow his or her family, social, or other relationships, to influence his or her judicial conduct or judgment.
II. You have the right to have a judge who performs his or her judicial functions with impartiality and diligence.
III. You have a right to have a judge who is faithful to the law and maintains professional competence, and who is unswayed by partisan interest, public clamor and fear of criticism.
IV. You have the right to have a judge who maintains order and decorum in the proceedings before him or her.
V. You have the right to have a judge who is patient, dignified and courteous to you, to witnesses, to attorneys and to

others with whom he/she deals in an official capacity, and who requires similar conduct of lawyers, of his or her staff, court officials, and others subject to his or her discretion and control.

VI. You have the right to have your position heard by a judge, according to law.

VII. You have the right to have a judge promptly dispose of the business of the court.

VIII. You have the right to have the judge disqualify himself or herself in a proceeding in which his or her impartiality might reasonably be questioned, including but not limited to circumstances where the judge has personal bias or prejudice concerning a party, or personal knowledge of disputed evidentiary facts concerning the action or proceeding.

IX. You have the right to have the judge determine a motion for interim maintenance or child support within thirty days of the date of submission, or within the legally stated time, according to the statutes in your state.

X. You have the right to be treated fairly and with respect by a judge, regardless of your gender, race, creed, color, national origin or disability.

If at any time you believe that a judge has engaged in improper conduct, or has given the appearance of impropriety, or has otherwise violated your rights, you can report the matter to the State Commission on Judicial Conduct, which oversees judicial discipline.

10. MODERNIZE THE MANAGEMENT OF CASES

The court bureaucracy itself is in bad need of modernization to bring its procedures in line with the twenty-first century. Whitney North Seymour Jr., a former U.S. attorney and past president of the New York State Bar, has a very helpful, common-sense suggestion: Get court clerks to use appointment books and telephones, rather than make fifty or so lawyers wait—and charge their clients—while the judge confers about the status of each case. According to Mr. Seymour, potential savings to the court and to litigants would be $2,000 to $10,000 a case.

He also suggests videotaping all trials. "Stenographic court reporters are an anachronism in this electronic age. Tapes can record faster, more accurately and at much lower cost. . . . Possible savings: $5,000 to $15,000 per appeal," Mr. Seymour wrote in a *New York Times* op-ed piece.[13]

Also, the courts should be consolidated so that a divorce case, with the various issues involved, receives attention from start to finish in the same court with the same judge. This would prevent abusive, scattershot litigation with different judges, and would provide continuity and maximum efficiency. The 1993 New York Milonas Report stated: "It is an unfair burden for the parties to litigate in two courts, and consumers and attorneys reported that some actions were instituted in the second court merely to delay an ongoing action. This view is consistent with caseload statistics, which demonstrate that Family Courts statewide would be hard-pressed to absorb additional cases."[14]

11. IMPROVE THE JUDICIAL MANAGEMENT OF CASES

While these pages have focused on the abuses in divorce court, the problems of expense and delay are found throughout the civil court system. On behalf of corporate America, the U.S. Congress has intervened by enacting the Civil Justice Reform Act and the Judicial Improvements Act of 1990, to force the judiciary branch of government to reduce the cost and delay to litigants in federal civil court.

One of the law's major provisions requires judges to improve the management of their cases. It requires early, active intervention by judges to assess and plan the progress of each case, and to ensure compliance with discovery requests.[15] These reforms, which now apply only to the federal courts, should be adopted for state court operations too.

Judges need to use their judicial sanctioning authority and

punish attorneys who abuse court processes on behalf of their clients, such as deliberately and knowingly presenting false information to the judge to discredit the wife. If the methods of appointing/electing judges were depoliticized, judges would no longer fear punishing abusive attorneys. Attorneys can presently act with impunity, disregarding the laws of this land, because judges do not use the powers available to them, such as fining outlaw attorneys. Judges need to start imposing sanctions on Rambos and Rambettes.

12. ALLOW CLIENTS TO ATTEND THEIR OWN COURT CONFERENCES

Lawyers and judges frequently argue that clients are "too emotional" to attend their own conferences, but there are three good reasons to eliminate the secrecy and allow clients in. First, keeping clients out is arguably an infringement of the client's constitutional right to be a party to his or her own proceedings. Second, this secrecy does not benefit the client but greatly benefits the judge and lawyers by allowing them to work out quick deals not necessarily in the client's interest and without the client's direct knowledge. Third, this one-sided arrangement also works against the principle that a well-informed client can make well-informed decisions. Clients can't rely on their lawyers to represent the client's interests at these secret conferences, because the lawyer is influenced by the judge, who may be more concerned with disposing of the case than solving the issues involved.

13. ALLOW CLIENTS TO CHANGE JUDGES WHO MAKE UNLAWFUL RULINGS

A client who is forced to appeal a judge's wrongful decision is not helped when the appellate judge returns the client to the same judge to rehear the case. The client should be entitled to a new judge, yet in many if not most states, a client is stuck with the same judge no matter how many times that judge has erred in his or her decisions on that client's case.

*   *   *

The idea of this package of reforms is to shift the balance from a lawyer-centered system to a consumer-driven system, specifically by making lawyers and judges accountable to public scrutiny. But making divorce court consumer-friendly is easier said than done. These reforms have little if any chance of passing because the very people who would have to enact the laws are, by and large, lawyers with a vested interest in preserving the status quo. As Professor Geoffrey Hazard warned, "Change is not going to come from within the system."[16] Therefore, it is up to citizens to act.

There are other, more extreme solutions to the problems in divorce court. One would involve abolishing the entire system for people in divorce. It would require marriage contracts that would diminish the need for much potential litigation in court, while retaining the rights of both parties, at the least expense. It's an ancient idea that seems, in many ways, far more advanced than our present system.

The idea of a written marriage contract dates all the way back to Hammurabi's code 4,000 years ago, decreed by the King of Babylonia. Ancient Jewish culture also had a marriage contract, known in the Talmud as a *ketubah*, that placed great value on protecting women after divorce. According to Jewish historians, the essence of the ketubah was to spell out the financial responsibilities of the husband and the wife—in marriage *and divorce*. Of special interest here is one of the main terms outlined in the agreement, explained by Adin Steinsaltz in the book *The Essential Talmud*[17]:

> One basic condition in the ketubah is the husband's guarantee to pay a certain sum on divorcing his wife or if he should die before her. . . . In ancient times, a sum of money or a precious object of equal value was set aside for this purpose, and the husband was forbidden to make use of it. Simeon Ben Setah thought this encouraged husbands to divorce their wives without giving the matter due consideration, since the ketubah was ready

for this eventuality at any time. He therefore amended the ruling so that the sum of the ketubah was calculated as part of the husband's assets; therefore, any man wishing to divorce his wife was first obliged to produce this sum, thus having respite to reconsider his actions.

In many ways, the ancient ketubah makes our own present system seem backward and barbaric by comparison. In ancient Jewish life, if the husband wanted to leave his wife, he would have to be responsible for providing for her after the marriage. Compare that to modern America where many judges would rather have women go on welfare than require alimony for those in need. Not that the ketubah ignored women's responsibilities to the marriage either, as Steinsaltz explains: "[The husband] is entitled to enjoy the profits of the assets she brings with her from her parental home. . . although he has no ownership rights thereof. She is obliged to work in order to help support the family. . . ."[18]

A marriage contract should not, however, be confused with a prenuptial agreement, which is an individual arrangement usually controlled by the party with the most financial resources. A marriage contract is uniform for everyone, a standardized agreement. The responsibilities of both parties are delineated in a marriage contract—which does not favor either gender, but takes into account the real differences that women and men bring into the marriage. A marriage contract could spell out financial provisions after marriage for whichever party took primary care of the children during the marriage. The house would go to that person, not to the person who litigated the hardest using the most resources, as is currently the trend.

Imagine our society replacing all the complicated legal rituals and insufferable procedures in divorce court with one piece of paper signed at the time two people commit to marriage. If the husband wanted a divorce, the financial responsibilities would have been outlined at the outset of the marriage. If the wife were seeking the divorce, she would have to share her assets as well.

What about complexities or special difficulties that arise in some divorces? This is where the second solution, a therapeutic treatment model, comes into play. Whereas in the adversarial system the divorcing couple's lawyers' primary focus is on taking sides and discrediting each other, the therapeutic model is concerned with diagnosing the family's needs and special problems during the throes of its disintegration in order to arrive at practical treatment solutions to best serve the family members during and after the crisis. If this model were to be adopted for use in divorce, a special panel comprised of members specially trained in handling complex matters that arise in divorce would be assigned to each case. The panel would include a team: a financial planner, and, if needed, an investigative accountant, and doctors or counselors trained in identifying alcoholism, child abuse, domestic violence, and the like. This panel would conduct a neutral investigation, a fact-finding mission, and any doctors or counselors on the panel would give the family's problems the same meaningful attention that treatment units give patients in a hospital.

The team would analyze the facts in the case, and issue a treatment plan in order to minimize economic disruption and create ongoing financial stability for the family members after the divorce. A specially trained team manager would oversee the process, consulting with a specially trained judge, who had been screened and trained to handle these kinds of cases. Together they would arrive at a decision. The key requirements for making this model work are the expertise of the fact-finding professionals, the supervisory experience of the team manager and judge, and the use of modern financial planning techniques to arrive at an accurate assessment of the family members' economic situation and needs. Just as you would not want an inexperienced intern who had never performed surgery before to be in charge of your heart operation, you would not want a first-year student of social work to look into charges of child sexual abuse or economic fraud in the divorce.

This fact-finding approach, however, should not be confused with mediation, in which a third party tries to negotiate an out-of-court settlement between the husband and wife. The difference between the two is very significant. Instead of offering boilerplate compromises, as mediators sometimes do, a divorce panel would make recommendations based upon a family's unique situation. For example, if a man has abandoned the family and filed for divorce, a mediator might suggest joint custody of the children as a compromise because it's one quick way of satisfying the man's desire to pay the least amount of child support. After all, mediators are trained and required simply to help the couple reach a compromise, so they might advocate joint custody without knowing or being concerned about its effects on children. A divorce panel's recommendations, however, would take into account the social and psychological implications of various custody arrangements. The problems of joint custody are well known among mental health professionals: it's disruptive to children and prolongs the conflict between high-conflict parents. The fact-finders on the divorce panel would provide detailed information on the child's situation, including who takes care of the child and whom the child considers the nurturing parent. The same precision, knowledge, and care that goes into a medical diagnosis would go into the family diagnosis.

For many families, a marriage contract would be a realistic and inexpensive alternative to the present system, and there are many persuasive arguments in its favor. For those families with complicated and severe problems, a team of specially trained experts could be called in. When a marriage license is $25, why should a divorce cost $20,000, or $2 million for that matter? With a standardized marriage contract, a couple would know what was expected of each of them. Such a marriage contract would do all the work of lawyers and judges combined, and rid society of the monstrous labyrinth that the divorce court system has become. Imagine the courts suddenly unburdened of one third to one half of all civil litigation. Imagine husbands and wives who actually had a ready plan that honored their rights and preserved their security, in the event of divorce.

❧ 12 ❧

A PRACTICAL GUIDE
FOR WOMEN
CONSIDERING DIVORCE

THE DAILY workings of the divorce court system are not subject to any independent oversight, so you must learn how to protect yourself from the possible pitfalls. Until uniform safeguards are established for consumers of legal services, you need to take precautions to dodge the legal and financial grenades that lawyers, judges, and the system might throw in your path. Here, then, are some actions you as a consumer can take to protect yourself.

I. LEARN YOUR RIGHTS

The wise know that knowledge is power. The more you know about your rights, the less opportunity a lawyer or judge will have to trample on them. I conceived of and created a Bill of Rights for Divorce Clients, in the New York City Department of Consumer Affairs' *Women in Divorce* report, specifically to inform divorce clients of their rights. The following year, on November 30, 1993, New York's Chief Judge Judith Kaye ordered every lawyer in New York who handles divorce cases to give the adopted version of this statement to prospective clients before the retainer is signed.[1]

Unfortunately—perhaps inevitably—some lawyers began using the statement not to educate clients but to promote their own self-serving demands. A front-page story carried in the *New York Law Journal* described how lawyers were including outrageous provisions in the statement, such as the lawyer's right to abandon a case if payment was more than five days late.[2] Judge E. Leo Milonas, then the top court administrator, and chair of the commission that examined lawyer misconduct in divorce actions, subsequently cracked down with a follow-up rule that now requires lawyers to present a standardized statement of client rights, as outlined by the court administration.

Study and learn this abridged version of the adopted bill of rights for clients before you sign on the dotted line. Every divorce client in the United States has the legal right to set the conditions outlined in this bill of rights—with the exception of #13—the right to mandatory arbitration of fee disputes, which is not available in most states. Unless you live in New York, currently the only state that has codified these rights into formal court rules, you must make sure that you set forth these conditions with your lawyer in a written retainer agreement (explained later in this chapter). It is up to you to use this statement as a tool to give you more control in dealings with your lawyer.

In italics are those rights that appear in the original Consumer Affairs report but were eliminated from the court's version.

THE BILL OF RIGHTS
FOR DIVORCE CLIENTS

1. You are entitled to a written retainer agreement which must set forth, in plain language, the details of the fee arrangement. At your request, and before you sign the agreement, you are entitled to have your attorney clarify in writing any of its terms, or include additional provisions.

2. You are entitled to know the approximate number of attorneys and other legal staff members who will be working on

your case at any given time and what you will be charged
for the services of each.

3. You are under no legal obligation to sign a confession of
judgment or promissory note, or to agree to a lien or mortgage on your home to cover legal fees. Your attorney's
written retainer agreement must specify whether, and
under what circumstances, such security may be requested.[3]

4. In no event may such security interest be obtained by your
attorney without prior court approval and notice to your
adversary. An attorney's security interest in the marital residence cannot be foreclosed against you.

    *You are under no legal obligation to waive your rights to
    dispute a bill for legal services.*

5. You are entitled to know in advance how you will be asked
to pay legal fees and expenses, and how the retainer, if any,
will be spent.

    *If your lawyer agrees to lend or advance you money for
    preparing your case, you have the right to be informed peri-
    odically how much money your lawyer has spent on your
    behalf. You also have the right to decide, after consulting
    with your lawyer, how much money is to be spent to prepare
    a case. If you pay the expenses, you have the right to decide
    how much to spend.*

6. You are entitled to receive a written, itemized bill on a regular basis, at least every 60 days.

7. You are expected to review the itemized bills sent by
counsel, and to raise any objections or errors in a timely
manner. Time spent in discussion or explanation of bills
will not be charged to you.

8. You are expected to be truthful in all discussions with your
attorney, and to provide all relevant information and documentation to enable him or her to prepare your case com-
petently.

9. You are entitled to be kept informed of the status of your
case, and to be provided with copies of correspondence and

documents prepared on your behalf or received from the court or your adversary.

10. You have the right to be present in court at the time that conferences are held.

    You have a right to be present at court conferences relating to your case that are held with judges and attorneys, and you also have the right to bring a family member or a friend to all court proceedings, unless a judge orders otherwise.

11. If you entrust money to an attorney for an escrow deposit in your case, the attorney must safeguard the escrow in a special bank account. You are entitled to a written escrow agreement, and may request that one or more interest-bearing bank accounts be used. You also are entitled to a written receipt and a complete record concerning the escrow. When the terms of the escrow agreement have been met, the attorney must promptly make payment of the escrow to all persons who are entitled to it.

12. If an action or proceeding is pending, the court may give your attorney a "charging lien," which entitles your attorney to payment for services already rendered at the end of the case out of proceeds of the final order of judgment.

13. In the event of a fee dispute, you may have the right to seek arbitration. Your attorney will provide you with the necessary information regarding arbitration in the event of a fee dispute, or upon your request.[4]

One provision that was added to the state's version of the bill of rights is dangerous to clients. It gives the attorney the right to withdraw from the case before the work is complete, using language that reads, "Your attorney's written retainer agreement must specify under what circumstances he or she might seek to withdraw as your attorney for nonpayment of legal fees." Consumers would be well advised to add to the terms of the written retainer agreement the provision that the lawyer agrees not to abandon the case because of lack of payment, once he or she has agreed in writing to take the case. The attorney is still protected because the attorney can legally claim fees owed at the end of the case, regardless of whether the case is brought to trial or results in a negotiated settlement agreement. It should be noted that in federal court, once an attorney takes a case, the attorney can't back out if his or her fee demands aren't met. The attorney in federal court is required to bring the case to conclusion. Why shouldn't divorce lawyers be held to the same standard?

Your attorney *does not* have the right to do the following:

- Obtain a bonus from you at the end of the case. Make sure your written retainer agreement does not include the agreement to provide a bonus.
- Withdraw from your case without just cause, and the attorney must seek formal approval from the judge, who determines if the attorney's cause for withdrawing is justified.
- Demand a nonrefundable retainer.
- Betray any confidences, or breach attorney/client privilege, that could prejudice your case to the judge or to the other side.
- Force you to settle. You have a right to have your case heard before a judge or designated judicial officer, unless you live in a state requiring mandatory mediation.

II. LEARN HOW TO SELECT AN ATTORNEY

Choosing an attorney is a dilemma. It is difficult for the consumer to distinguish the good ones from the corrupt or incompetent ones. The problem is exacerbated by laws in most states that keep most attorney complaints confidential. Furthermore, misconduct is rarely punished.

So where should you begin? The *Martindale Hubbell Law Directory* is a guide that supplies biographies and addresses of attorneys, and can be used as a starting point; however, the directory is not very practical for consumers. The book doesn't list complaints against particular attorneys and it includes no information provided by clients, satisfied or otherwise. Legal reform groups might offer attorney references, but again, you need to be cautious, because some attorneys use the organizations to lure customers. Therefore, the savvy consumer has to seek creative solutions for selecting an attorney:

1. Make a background check on the potential attorney you select. You can do this by joining one of the several grassroots organizations that have been formed in response to lawyer abuse. You might want to check the Internet for electronic bulletin boards and discussion groups about attorneys. (See Appendix II for a listing.) Talking to the members about their attorney experiences can be useful. Compare notes. You'll quickly find out if the attorney's reputation is matched by client satisfaction or dissatisfaction. If none of these groups is available where you live, you'll have to resort to a more unconventional method. In most states matrimonial records aren't sealed to the public, so you can go to the courthouse and look up litigants' and attorneys' names, which are listed in the case files. Then call up a few litigants who have used the same attorney and ask them for their opinions. If you live near a university, you may also obtain names of lawyers by contacting law professors who are known to be interested in women's rights and asking them for help.

2. Forget about using the local bar association as a reference. The bars don't keep track of complaints against attorneys and offer no mechanism for screening. Some bar associations offer lawyer referral services, but the majority of these also do not actively screen for complaints.[5] Instead check with the local grievance committees. Turn to Appendix 1 to get the address and phone number. Remember, most complaints against attorneys don't reach the stage of formal investiga-

tion, where the charge is then made public. Complaints involving garden-variety overcharging, such as padding the bill, are not even investigated. If the attorney is privately admonished, this too is kept confidential, except in Oregon, Florida, and West Virginia, which have opened complaint records to the public.

When you check to see if the prospective lawyer is under investigation for misconduct by the disciplinary committee, they might not tell you because an attorney remains "in good standing" until there is a final disposition. Complaints by consumers are confidential, so asking if there is a complaint against the attorney is futile. If you know a formal complaint by the agency, itself, has been filed, then you might be able to find out.

3. Take a friend to the interview with the prospective attorney. A trusted friend can provide support and feedback, and be your eyes and ears when you are in distress. Most literature warns clients to be "professional" and "businesslike" in dealing with their attorneys, but this is unrealistic advice in a divorce case where a person's life is being uprooted and a child or a home can be at stake. A woman who is describing her abandonment might start crying. This is understandable. A friend can provide objectivity that you may lack during the interview.

4. Understand the inherent limitations of the first interview. Oral communication with the attorney at the consultation meeting is no accurate gauge of the attorney's future performance. All attorneys want to put on their best show in order to draw business. An attorney who makes promises to fight for you may turn to Jell-O in front of a judge whose main concern is to dispose of your case. That same attorney might tell you to give in, rather than his or her risking the judge's displeasure. Attitudes of bravado and macho are just appearances, which have little to do with actual performance.

High-profile attorneys, known as rainmakers, are no safe bet either. The attorney pontificating on a national television show is the firm's designated salesperson. This rainmaker most likely will hand your case over to an associate, who may or may not adequately know the law. The rainmaker's status or credentials have little to do with actual performance, particularly if you are not a wealthy celebrity, but the average Joe or Josephine looking for a hardworking legal advocate.

And remember, an attorney can't legally be held to his or her word in any verbal communication, unless you tape-record it. National Coalition for Family Justice leader Monica Getz's favorite adage comes to mind: "The system goes by proof, not truth." Notwithstanding the limitations of oral promises, here are some smart questions to ask during the first interview:

1. What other cases like mine have you handled? How many?
2. If this litigation goes to trial, are you experienced as a courtroom litigator? Or are you better as a negotiator?
3. How many lawyers will be handling my case? What are their rates? Will you be the main person doing the day-to-day work?
4. Can you give me a ballpark estimate of how legal fees might accrue in the best and worst case scenario? (If your lawyer won't answer this question, it's a clue for you to look elsewhere. Most attorneys know how much the case will cost because they figure out the potential profit to them before they decide to take your case.)
5. Will you ask the judge to grant legal fees? (If you are a dependent spouse and your husband controls the marital estate, your lawyer should ask the judge to award legal fees.)
6. If the judge does not grant legal fees will you wait until the divorce proceeding is completed for your payment?
7. Will you send me copies of correspondence and the court documents on a regular basis, or as developments occur?

8. How much is the retainer fee? Will you notify me as soon as the retainer fee has been exhausted?

During the initial interview, see how the attorney reacts to the idea of your negotiating some of the terms mentioned in the retainer agreement. The real litmus test is getting an attorney to commit on paper to what he or she promises you orally. A retainer is a written contract that is legally binding, and it will protect you. It also helps separate the chaff from the wheat. For example, if the prospective attorney agrees verbally not to sue to collect fees, put that promise in writing and add it as a provision to the retainer agreement. If the attorney agrees in writing not to sue you if the fee surpasses the maximum budget you set for handling the divorce, that's a good indication that you are working with someone who will honor your goals. If your attorney is unwilling to negotiate with you at the beginning of the relationship, there is no reason to believe he or she will be any more cooperative in the future. If you get a huffy or irritated response, just think of how he or she will act down the road when you ask him or her to respect your decisions. It is better to find out sooner rather than later—before it is too late.

Finally, you should also ask the attorney to agree to a model retainer agreement that includes the consumer-friendly provisions outlined below.

III. LEARN HOW TO NEGOTIATE A RETAINER AGREEMENT

Retainer agreements outline the terms of the representation. Unfortunately, most retainers are written to benefit the lawyer more than the client. Legalese obscures important provisions that could be financially harmful to you.

To avoid problems, don't sign anything without carefully looking it over. Take the retainer agreement home and study it. Make sure you understand everything. Most importantly, remember that you have the right to negotiate the terms and to set forth conditions that are favorable to you. You have the right to negotiate the retainer fee, just as you have the right to negotiate the terms of any standard contract.

New York now requires lawyers to provide a relatively understandable and fair retainer agreement that eliminates one-sided benefits to lawyers. If you don't live in New York, you must take extra care to be sure your agreement is consumer-friendly.

The agreement should include the following standard information:

1. Names and addresses of the parties entering into the agreement
2. Nature of the services to be rendered
3. Amount of the advance retainer, if any, and what it is intended to cover
4. Amount of the hourly rates for the attorney, the associate, and the paralegal

The following consumer-friendly provisions should also be included in the retainer:

- If for any reason you [the client] decide to discontinue my services, I [the attorney] will return any unused portion of the retainer. I will release your file to you immediately upon receipt of any payment due.
- I [the attorney] will keep you informed as to the status of your case, and agree to explain the laws pertinent to your situation, the available course of action, and the attendant risks. Copies of all papers will be supplied to you [the client] as they are prepared, and if there is a charge for these materials it will be included in your monthly bill.
- There is to be no change in the provisions of this agreement unless it is made in writing and signed by both of us.
- Neither of us will make any agreement or settlement without the knowledge or consent of the other.

- It is understood that I [as your attorney] will not ask you to sign a confession of judgment or a promissory note, nor will I place any liens on your property in order to secure legal fees.
- It is understood that I [as your attorney] will ask the court to award legal fees, if you are a financially needy spouse and the parties' financial conditions warrant the award.

Legal Awareness of Westchester, Inc. (LAW)[6], offers some helpful tips on what words and phrases to avoid in retainer agreements:

- Be careful when the agreement says the fee will be based on "results obtained." This is like a blank-check agreement that means your attorney could demand more fees beyond the retainer and hourly rates, on the grounds that you came out ahead in your divorce. Be careful for sentences such as "the ultimate fee will be based upon time spent plus additional amounts based upon results achieved." Or "may be an additional charge based on the complexity of the case. . . ." Make sure these kinds of sentences are deleted from the retainer before you sign it. It is interesting to note that in at least one state, Oklahoma, bonuses have been struck down as unacceptable by the courts.
- Be on the lookout for the phrase "Thank you for hiring *the firm* of. . . ." According to LAW, this can mean that the attorney you interviewed may not be the attorney assigned to your case. "This is especially true in large firms with a 'big name' partner," states the LAW literature. The phrase is acceptable, but you have a right to know who will be handling your case.
- Remember to make sure you fully understand the agreement before you sign on the dotted line. If you have any questions about any of the provisions in the retainer, find out what they mean before you sign it. The legal reform organizations listed in Appendix II of this book can help you.

IV. LEARN HOW TO FILE A GRIEVANCE

If you believe your attorney has engaged in misconduct in your case, you can file a complaint with the local grievance or disciplinary committee that regulates lawyer conduct. There's also nothing to stop you from filing a grievance against the opposing side's attorney, if you believe that attorney has engaged in dishonest or deceptive conduct that was intentionally harmful. Based on the committee's assessment of the case, possible punishments range from private admonition to public censure, suspension, or even disbarment. However, don't get false hopes about what you can expect. You can't get your money back by filing a complaint. The grievance committees don't give refunds. Furthermore, according to the statistics, chances are that your complaint will be dismissed. And if you file a complaint, the action will place you and your attorney in an adversarial position and you'll have to prepare yourself to find a new attorney.

Despite these discouraging facts, however, there are important reasons to file a grievance. For one thing, if the attorney's record shows a pattern of complaints, there's a better chance the grievance committee will take appropriate disciplinary action. If no one complains, the grievance committee can't take action. Second, your attorney will have to respond in writing to the complaint. Attorneys hate having to respond to charges of misconduct. Holding your attorney accountable for his or her misconduct empowers you. Also, the attorney might start to behave better when his or her actions are under official scrutiny. Finally, filing a complaint can strengthen your argument that you had a good cause for firing your attorney and therefore shouldn't be required to pay fees, writes Kay Ostberg in the book *Using a Lawyer*.[7]

If you do contact the grievance committee, you will receive a complaint form to fill out. Provide a summary of your complaint. Enclose copies of the documents that support your claims. (It is very important to keep records and documents to be able to back up your claims.)

After you complete the form and send it back, your complaint will be forwarded to your lawyer for his or response. The committee will then forward you a copy of that response, for rebuttal. At the end of this stage of the bureaucratic paper shuffle, most complaints are dismissed. If this happens, you should not automatically conclude that your complaint was not legitimate. The attorney might receive a private warning, if a violation has occurred, but in most states this lesser punishment is kept secret from the consumer.

In another common scenario in which complaints are summarily dismissed, the attorney has committed wrongdoing but the committee will not acknowledge it as such because of their subjective interpretation of certain categories of complaints, like fee deception. For example, although there is a disciplinary rule in every state that prohibits lawyers from engaging in dishonest and deceptive conduct, the grievance committees generally don't punish attorneys for small-scale overbilling based on one complaint. Such a complaint won't warrant further investigation unless there are multiple complaints over the years that show gross overbilling.

In cases of clear-cut criminal behavior such as embezzlement of funds, the committee will probably further investigate the attorney. If the disciplinary agency decides there is probable cause that your lawyer is a thief or a cheat by criminal standards, the committee will hold a hearing that somewhat follows the procedure of a trial. The accused lawyer will most likely have hired legal representation to shepherd him or her through the process. The grievance agencies don't often tell consumers what to expect at the hearings, so it would be wise to ask them, or check with one of the groups listed in Appendix I or II to prepare yourself for the hearing.

If the attorney is found guilty and disbarred, then you have a chance of claiming lost funds from an agency called Lawyers' Funds for Client Protection. Every state, with one current exception, has such an agency. You can check in Appendix I to find the phone numbers. You can also get the address and phone number by calling your local bar association, your local courthouse, or the American Bar Association's Center for Professional Responsibility in Chicago.

You can also file a complaint against your judge, if you believe he or she has engaged in misconduct or action unbefitting a judge. Each state has an ethics commission that looks into allegations of judicial misconduct. The same warnings apply. If you file a complaint, the judge might engage in retribution against you, if your case is active. You need to consider the benefits and the risks. (See Appendix I for the phone numbers of the judicial commissions.)

V. IF THINGS HAVE REALLY GOTTEN OUT OF HAND. . .

The following guidelines are for those clients who feel they are being seriously exploited or misled by their attorneys. Some of these measures may sound extreme, but extreme solutions are needed for extreme problems. Here they are:

1. *Keep written records of your contact with your attorney.*

   Note the calls you make and receive, and the length of the conversations. This log book may be used in the future as evidence you need in a malpractice case or fee hearing dispute.

2. *Tape-record your phone calls.*

   If you believe your lawyer is lying to you, deliberately misinforming you, or using rough, obscene, or intimidating language with you, record the phone call. The system requires this proof to back up your claims so that it's not just your word against your attorney's. You can do this if you live in a state such as New York where recording conversations is legal, as long as one party is aware the conversation is being recorded. You don't have to tell your attorney you are recording the call. However, if you live in a state that requires both parties' awareness of being recorded, you will have to tell your attorney you are recording the call. You can find out if it's legal by contacting the editor of your local newspaper, who would know the law, since reporters sometimes record their conversations. There are two ways to tape-record calls. You can either buy an answering machine that is equipped to record calls, or if you have a tape recorder, you can purchase a telephone-jack pickup. This is a suction-cup device that acts like a microphone and attaches from the ear part of the telephone receiver to the microphone jack of a tape recorder. These devices are very inexpensive (costing about $4) and can be purchased at stores like Radio Shack.

3. *Take a witness to meetings and to court.*

Don't make the mistake of going to the lawyer's office alone if you think he or she is going to use pressure tactics to intimidate you into doing something you don't want to do. If you are at a settlement negotiation and your lawyer pressures you to sign away your rights, if you are alone, you won't have any proof that you were coerced. If you have a witness present to take notes, it is more difficult for the attorney to lie.

4. *Go wired.*

If you believe there is serious criminal corruption in your case, and you have reason to fear you will be coerced, you may want to secretly tape the meeting. A microcassette tape recorder can be easily hidden in your jacket pocket and a small microphone attached under your blouse. At New York City's Department of Consumer Affairs, investigators often wire themselves to catch deceptive business practices. Until the government starts taking a proactive look at divorce court deceptions, the consumer has to take these extreme measures supply the proof to law enforcers.

5. *Inform the administrative judge.*

This advice comes by way of Adria Hillman, a legal reformer and seasoned Manhattan divorce attorney.[8] Ms. Hillman says that if your attorney won't return your calls, and you don't know where you stand on your case, you should inform the administrative judge of your circumstances. Each court has an administrative judge who oversees the proceedings and personnel at court. You can request a meeting. Ms. Hillman also suggests that you request a conference with the judge who has been assigned to your case. Even if you are not going to trial and want to settle your case, there will be a judge, as a formality, who will have to authorize the divorce. You can request a meeting and tell the judge that you don't know where your case stands. If the judge ignores your request, you can ask for a meeting with the judge's supervisor. If that doesn't work, each court system has a top administrator you can contact. Even if the administrative judge does not show any reaction to what you are saying, don't be fooled. Once made aware of a problem, he or she may take informal measures to correct it in order not to draw any more negative attention to the situation.

6. *Ask for a court reporter at any and all court hearings.*

Court proceedings need to be documented in the event that the judge erred and you have to appeal a decision to a higher court. This suggestion applies to all major hearings, not just to problematic ones.

VI. LEARN HOW TO HANDLE FEE ARRANGEMENTS

As you have learned by now, there are any number of deceptive billing practices by which clients can be defrauded of their assets. Lawyers can inflate the number of hours actually worked on the case, bill for unnecessary services, misquote their hourly rates, and charge lawyer time for nonlawyer services. For example, a divorce attorney in San Diego, California, told his client that his hourly rate was $150, but when the client got the bill she saw that it reflected a rate of $175 per hour. When the client pointed this out to her lawyer, he agreed to adjust the bill to the lower rate. For that reason, it is very important to keep track of your bills and to learn to understand what the charges mean. Here, then, are some helpful tips.

• Always be sure to get an itemized bill. You have the right to ask for an explanation of the basis of the charges, according to the attorneys' ethics code. In other words, you have the right to an itemized bill. If your attorney tells you otherwise, he or she is misinforming you. If the bill is illegible, or is garbled in a computer printout, don't accept it. Demand a legible, readable bill that shows what you owe in dollars and cents.

Carefully examine the explanations of charges. Be wary of vagueness. If an attorney bills you for thirty-five hours of "legal research," that is unacceptable. The attorney is obligated to describe the specific legal research that was done.

Also beware of large bills that show mostly phone calls. One of the easiest overbilling maneuvers is to charge for unnecessary or excessive phone calls. Your lawyer may be discussing golf with your husband's lawyer and then charge you for the call. Billed phone calls should result in progress in the case, such as a proposed settlement agreement. Little work is accomplished in routine phone calls. Look also for phone calls made by secretaries and paralegals that are billed as attorney calls at attorney rates.

If substantial assets or a custody dispute is involved, your attorney will have to do substantial work, such as filing certain papers, to make sure your rights are defended, and these charges can add up. For example, if you believe your husband has hidden money, your attorney might have to access certain computer data banks, such as Info-trak and Nexius, to track assets. This kind of work leaves a paper trail behind showing what the lawyer actually worked on. Another reason to be careful of bills listing many phone calls is that your lawyer may not be handling your case properly. If after six months your bills have shown mainly phone calls, this may be the case.

Examine all the initials listed next to the charges on the bill. These initials represent the names of law office staff working on your case. Have you authorized them—especially the number of attorneys listed—to work on your case? Do you recognize their names? If not, you might not have to pay for their services, or maybe you can negotiate the bill downward on the basis that you did not authorize them to do the work.

- If you are challenging the bill, *do it in writing*. Many judges believe you are giving up your right to challenge the bill if you don't prove in writing that you objected to the fees when you received the bill. Send a *certified* letter. This will document the facts. An alternative solution may be to pay what you think you owe and mark the receipt to the attorney PAID IN FULL, making sure to state in writing the reasons for your action. This action, however, won't legally protect you from having your former attorney sue you to collect. It just gives you a little extra protection by showing that you disputed the amount of the bill.

- Hire an auditing firm to analyze the bill. If there is a substantial amount at stake—$75,000 or $100,000—it may well be worth it to have your bill professionally audited. There are several firms that specialize in legal audits and can detect overcharging. Philadelphia-based Legalgard is one of the oldest, and their lawyers have been used as expert witnesses in legal fee lawsuits in divorce cases. These firms, of course, charge for their services, and you will want to find out how much they charge so that you can know if the audit would be economically beneficial.

VII. LEARN HOW TO ENSURE YOUR FINANCIAL RIGHTS

In middle-class divorces, where there are substantial assets and/or children involved, a good lawyer is really functioning as a financial expert. Therein lies the problem. Lawyers do not get special training as financial analysts, and the woman pays for her lawyer's ignorance. For example, according to the Pension Rights Center, many lawyers simply do not know about the pension laws in their states, thereby causing women to lose their pension rights—one of the causes of poverty in older divorced women, according to a Brandeis University study[9].

A new field has recently emerged that takes the guesswork out of women's economic rights. Financial consultants can calculate the financial value of the woman's contribution to the marriage. Using economic data and government indicators, they can help her get the most equitable settlement and spousal and child support.

One such consultant, Cicily Carson Maton, who heads the Chicago-based firm Aequus, says there are many relevant criteria that go into computing a woman's needs after the divorce, which lawyers do not take into account. For example, she uses several economic indicators, such as the rate of inflation and government figures on the cost of raising children, to figure out future costs of raising a child. She also values the custodial parent's (usually the mother's) services to the welfare of the child, to assess her contributions to child-rearing. This factor should be considered in the settlement offer or in the judge's determination of the woman's potential share of the estate.

To get an idea of how a wife's services would be broken down in the commercial marketplace, Maton has calculated the market value of those services. Her calculations are based on an analysis of economic data. Maton calculates that to replace the services of an average mother who takes care of four children, it would cost $32,431 for one year (based on March 1993 figures). Here's a sampling of how she breaks it down:

JOB PERFORMED	HOURS PER WEEK	EQUIVALENT MARKET JOB	WAGE PER HOUR	VALUE PER WEEK
I. Buyer, food & household	8.29	Purchasing Agent	$14.77	$122.45
II. Physical care of family	.73	Nurse	$13.18	$9.59
III. Seamstress	7.27	Seamstress	$10.68	$77.65

The benefit of a qualified financial planner is that it adds a measure of protection to make sure your financial rights are honored by your lawyer.

VIII. JOIN A SUPPORT GROUP

Support groups can help provide information and feedback as well as emotional support. You will learn you are not alone, and it's easier to find answers when you have others to talk to than when you are isolated. See Appendix II for resources to help you contact a local group.

IX. PREPARE YOURSELF BY ATTENDING A DIVORCE COURT HEARING

Go to see for yourself how the day-to-day operations of a courtroom work. See how the lawyer and judge act to get an idea of what you may expect. Courtroom activities can be a real eye-opener, and understanding how things work in court will help you know how to proceed with your own case. Your court hearing will be less intimidating to you if you are familiar with the surroundings, formalities, and procedures.

X. ASK YOUR MINISTER OR RABBI TO INTERVENE

This suggestion comes by way of Legal Ethics professor Geoffrey Hazard, who firmly believes that our religious organizations should take an active role in protecting women and men from potential abuses by lawyers in divorce litigation. A member of the clergy can be a highly effective intermediary between you and your lawyer. He or she can intervene on your behalf, if you give your lawyer written permission to discuss your case. If your minister or rabbi is not familiar with the kinds of abuses you are experiencing, ask him or her to read this book, or to contact one of the groups listed in Appendix II for a better understanding.

XI. GET YOURSELF COUNTED

If you have experienced financial exploitation by your lawyer, an unfair custody battle, or any of the patterns of abuse described in this book, you can get yourself counted as part of an ongoing effort to collect documentation to present to federal legislators to help get reforms enacted. If you are interested in participating in this study, you will need to supply proof of your claims. Look for *Divorced from Justice: The Bulletin* on the Internet for more about this study. See Appendix II for more information.

☙ 13 ☙

A NOTE TO THE READER

As you are reading these words, acts of injustice and mistreatment are being committed against American women in divorce proceedings. At this very moment, their liberties and rights are being threatened *by the public officials in charge of helping them.*

The mechanisms of oppression are as diverse as lawyers are creative—custody threats and financial and emotional coercions of every stripe ensure subjugation of the many by the few. Each and every American who cherishes democracy must ask him or herself: Who profits from divorce? Who nurtures the present system, which extols the virtue of economic independence for women while at the same time depriving them of their most basic legal rights? Who grows rich on the agony of families breaking apart? On the impoverishment of middle-class women after divorce?

In the answers to these questions the truth is exposed, and the real troublemakers stand bared. These culprits possess much power. It will take a huge coalition to restore the justice system to the people. Lone voices, though valiant, do not have a chance; they are like twigs waiting to be broken.

The late Heather Saville-Hyde, from California, who fought the secrecy of the court (see Chapter 8), was one such valiant voice, crushed in the end. This English-born, formerly upper-middle-class woman became unnecessarily destitute at the age of sixty-six after her divorce. She was a highly articulate spokesperson on the issue of divorcing women's rights, who knew her own rights had been violated by the California court system. But this knowledge alone was not enough. There were many alleged irregularities in her case, all typical of the patterns I have seen over and over again. By her own account she spent over $300,000 on lawyers, whom she hired to protect her rights. According to her son, her last lawyer billed her $180,000 for just eighteen months of work, with no perceptible results.

She would never see justice. I was shocked to learn of her sudden death in a letter from her son, Peter Hunt. It read in part:

> Tragically, my mother was struck by a car and killed while crossing the street August 1, 1994. And while it is only speculation, the tens of thousands of uncollectable dollars awarded to my mother by the court would have allowed her to purchase a car and avoid running all her errands on foot. She died with three dollars in her account and four in her purse. My father to date has escaped his financial obligations by living in another state.
>
> I share much of my mother's frustration. Unfortunately, she did not learn how to manipulate the legal system as she herself was manipulated. For those uninitiated, it may be natural to equate justice with the court. However, as your cleverly worded title suggests, the *legal system* is not the *justice system*. My mother could not accept this, and I watched as the legal system consumed all that she had and all that she was.

The circumstances surrounding the fatal accident were a direct result of Heather's new condition of poverty after divorce. Heather had phoned her son to pick her up from a public telephone booth on the side of the road. She had no transportation, and had walked to a store. With no car, she had no way of getting home. Her son told me that when he arrived at the telephone booth, she wasn't where she'd said she would be. A short distance away, he saw people gathered looking at something beside the road. As he slowly drove by, he stopped, suddenly realizing it was his mother, lying crumpled up in a heap on the pavement.

After receiving the news of Heather's passing, I reread a letter she had written to me dated October 21, 1992. She had been in correspondence with me because there was nowhere else to turn. Heather was not a masochist. She did not become poverty-stricken because of some character flaw. She knew all too well what had happened to her, and from whence her poverty and oppression stemmed. In her letter, she spoke about how the system betrays the interest of the people, and the need to organize and protest. She wrote:

> We are totally at the mercy of lawyers and the groups they represent *AND HAVE NO ONE AT ALL GUARDING OUR INTERESTS*. This is a totally insupportable and unacceptable situation. Is it any wonder we're being exploited? We have become the pawns of these powerful tyrants as a result of our own failure to coalesce and to assert our power of numbers and, above all, the power of right! We need to join the ranks of others to rally and demonstrate and petition. . . and we should be ready to do that at the next election and maybe before. It's a pity we were not organized enough to add our voices to the general clamor of dissent today.

Heather could not fight the system alone. She died trying, though. In her last years she was continually in touch with California legislators, trying to get reforms enacted. Perhaps her message can still make a difference. Our legal system *can* become a justice system. It's up to each one of us, together, to determine ultimately which it will be.

ADDENDUM

IN THE FOUR YEARS following the release of the New York City Department of Consumer Affairs report, *Women in Divorce: Lawyers, Ethics, Fees and Fairness,* New York's top judicial and state officials have begun to address some of the problems that have eroded New York's judicial system, and have enacted some significant reforms. The Milonas Committee made recommendations—mirroring those in the Consumer Affairs report—that became new court rules in November 1993. That same year, the New York Assembly's Standing Committee on the Judiciary held public hearings on New York's lawyer disciplinary system that exposed deep deficiencies in the system. By 1995, officials concluded their eighth public hearing over the course of three years on the topics of improving lawyer ethics and professionalism. These efforts, however, cannot realistically be expected to curb the legal abuses pervading the divorce industry in New York. As long as officials keep ignoring the underlying problem of lawyers who use sophism to creatively skirt around the law and avoid the truth-seeking process, and think nothing of destroying families in the process, distrust in our government will continue to grow.

After divorce lawyers complained of being unfairly singled-out for investigation, New York Chief Judge Judith Kaye appointed this latest committee, The Committee on the Profession and the Courts (known as the Craco Committee, after chairman Louis A. Craco), to investigate law practice in other areas. In the high-minded rhetoric that now fills the latest report, the committee suggested sending law graduates to more seasoned members of the bar for training in management skills. Unfortunately, as you will recall from the introduction of this book, a major malpractice study commissioned by the American Bar Association reveals that the family law lawyers with the most experience had proportionally far more complaints against them, than the least experienced.

The Craco Committee also proposed allowing public access to complaint records against attorneys who are formally charged with misconduct by the disciplinary committees. New York attorneys worry that their reputations will be damaged if the complaint records are even partially opened, but their worries seem unfounded given that most complaints against attorneys do not result in formal charges.

The committee also called for yet another investigation into divorce court, saying that family law, along with workers' compensation, received more criticism from professionals and laypeople than any other area of law.

Taken together, these three reforms seem about as effective as applying an eye-dropper of water to a house on fire. But what can really be expected when all these committees charged with looking into ethics have been composed exclusively of lawyers and judges, and when the people affected by their work have not been allowed to participate on the committees?

To their credit, however, the committee did recommend adopting Federal Rule 11. Federal Rule 11 requires attorneys to certify that they investigated the facts and the law before signing documents presented to the court. The attorneys are supposed to investigate to the best of their abilities, that the allegations and documents they present are actually true. If an attorney is found to violate Federal Rule 11, a judge can impose financial penalties on the lawyer. This is a good first step toward stopping unethical lawyers whose goal is to avert the truth-seeking process in order to win their cases. Federal Rule 11, would, presumably, deter frivolous actions and lying by attorneys.

For example, Madeline Bennett, author and advocate, recalled one case in which the divorce lawyer representing a father claimed in court documents that a child's mother "was sending the child to school in tatters." But in actuality, "The child was always well-dressed except for the day following the father's overnight visitation, according to the testimony of school officials," Bennett explained.[1] Under Federal Rule 11, the judge could have imposed a penalty on the lawyer for not making sure of the facts before presenting them in claims against the mother. The only problem with this rule is enforcement. There is no way of predicting which judges would enforce Federal Rule 11 and which judges, because of their strong connections to certain attorneys, wouldn't. How can the public trust them to enforce more laws when they don't bother to obey existing laws?

While officials attempt to restore public confidence to the judiciary, their words seem so far away from the daily ordeals of mothers and children facing atrocious legal abuse. Here is an ongoing story with no end yet in sight:

One Friday in the winter of 1996, a mother, age thirty-three, a successful career woman, went to visit her children at their grade school. That day, she was like any other devoted mother, waiting for her children, standing in the rain in front of one of the public schools in Manhattan, only this mother and her sons had not had any physical contact for six months. She had already lost custody of her three- and five-year-old sons, but not because she was a bad mother. In fact, the judge presiding over the case had said repeatedly in his decision that she was a fit mother. But the judge had granted custody to the father after deciding that the mother was an angry woman. When one journalist discovered that the mother's anger wasn't apparent after scouring 1,000 pages of court documents, she questioned the judge. He was quoted as saying that he could tell the mother was angry *because of her body language* in court.

After the mother lost custody, she temporarily lost her right even to visit her children too. Her legal right to present evidence to the judge was denied. Now, however, the mother was just looking forward to the day this temporary order expired, when her normal visitation schedule with her children was supposed to resume. But Thanksgiving, Christmas, her son's birthday, all passed, and each time she attempted to see her boys, as was her legal right, her-ex husband would not make the children available to her. Then the law firm that was representing the children's father went even further to keep the mother from seeing her children. On January 19, the father's lawyer wrote a letter to the school principal warning her that the mother was not permitted to visit her children at the school because of a court order. The principal was convinced by the attorney. In reality no such order was in effect, because it had already expired. Unfortunately, as is often the case, reality was immaterial in the court system. Often, only what the lawyers and judges say has power and consequence. The school principal believed the lawyer and secretly whisked the children out of the school through a side entrance. The mother was left alone in the principal's office, unaware that her children had already left the school. The mother returned to her apartment, where she broke into tears, not knowing what to do or where to turn.

Strictly speaking, what the husbands' lawyers did was not technically illegal. Lawyers who were consulted on the facts in this case agreed that because the temporary visitiation order had expired, the woman indeed had the legal right to see her children. But these lawyers cautioned that the husband's attorneys' could rightfully claim that they too were correct in denying visitation, according to their own interpretation of the same documents.

The damage done to children of divorce because of evil in our courtrooms cannot be assessed in monetary terms. Since being separated from his mother, witnesses say the eldest son in the case cited above has developed a severe facial tic. When the authories were notitifed about these goings-on described above they reacted as might be expected; they did nothing. No official has been willing to come forward to inform the school principal that the order has indeed expired, or to see to it that the children get to see their mother.

So while the new reforms in New York are commendable, there's a long way to go. Wrenching young children from their nurturing parents is still routine. Lawyers and judges who actively destroy the bonds of love between primary parents and their children seem unaware of the effects on the children. Our courts are creating a new generation of distrusting people, who know that government does not care about justice or the truth.

On another front, Manhattan's local divorce court industry was thrown into chaos in late 1995, when the court administration transferred the three divorce court judges that handle the bulk of Manhattan divorce cases and replaced them with outsiders unfamiliar with the modus operandi of Manhattan's matrimonial courthouse/clubhouse.

The official explanation given by the court administration for the transfers was that the judges needed a rest from the stressful job of presiding over divorce cases, but unofficial explanations were more readily accepted. Allegedly, Norman Sheresky and a group of powerful divorce lawyers had met with Judge Stanley Ostrau (as you may recall, he is the administrative judge mentioned in Chapter 9) to complain that one of the divorce court judges, Justice Phyllis B. Gangel-Jacob, was biased against male clients. Justice Gangel-Jacob had recently earned the attention of the nation when she jailed Jeffrey Nichols, who had deprived his children of $560,000 in child support payments.

Another unofficial explanation for Gangel-Jacob's transfer is that she was reportedly trying to curb lawyer fee-gouging and had questioned the practice of certain divorce lawyers who bring associates to court on trivial matters, billing the client for two lawyers when one lawyer would have sufficed. Whatever the reason, the lawyers' complaints to the administrative judge worked. Gangel-Jacob was transferred out. This action sent the message that lawyers privately control the selection of judges in Manhattan's clubhouse/courthouse. Gangel-Jacob was allowed to continue her term to the end of the year. When it was time for her to leave the matrimonial bench, however, the court administration made a surprise announcement that sent quite another message back to the lawyers. Administrators transferred out the other two judges, David B. Saxe and Lewis R. Friedman. (Friedman, the newest matrimonial judge, had only been on the matrimonial bench for two years when he was transferred out.)

The cliquey matrimonial bar was more than a little shaken up by the transfer of Saxe and Friedman. Lawyers became very nervous over not knowing yet how to manipulate the newcomer judges to preserve the custom of charging astronomical legal fees in Manhattan. The *New York Times* explained why the transfers were causing such a panic in the matrimonial bar: "The matrimonial part is an intimate little viper's nest, where a lawyer's survival skills must include the art of fine-turning a case to play to the quirks of whichever judge hears it. . . . Judges have almost untrammeled power over the outcome of a contested divorce and they can also order the spouse with the deeper pockets to pay for the other spouse's lawyer." The rule of law should have continuity based on faithful practice of the law, but the kind of divorce law practice described above is based on personalities, connections, and power players.

The self-serving interests of the legal profession are not just damaging to individual women and children; they are corroding the government institutions of our democracy. While the court culture remains unresponsive and inimical to the needs of citizens, the question of how to make the system more responsive is quietly being answered. An extremist movement to scuttle the judicial system has now swept through 11 states, and this movement is growing, according to recent news accounts. These people have given up hope on restoring public confidence in the judicial system. They are literally taking the law into their own hands.

In Pennsylvania, where judicial corruption has been alleged at both the highest and lowest levels, the anti-judicial movement is gaining ground. Supporters are establishing their own private courts. "We're just looking for justice," one court supporter was quoted as saying. "The court of Common Pleas is rigged, so we've realized that we've got to look someplace else." The adherents maintain they are not bound by the decisions of the system, including those in divorce court. Instead they hold their own "court" and all decisions are made, not by a judge, but by a twelve-member jury. At one of these "court" hearings, they declared a custody decision involving a woman and her four children null and void and ordered the state court to "cease and desist in any further actions on the case."

One frightened editorial writer in Pennsylvania's *Daily Local News* recognized the danger: "This is the stuff of which civil war is made. Look at the trouble spots in the world—Bosnia, Somalia and the rest. What is wrong in those places is that the rule of law has disintegrated. . . . [The] appearance in Chester County of a so-called 'common law court' is a threat to property and freedom of everyone." The writer added: "This is not to say that our courts are perfect. Various legal reform movements are motivated by the sense that our courts are dominated by money, connections and high-powered, predatory attorneys." What the writer was fearing was that people are beginning to resort to anarchy, and this is clearly dangerous terrain for any democratic union. What the writer didn't ask was this: Has the rule of law already disintegrated under the current system?

The corruption of our courts and the abuse and neglect of ethics and law puts ammunition into the guns of these anarchists who want to shoot down the government. Who is going to get the last word?

APPENDIX I

Addresses and Telephone Numbers of Lawyer Disciplinary Agencies, Lawyer Funds for Client Protection, and Judicial Commissions

- To find out where to file a complaint against a lawyer in your state, look for **L**.
- To call for reimbursement in case of lawyer theft, look for **$**.
- To complain about a state judge, look for **J**.

ALABAMA
L   Alabama State Bar
    Center for Professional
    Responsibility
    415 Dexter Avenue
    P.O. Box 671
    Montgomery, AL 36104
    (205)269-1515
$ Lawyers' Funds for Client
    Protection
    (334)269-1515
J   Judicial Inquiry Commission
    800 South McDonough
    Street, Suite 201
    Montgomery, AL 36104
    (334)242-4089

ALASKA
L   Alaska Bar Association
    510 L Street, Suite 602
    P.O. Box 100279

Anchorage, AK 99510-0279
(907)272-7469
$ Lawyers' Funds for Client
    Protection
    (907)272-7469
J   Commission on Judicial
    Conduct
    310 K Street, Suite 301
    Anchorage, AK 99501
    (907)272-1033

ARIZONA
L   State Bar of Arizona
    111 W. Monroe #1800
    Phoenix, AZ 85003-1742
    (602)340-7241
$ Lawyers' Funds for Client
    Protection
    (602)340-7284
J   Commission on Judicial
    Conduct

1501 W. Washington Street,
Suite 229
Phenix, AZ 85007
(602)542–5200

ARKANSAS

L Supreme Court of Arkansas
   Committee on Professional
   Conduct
   Justice Building
   625 Marshall
   Little Rock, AR 72201
   (501)376–0313
$ Lawyers' Funds for Client
   Protection
   (501)376–6655
J Judicial Discipline and Dis-
   ability Commission
   Tower Building—Suite 1060
   323 Center Street
   Little Rock, AR 72201
   (501)682–1050

CALIFORNIA

L State Bar of California
   Office of the Chief Trial
   Counsel
   1149 S. Hill Street, 10th
   Floor
   Los Angeles, CA 90015
   (213)765–1000
   San Francisco Office
   555 Franklin Street
   San Francisco, CA 94102
   (415)561–8200
$ Client Security Fund
   (213)765–1161

J Commission on Judicial
   Performance
   101 Howard Street, Suite 300
   San Francisco, CA 94105
   (415)904–3650

COLORADO

L Colorado Supreme Court
   Office of the Disciplinary
   Counsel
   Dominion Plaza Building
   600 17th Street, Suite 510
   South
   Denver, CO 80202–5435
   (303)893–8123
   (Colorado has discontinued
   its security fund.)
J Commission on Judicial
   Discipline
   1301 Pennsylvania Street,
   Suite 260
   Denver, CO 80203–2416
   (303)861–1111

CONNECTICUT

L Connecticut Statewide
   Grievance Committee
   287 Main Street, 2nd Floor,
   Suite 2
   East Hartford, CT 06118–1885
   (203)568–5157
$ Lawyers' Funds for Client
   Protection
   (203)721–0025
J Judicial Review Council
   30 Trinity Street
   P.O. Box 260099

Hartford, CT 06126-0099
(203)566-5424

DELAWARE

L Delaware Office of Disciplinary Counsel
200 West Ninth Street, Suite
300-A
P.O. Box 472
Wilmington, DE 19899
(302)571-8703

$ Lawyers' Funds for Client
Protection
(302)652-2117

J Court on the Judiciary
P.O. Box 476
Dover, DE 19903
(302)739-4155

DISTRICT OF COLUMBIA

L District of Columbia Board
on Professional
Responsibility
515 Fifth Street, N.W.,
Building A, Room 127
Washington, DC
20001-2797
(202)638-1501

$ Lawyers' Funds for Client
Protection
(202)737-4700 ext. 237

J Commission on Judicial
Disabilities and Tenure
515 Fifth Street, N.W.,
Building A, Room 312
Washington, DC 20001
(202)727-1363

FLORIDA

L The Florida Bar
650 Apalachee Parkway
Tallahassee, FL 32399-2300
(904)561-5600

$ Lawyers' Funds for Client
Protection
(904)561-5812

J Judicial Qualifications
Commission
The Historic Capitol, Room
102
Tallahassee, FL 32399-6000
(904)488-1581

GEORGIA

L State Bar of Georgia
800 The Hurt Building
50 Hurt Plaza
Atlanta, GA 30303-2934
(404)527-8720

$ Lawyers' Funds for Client
Protection
(404)527-8732

J Judicial Qualifications
Commission
77 East Crossville Road,
Suite 206
Roswell, GA 30075-3085
(404)587-5208

HAWAII

L Supreme Court of Hawaii
Office of Disciplinary
Counsel
1164 Bishop Street, Suite 600

Honolulu, HI 96813
(808)521-4591
$ Lawyers' Funds for Client
Protection
(808)599-2483
J Commission on Judicial
Conduct
P.O. Box 2560
Honolulu, HI 96804
(808)549-4790

IDAHO

L Idaho State Bar
P.O. Box 895
525 West Jefferson
Boise, ID 83701-0895
(208)334-4500
$ Lawyers' Funds for Client
Protection
(208)342-8958
J Judicial Council
P.O. Box 16488
Boise, ID 83715
(208)344-8474

ILLINOIS

L Attorney Registration and
Disciplinary Commission
of the Supreme Court of
Illinois
One Prudential Plaza
130 East Randolph Drive,
Suite 1500
Chicago, Il 60601
(312)565-2600,
(800)826-8625

$ Lawyers' Funds for Client
Protection
(312)565-2600
J Judicial Inquiry Board
100 West Randolph Street,
Suite 14-500
Chicago, IL 60601
(312)814-5554

INDIANA

L Indiana Supreme Court Disciplinary Commission
1150 W. Washington Street,
#1060
Indianapolis, IN 46204-3417
(317)232-1807
$ Lawyers' Funds for Client
Protection
(317)639-5465
J Commission on Judicial
Qualifications
115 W. Washington Street,
#1080
Indianapolis, IN 46204-3417
(317)232-4706

IOWA

L Iowa State Bar Association
Committee on Professional
Ethics and Conduct
521 East Locust Street, 3rd
Floor
Des Moines, IA 50309-1939
(515)243-0027
$ Lawyers' Funds for Client
Protection
(515)246-8076

J   Commission on Judicial
      Qualifications
    State Capitol
    Des Moines, IA 50319
    (515)281-5241

KANSAS

L   Supreme Court of Kansas
    3706 S.W. Topeka Blvd.,
      #100
    Topeka, KS 66609
    (912)296-2486
$ Lawyers' Funds for Client
      Protection
    (913)296-3229
J   Commission on Judicial
      Qualifications
    Kansas Judicial Center,
      Room 374
    301 S.W. 10th Avenue
    Topeka, KS 66612-1507
    (913)296-3229

KENTUCKY

L   Kentucky Bar Association
    514 West Main Street
    Frankfort, KY 40601-1883
    (502)564-3795
$ Clients' Security Fund
    (502)564-3795
J   Judicial Retirement and
      Removal Commission
    P.O. Box 21868
    Lexington, KY 40522-1868
    (606)233-4128

LOUISIANA

L   Louisiana State Bar
      Association
    Office of Disciplinary
      Counsel
    601 St. Charles Avenue, 4th
      Floor
    New Orleans, LA 70130
    (504)523-1414
$ Lawyers' Funds for Client
      Protection
    (504)566-1600
J   Judiciary Commission of
      Louisiana
    301 Loyola Avenue, Room
      109
    New Orleans, LA 70112-1887
    (504)568-5747

MAINE

L   Maine Board of Overseers of
      the Bar
    97 Winthrop Street
    P.O. Box 1820
    Augusta, ME 04332-1820
    (207)623-1121
    (Maine does not have a secu-
      rity fund.)
J   Committee on Judicial
      Responsibility and
      Disability
    P.O. Box 8058
    Portland, ME 04104-8058
    (207)780-4364

MARYLAND

L   Attorney Grievance Commission of Maryland
    100 Community Place, Suite 3301
    Crownsville, MD 21032–2027
    (410)514–7051

$ Lawyers' Funds for Client Protection
    (410)543–8410

J   Commission on Judicial Disabilities
    University of Baltimore Law School
    Charles Street at Mount Royal
    Baltimore, MD 21201
    (410)625–3086

MASSACHUSETTS

L   Massachusetts Board of Bar Overseers
    Office of the Bar Counsel
    75 Federal Street, 7th Floor
    Boston, MA 02110
    (617)357–1860

$ Lawyers' Funds for Client Protection
    (617)357–1860 ext. 51

J   Commission on Judicial Conduct
    14 Beacon Street, Suite 102
    Boston, MA 02108
    (617)725–8050

MICHIGAN

L   Michigan Attorney Grievance Commission
    Marquette Building, Suite 256
    243 West Congress
    Detroit, MI 48226
    (313)961–6585

$ Lawyers' Funds for Client Protection
    (517)372–9033 ext. 3010

J   Judicial Tenure Commission
    211 West Fort Street, Suite 1410
    Detroit, MI 48226
    (313)256–9104

MINNESOTA

L   Minnesota Office of Professional Responsibility
    25 Constitution Avenue, Suite 105
    St. Paul, MN 55155–1500
    (612)296–3952

$ Lawyers' Funds for Client Protection
    (612)296–3952

J   Board on Judicial Standards
    2025 Centre Pointe Blvd., Suite 420
    Mendota Heights, MN 55120
    (612)296–3999

MISSISSIPPI

L   Mississippi State Bar
    643 North State Street
    P.O. Box 2168
    Jackson, MS 39225–2168
    (601)948–4471

$ Lawyers' Funds for Client
 Protection
 (601)948-4471

J Commission on Judicial
 Performance
 P.O. Box 22527
 146 East Amite Street
 Jackson, MS 39225-2527
 (601)359-1273

MISSOURI

L Missouri Supreme Court
 Office of Chief Disciplinary
 Counsel
 3335 America Avenue
 Jefferson City, MO 65109
 (314)635-7400

$ Lawyers' Funds for Client
 Protection
 (314)635-4128

J Commission on Retirement,
 Removal and Discipline
 6933 Hampton Avenue
 St. Louis, MO 63109
 (314)352-6944

MONTANA

L State Bar of Montana
 P.O. Box 577
 Helena, MT 59624
 (406)442-7660

$ Lawyers' Funds for Client
 Protection
 (406)442-7660

J Judicial Standards
 Commission
 Justice Building, Room 315

215 North Sanders
 Helena, MT 59620-3002
 (406)444-2608

NEBRASKA

L Nebraska State Bar
 Association
 P.O. Box 81809
 Lincoln, NE 68501
 (402)475-7091

$ Lawyers' Funds for Client
 Protection
 (402)475-7091

J Commission on Judicial
 Qualifications
 State Court Administrator
 1220 State Capitol
 P.O. Box 98910
 Lincoln, NE 68509
 (402)471-3730

NEVADA

L State Bar of Nevada
 201 Las Vegas Blvd. South,
 #200
 Las Vegas, NV 89101-6579
 (702)382-2200

$ Lawyers' Funds for Client
 Protection
 (702)382-2200

J Commission on Judicial
 Discipline
 P.O. Box 48
 Carson City, NV 89702
 (702)687-4017

NEW HAMPSHIRE

L   New Hampshire Supreme
      Court
    Professional Conduct
      Committee
    4 Park Street, #304
    Concord, NH 03301
    (603)224-5828

$ Lawyers' Funds for Client
      Protection
    (603)224-6942

J   Committee on Judicial
      Conduct
    Frank Rowe Kenison
      Supreme Court Building
    P.O. Box 1476
    Concord, NH 03301-1476
    (603)271-2646

NEW JERSEY

L   Office of Attorney Ethics
    Supreme Court of New Jersey
    Hughes Justice Complex,
      CN-963
    25 West Market Street
    Trenton, NJ 08625
    (609)292-8750

$ Lawyers' Funds for Client
      Protection
    (609)984-7179

J   Advisory Committee on
      Judicial Conduct
    Hughes Justice Complex, 7th
      Floor, North Wing
      CN-037
    Trenton, NJ 08625
    (609)292-2552

NEW MEXICO

L   Disciplinary Board of the
      Supreme Court of New
      Mexico
    400 Gold S.W. #800
    Albuquerque, NM
      87102-3261
    (505)842-5781

$ Lawyers' Funds for Client
      Protection
    (505)843-8765

J   Judicial Standards Commis-
      sion
    2539 Wyoming, N.E. #A
    Albuquerque, NM 87112
    (505)841-9438

NEW YORK

L   (covering Bronx and New
      York Counties)
    First Judicial Department
    Departmental Disciplinary
      Committee
    41 Madison Avenue, 39th
      Floor
    New York, NY 10010
    (212)685-1000

    (covering Kings, Queens, and
    Richmond Counties)
    Second Judicial Department
    Second and Eleventh Judicial
      District Grievance Com-
      mittees
    Municipal Building—12th
      Floor
    210 Joralemon Street

Brooklyn, NY 11201
(718)624-7851

(covering Dutchess, Orange,
Putnam, Rockland, and
Westchester Counties)
Second Judicial Department
Ninth Judicial District Griev-
 ance Committee
Crosswest Office Center,
 Suite 200
399 Knollwood Road
White Plains, NY 10603
(914)949-4540

(covering Nassau and Suffolk
Counties)
Second Judicial Department
New York State Grievance
 Committee
Tenth Judicial District
6900 Jericho Turnpike, Suite
 LL-102
Syosset, NY 11791
(516)364-7344

(covering Albany, Broome,
Chemung, Chenango,
Clinton, Columbia, Cort-
land, Delaware, Essex,
Franklin, Fulton, Greene,
Hamilton, Madison, Mont-
gomery, Otsego, Rensselaer,
St. Lawrence, Saratoga,
Schenectady, Schoharie,
Schuyler, Sullivan, Tioga,
Tompkins, Ulster, Warren,

and Washington Counties)
Third Judicial Department
Committee on Professional
 Standards
Alfred E. Smith Office Bldg.,
 22nd Floor
P.O. Box 7013
Capitol Station Annex
Albany, NY 12225-0013
(518)474-8816

(covering Herkimer, Jef-
ferson, Lewis, Oneida,
Onondaga, and Oswego
Counties)
Fourth Judicial Department
Fifth District Grievance
 Committee
465 South Salina Street, #106
Syracuse, NY 13202
(315)471-1835

(covering Cayuga, Liv-
ingston, Monroe, Ontario,
Seneca, Steuben, Wayne, and
Yates Counties)
Fourth Judicial Department
Seventh District Grievance
 Committee
1002 Union Trust Building
19 West Main Street
Rochester, NY 14614
(716)546-8340

$ Lawyers' Funds for Client
 Protection
(518)474-8438

J   Commission on Judicial
    Conduct
    801 Second Avenue
    New York, NY 10017
    (212)949-8888

NORTH CAROLINA
L   North Carolina State Bar
    208 Fayetteville Street Mall
    P.O. Box 25908
    Raleigh, NC 27611
    (919)828-4620
$ Lawyers' Funds for Client
    Protection
    (919)828-4620
J   Judicial Standards
    Commission
    P.O. Box 1122
    Raleigh, NC 27602
    (919)733-2690

NORTH DAKOTA
L   Disciplinary Board of the
    Supreme Court of North
    Dakota
    P.O. Box 2297
    Bismarck, ND 58502-2297
    (701)328-3925
$ Lawyers' Funds for Client
    Protection
    (701)255-1404
J   Judicial Conduct
    Commission
    P.O. Box 2297
    515½ East Broadway, #101
    Bismarck, ND 58502
    (701)224-3348

OHIO
L   Office of the Disciplinary
    Counsel of the Supreme
    Court of Ohio
    175 South 3rd Street, Suite 280
    Columbus, OH 43215-5134
    (614)461-0256

(covering Summit County)
Akron Bar Association
90 South High Street
Akron, OH 44308
(216)253-5007

(covering Hamilton
County)
Cincinnati Bar Association
35 East 7th Street, #800
Cincinnati OH 45202-2411
(513)381-8213

(covering Cuyahoga County)
Cleveland Bar Association
113 St. Clair Avenue, 2nd Floor
Cleveland OH 44114-1253
(216)696-3525

(covering Franklin County)
Columbus Bar Association
175 S. Third Street
Columbus, OH 43215-5193
(614)225-6053

(covering Montgomery
County)
Dayton Bar Association
600 One First National Plaza

Dayton, OH 45402–1501
(513)222–7902

(covering Lucas County)
Toledo Bar Association
311 N. Superior Street
Toledo, OH 43604
(419)242–9363
$ Lawyers' Funds for Client
   Protection
   (614)221–0562
J See first listing "L" (Office of
   the Disciplinary Counsel
   of the Supreme Court of
   Ohio).

OKLAHOMA
L Oklahoma State Bar
   Association
   1901 North Lincoln Blvd.
   P.O. Box 53036
   Oklahoma City, OK 73152
   (405)524–2365
$ Lawyers' Funds for Client
   Protection
   (405)524–2365
J Council on Judicial
   Complaints
   1915 North Stiles, #305
   Oklahoma City, OK 73105
   (405)521–2450

OREGON
L Oregon State Bar
   P.O. Box 1689
   5200 S.W. Meadows Road
   Lake Oswego, OR

97035–0889
(503)620–0222
$ Lawyers' Funds for Client
   Protection
   (503)620–0222 ext. 320
J Commission on Judicial Fitness and Disability
   P.O. Box 9035
   Portland, OR 97207
   (503)241–2300

PENNSYLVANIA
L Disciplinary Board of the
   Supreme Court of
   Pennsylvania
   Union Trust Building, #400
   501 Grant Street
   Pittsburgh, PA 15219–4407
   (412)565–3173
$ Lawyers' Funds for Client
   Protection
   (717)691–7503
J Judicial Conduct Board
   225 Market Street
   Harrisburg, PA 17101
   (717)234–7911

RHODE ISLAND
L Disciplinary Board of the
   Supreme Court of Rhode
   Island
   Fogarty Judicial Annex
   24 Weybasset Street
   Providence, RI 02903
   (401)277–3270

$ Lawyers' Funds for Client
Protection
(401)421–5740

J Commission on Judicial
Tenure and Discipline
J. Joseph Garrahy Judicial
Complex
One Dorrance Plaza
Providence, RI 02903
(401)277–1188

SOUTH CAROLINA

L South Carolina Board of Commissioners on Grievances
and Discipline
P.O. Box 11330
Columbia, SC 29211
(803)734–2038

$ Lawyers' Funds for Client
Protection
(803)799–6653

J Board of Commissioners on
Judicial Standards
P.O. Box 50487
Columbia, SC 29250
(803)734–1965

SOUTH DAKOTA

L State Bar of South Dakota
222 E. Capitol
Pierre, SD 57501–2596
(605)224–7554

$ Lawyers' Funds for Client
Protection
(605)224–7554

J Commission on Judicial
Qualifications

P.O. Box 507
Madison, SD 57042–0507
(604)256–5285

TENNESSEE

L Board of Professional
Responsibility of the
Supreme Court of
Tennessee
The Oaks Tower, #730
1101 Kermit Drive
Nashville, TN 37217
(615)361–7500

$ Lawyers' Funds for Client
Protection
(615)741–3096

J Court of the Judiciary
100 Supreme Court Building
7th and Charlotte
Nashville, TN 37243–0606
(615)741–2681

TEXAS

L State Bar of Texas
P.O. Box 12487
Austin, TX 78711
(800)204–2222

$ Lawyers' Funds for Client
Protection
(512)463–1463

J State Commission on Judicial Conduct
P.O. Box 12265, Capitol Station
Austin, TX 78711
(512)463–5533

UTAH

L   Utah State Bar
    Office of Attorney Discipline
    645 South 200 East
    Salt Lake City, UT 84111
    (801)531-9110
$ Lawyers' Funds for Client
    Protection
    (801)531-9077
J   Judicial Conduct Commission
    3760 Highland Office Plaza,
        #400
    3760 Highland Drive
    Salt Lake City, UT 84106
    (801)273-3363

VERMONT

L   Professional Conduct Board
    of the Supreme Court of
    Vermont
    Office of Bar Counsel
    59 Elm Street
    Montpelier, VT 05602
    (802)828-3368
$ Lawyers' Funds for Client
    Protection
    (802)223-2020
J   Judicial Conduct Board
    P.O. Box 796
    White River Junction, VT
        05001
    (802)295-5631

VIRGINIA

L   Virginia State Bar
    Eight and Main Building
    707 East Main Street, #1500

Richmond, VA 23219-2803
(804)775-0500
$ Lawyers' Funds for Client
    Protection
    (804)775-0524
J   Judicial Inquiry and Review
    Commission
    P.O. Box 367
    Richmond, VA 23203-0367
    (804)786-6636

WASHINGTON

L   Washington State Bar
    Association
    500 Westin Building
    2001 Sixth Avenue
    Seattle, WA 98121-2599
    (206)727-8207
$ Lawyers' Funds for Client
    Protection
    (206)727-8232
J   Commission on Judicial
    Conduct
    P.O. Box 1817, EW-14
    Olympia, WA 98507
    (360)753-4585

WEST VIRGINIA

L   West Virginia State Bar
    210 Dickinson Street
    Charleston, WV 25301
    (304)558-7999
$ Lawyers' Funds for Client
    Protection
    (304)558-7993

J Judicial Investigation Commission
P.O. Box 1629
Charleston, WV 25326–1629
(304)558–0169

WISCONSIN
L Wisconsin Board of Attorneys' Professional Responsibility
110 East Main Street, #410
Madison, WI 53703–3383
(608)267–7274
$ Lawyers' Funds for Client Protection
(608)257–3838
J Judicial Commission
110 East Main Street, #606

Madison, WI 53703–3328
(608)266–7637

WYOMING
L Wyoming State Bar
500 Randall Avenue
P.O. Box 109
Cheyenne, WY 82003–0109
(307)632–9061
$ Client Security Fund
(307)632–9061
J Judicial Supervisory Commission
Supreme Court Building, Room 110
Cheyenne, WY 82002
(307)777–7581

APPENDIX II

Organizations and Resource Numbers

GET YOURSELF COUNTED
In 1995, the Illinois State Senate began collecting testimony from women and men who have experienced legal/court abuse in Illinois's divorce court system. Please send a letter documenting your experience to:

Illinois State Senator Kathleen K. Parker
Chair, Senate Legislative Inquiry Committee on Divorce Law and
    Procedure in Illinois
191 Waukegan Road, Suite 210
Northfield, IL 60093
(708)441-0077

A nationwide data collection effort is being conducted to document lawyer/court abuses for the purposes of reforming the system in family law cases. If you have experienced legal bashing, financial abuse by an attorney, misrepresentation, an arbitrary or cruel ruling by a judge, or related lawyer or judicial abuse, please document your experience in a letter and send it to the following address. If you provide backup documentation, such as court papers, that you wish to have returned to you, please remember to include a self-addressed stamped envelope. (Don't forget to include your e-mail address if you have one.)

Divorced From Justice
200 East 10th Street, Suite 618
New York, NY 10003
Send e-mail to: kwinner@divorcedfromjustice.com

SELF-HELP ORGANIZATIONS FOR WOMEN

National Coalition for Family Justice, Inc.

821 Broadway

Irvington-on-Hudson, NY 10533

(914)591–5753

With national headquarters in Irvington-on-Hudson, New York, this nonprofit self-help organization was formed by Monica Getz for families in divorce who have been abused by the legal/justice systems. The Coalition holds group meetings, provides information, offers volunteer support services such as court-watching, and works for legislative reform. Has newsletter. Has affiliate organization in Long Island, N.Y., and nationwide contacts.

National Coalition for Family Justice, Inc., Louisiana affiliate

P.O. Box 231173

New Orleans, LA 70183

(504)525–9580

The Louisiana affiliate is currently collecting data to document abuses in that state. Please send letters to the above address.

Fresno Alliance for Divorce Reform (California)

(209)435–5715

This grassroots organization for divorcing women holds monthly meetings, provides information on California laws, and offers volunteer support services, such as accompanying women to meetings with their attorneys. Has an affiliate organization in San Diego.

Michigan Alliance for the Rights of Children

P.O. Box 951

Fenton, Michigan 48430

(810)629-8554

This is a grassroots organization for women embattled in custody litigation.

Mothers on Trial

c/o 707 Riendas Street West

Toronto, Ontario M5T 2W6

(416)761-7734

A Self-help organization to provide support to women involved in the family system.

LEGAL ORGANIZATIONS

Justice for Children (JFC)
412 Main Street, Suite 400
Houston, TX 77002
(713)225-4357
fax: 713-225-2818

This national nonprofit child advocacy organization is headquartered in Houston, Texas, and works on behalf of abused or neglected children whose cases have been lost in the child welfare, family court, and/or criminal justice systems. Unlike other child advocacy organizations, which have been formed to prevent child abuse through education and social programs, JFC focuses on protecting the abused child once an initial report has been made to the authorities. Justice for Children currently has chapters in Texas, Utah, Indiana, California, Florida, South Carolina, and Michigan.

National Center for Protective Parents, Inc.
1908 Riverside Drive
Trenton, NJ 08618
(609)394-1506

The National Center for Protective Parents in Civil Child Sexual Abuse Cases is a nonprofit organization that provides legal assistance and resources to parents in divorce who have experienced "system failure" trying to protect their children from sexual abuse by the abuser/spouse. The organization also offers attorney training in exchange for pro bono representation. Has newsletter.

National Organization for Women (NOW) Legal Defense and
   Education Fund
Washington, D.C., office: (202)544-4470
New York office: (212)925-6635
(Does not supply help to individuals in family law cases.)
Resource Center on Child Protection and Custody
(800)527-3223
fax: 702-784-6160

Located in Reno, Nevada, the Resource Center provides information, materials, consultation, technical assistance, and legal research related to child protection and custody in the context of domestic violence.

Family Civil Rights Project
Policy Sciences Center Inc.
Conducts civil rights litigation
(212)964-6818
Jeremiah McKenna, Esq. is the director.

LEGAL AUDITING

Legalgard
Corn Exchange Building
123 Chestnut Street
Philadelphia, PA 19106
(800)525-3426

Legalgard is a company of auditors that specialize in legal billing issues in all areas of law. The company provides expert testimony where necessary, and has branches nationwide.

FINANCIAL PLANNING SERVICES

Aequus Financial Advisory Services
303 West Erie, Suite 311
Chicago, IL 60610
(312)664-4090

Aequus provides detailed financial analysis that can be used by individuals, lawyers, and the courts to establish financial needs for dependent families, during and after the divorce proceeding; also sells computer software to attorneys providing analysis that takes into account the variations in state laws.

Pension Rights Center
918 16th Street, N.W., Suite 704
Washington, DC 20006
(202)296-3776

The Pension Rights Center provides information about the various rules that apply to the division of pensions in divorce.

BATTERED WOMEN SERVICES

The following are state domestic violence crisis hotlines compiled by the National Resource Center on Domestic Violence. These are toll-free, 24-hour, crisis intervention phone lines. These 800 numbers will only work if called from within the state. Those noted as I&R are not crisis hotlines. They are for information and referral only. Call the Coalition numbers to find out how to obtain free court orders of protection if you or your children are in danger and cannot afford to hire a lawyer.

STATE	HOT LINE	COALITION
Florida	1-800-500-1119	904-668-6862
Georgia	1-800-643-1212(I&R)	404-524-3847
Illinois	1-800-241-8456	217-789-2830
Indiana	1-800-332-7385	317-641-1912
Iowa	1-800-942-0333	515-281-7284

STATE	HOT LINE	COALITION
Lousiana	1-800-837-5400	504-542-4446
Maryland	1-800-MD-HELPS	301-942-0900
Minnesota	1-800-646-0994	612-646-6177
New Hampshire	1-800-852-3388	603-224-8893
New Mexico	1-800-773-3645	505-246-9240
Nevada	1-800-500-1556	702-358-1171
New York	1-800-942-6906	518-432-4864
North Dakota	1-800-472-2911	701-255-6240
Ohio	1-800-934-9840	614-784-0023
Oklahoma	1-800-522-9054	405-557-1210
Rhode Island	1-800-494-8100(I&R)	401-723-3051
South Carolina	1-800-260-9293	803-254-3699
Tennessee	1-800-356-6767	615-386-9406
Virginia	1-800-838-8238	804-221-0990
Washington state	1-800-562-6025	206-352-4029
Wyoming (covers Nebraska also)	1-800-990-3877	307-235-2814

VISIT OUR WEB SITE ON THE INTERNET

For more information on women, children, and consumers dealing with the inner workings of the U.S. courts, visit us on the World Wide Web. Here's an easy-to-remember Web address (known as URL):

http://www.divorcedfromjustice.com

Compuserve, America OnLine, and Prodigy provide access to the Internet.

E-mail us at:

kwinner@divorcedfromjustice.com

If you don't have a computer, you can obtain access to the Internet through your local library. Also try your local community college or continuing-education center.

APPENDIX III

TESTIMONY OF: ELEANOR S. GOODWIN
BUTLER COUNTY, PA
FC 88–1161
BOOK 21 P. 369

Good afternoon and thank you for inviting me. First I would like to introduce myself—I am Eleanor Goodwin from Butler County. I filed for a divorce, PFA [Protection From Abuse] and an injunction to protect the multi-million dollar estate during the divorce proceedings on December 6, 1988.

As I speak today, I am no longer seeking a divorce. There will be no equitable distribution. Spousal support was awarded but never paid. My home valued in excess of 1 million dollars is gone, sold at sheriff sale. A second home sits in ruins awaiting the same fate. All of the assets acquired during a 10 year marriage are gone and yet, I NEVER RECEIVED ONE CENT!

I have over $98,000 in legal fees of which $83,000 remain unpaid, forcing me to file bankruptcy. I have been in two states and three countries and now I am in FEDERAL COURT because nothing was ever resolved by the Butler County Courts! I now have in excess of $300,000 in judgments filed against me, yet I was NOT responsible for most of these debts. I filed a complaint against my first attorney with the Disciplinary Board. He retaliated by accepting a foreclosure action naming me as a DEFENDANT to this action. He knew I was NOT. The Judge knew I was NOT, yet he refused to dismiss the complaint against me and a judgment was entered regardless. I filed a second complaint with the Disciplinary Board and that too was dismissed. My credit has been ruined, my life has been hanging in limbo for over 32 months, the marital assets are gone forever and I have lost all faith in the judicial system. A Supreme Court Judge proudly boasted, "PENNSYLVANIA IS THE GRANDDADDY OF THE RULES OF CIVIL

PROCEDURE." Well Pennsylvania, it is a sad commentary what you have allowed to happen. The stories we have heard today all tell of the abuses of those Rules and the devastating effects the citizens of this Commonwealth have endured in our courts. I am no different.

My husband was a self-made multi-millionaire who knew how to play the legal game. He could afford top notch legal counsel. He knew he could drag out litigation until I was defeated financially, emotionally and mentally. He knew the system could be manipulated and he became the Master. He knew the system DOES NOT WORK! He knew he could purge himself of contempt and continue to do whatever he wanted. He vowed I would receive "nothing" and he kept that vow until the end. He was killed in Butler County on May 11, 1991. Had this not happened I have to wonder if I would still be in the Butler County Courts another 32 months.

The nightmare began in Butler County when the first Judge denied the PFA, denied an injunction to protect the assets and further took no action when I asked to withdraw the divorce complaint, due to health problems my husband developed. Because Butler refused to take jurisdiction (which is inconsistent with the Rules of Civil Procedure as well as the PA Divorce Code), this allowed my husband to flee to Florida with most of the assets where he promptly filed for and was granted a divorce. I filed an appeal and the divorce was reversed and remanded to the lower court. This caused $31,000 in legal fees as my husband continued to file a total of 95 actions in Florida trying to obtain a divorce and gain jurisdiction. Florida refused to take jurisdiction citing PA *was* the proper forum and *should proceed*.

On December 8, 1988, *two days after* I filed for divorce in PA, my husband gave his son from a former marriage all stock in a real estate venture worth 1.5 million dollars without any consideration. This was clearly a fraudulent conveyance in an effort to defeat equitable distribution and should have been declared null and void. It was not. I filed an equity suit to protect my interests. This property was sold with the proceeds going into an escrow account. The attorneys opened the account, never told me how much money was in the account or where the account was! I have recently filed a suit in Federal court to have this resolved as his son, who was a party to the fraud, is now claiming all rights to the money.

In May, 1989 I was awarded spousal support. My husband refused to appear at the hearing, yet three days later filed exceptions and demanded a de novo hearing. As of May, 1991 a hearing was NOT held, support was NEVER paid. A hearing for contempt was scheduled for March, 1991. I appeared, my husband refused. I asked the hearings officer why he wouldn't put a judgment against property my husband owned and he replied "HE WASN'T TAUGHT THAT." He finally concluded by saying "YOU MAY END UP A PAUPER, YOU MAY SPEND SEVERAL THOUSAND DOLLARS, YOUR HEALTH WILL SUFFER, BUT DON'T GIVE UP, THE SYSTEM WORKS, THAT'S WHY I AM PAID BIG BUCKS!" Well the system didn't work as the support due was in excess of $50,000. Within two weeks of my husband's death, I was notified the matter should now be taken up with his estate and not the Domestic Relations Office.

I petitioned the Butler Courts to begin equitable distribution in May, 1989 while there were still assets. The Judge ordered briefs to be filed regarding jurisdiction which delayed the process further. My attorneys filed ours—my husband's attorney ignored the order and finally the Judge ignored it as well. In May, 1990 a Master was appointed. Hearings were scheduled but my husband refused to file the inventory and other financial information as well as appearing. This went on until September 20, 1990! I immediately filed exceptions and as of May, 1991 they were never heard. Unknown to me, the attorneys agreed by stipulation that the Master would be paid $110.00 an hour, which is contrary to the Local Rules of Court for Butler County, whereas the Rules state the Master shall be paid $40.00 an hour and not to exceed $150.00!

Prior to the equitable distribution hearing, I filed numerous petitions trying in vain to protect what I could. I petitioned that my husband's sons be named as additional defendants since he was using them to remove, sell and hide assets under their names and in bogus corporations. The Judge had the complaint "under advisement" for 15 months thereby allowing the assets to continue to be removed by my husband's sons at his direction.

In the interim I filed other petitions requesting injunctions to prevent my husband from raping the estate and to post a bond to protect my interests. The Judge stated he did not think my husband could post a bond! My husband continued to remove, sell, and hide assets. At one of the hearings the Judge waved his hand in the air and stated "THAT WAS YESTERDAY, WHAT DO YOU WANT?" *I WANTED THE ASSETS PROTECTED*! He cautioned my husband to stop. My husband ignored the order and again another petition was filed requesting contempt charges be brought. The Judge found him in contempt of court and allowed him to purge himself of this wrongdoing by posting $7500.00 with the prothonotary's office. This was to be used for equitable distribution. What an investment for my husband—he had removed over 1 million dollars of assets already! The $7500.00 was then used to pay the Master's fees. When my husband was killed, his attorney decided he should not have to file a claim against the estate. He could be paid with the balance of that money! The Judge thought that was fair and awarded him counsel fees. I RECEIVED NOTHING!

As of November, 1990 I was unable to afford an attorney and could not pay the ones I had previously. I was forced to act pro se. I petitioned for counsel fees and was denied. I petitioned the court then appoint me counsel. The Judge replied "THERE ARE SUBSTANTIAL MARITAL ASSETS, THEREFORE THIS PETITION IS DENIED." Yet this was the same Judge who found my husband in contempt for removing the marital assets a few months earlier! He knew I did not have access to the assets. It was not my choice to become a pro se litigant—it was the Courts by their refusal to adhere to the Rules of Civil Procedure and the PA Divorce Code when they refused to award counsel fees and when they refused to enforce spousal support for over two years! This is a blatant violation and it cannot not be ignored!

In December, 1989 an agreement was reached between my husband and myself, whereas he would give up the exclusive possession of *my* condominium in Florida that the Butler County Courts gave him. In return I would allow the sale of a property (that was fraudulently conveyed to his son) to proceed as long as the funds were held in escrow. My attorney assured me a court order was being prepared and not to worry. In May, 1990 my husband finally removed himself from the condo along with all of the built in appliances, the furniture and totally destroyed the interior, leaving the condo in foreclosure. I began filing petitions in November, 1990 to get my property back because my attorney would not do anything for 16 months already! Butler County ignored my petitions! In desperation I filed a petition for a pre-trial conference. The Judge answered "THIS COURT HAS NO INTEN-TIONS OF EVER HAVING A PRE-TRIAL CONFERENCE WITH YOU." I have lost a second home along with all of the equity I had in it. It is being foreclosed this month and I do not have the funds to again save it. Nor would the courts do anything to protect the property!

Perhaps William Gladstone said it best when he said "JUSTICE DELAYED IS JUSTICE DENIED." Throughout the 32 months I have been in the Butler County Courts I have found, with or without counsel, petitions are routinely ignored or denied regardless of the urgency or the merits. I have been deprived of the basic right to have my day in court, to be heard or to have my property protected! I have often said a bad decision is better than no decision. Without a decision from the courts you cannot go on. You are completely shut out of the due process which we are guaranteed under the Constitution of the United States! THIS IS NO FAULT IN PENNSYLVANIA TODAY AND IT DOESN'T WORK!

I have been an eyewitness to the greatest travesty of justice that a court can inflict on one person. I have felt as a hostage surely must feel being at the mercy of a malevolent captor. I have felt more abused by the very courts I sought refuge in than I did in an unhappy marriage that had to end. I feel I have been held hostage for 32 months and at the mercy of a Judge who has no regard or perhaps worse, knowledge of the Rules of Civil Procedure, the PA Divorce Code and the Consti-tution of the United States. He has abused his position under the guise of "discretion of the court" which is a cop out for incompetence and personal bias against certain litigants! WHERE ARE THE CHECKS AND BALANCES IN FAMILY COURT? WHERE DOES ONE GO TO GET EQUITY OR JUSTICE IF *NOT* THE COURTS? WHAT GOOD ARE THE RULES OR THE DIVORCE CODE IF THE JUDGES CAN ARBITRARILY ABANDON THEM AND RUN AMOK WITHOUT ANY ACCOUNTABILITY?

I would like to conclude by sharing with you the last day I was in the Butler County Courts. I was given a telefax that was forwarded to the Butler County Police Department from the Florida Police advising my husband intended "to kill me at the May 7, 1991 hearing and any police officer who attempted to stop him." I notified the Judge, the President Judge and District Attorney of Butler County by fax. THE FAX WAS IGNORED BY ALL OF THE ABOVE! I then called the District Attorney and demanded police protection as I knew my husband meant what he said. He had made death threats and attempts against me beginning in December, 1988 when I filed for a divorce. Upon entering the courthouse I was searched and led under armed guard to the courtroom. The Judge appeared briefly in what appeared to be a bullet proof vest and announced to the attorneys they should come into his chambers. I sat alone in the courtroom. His final decision—he would give the matters some thought and one of the attorneys should call him the following week!

FOUR DAYS LATER MY HUSBAND WAS KILLED IN A SHOOT OUT WITH POLICE IN BUTLER COUNTY. When they recovered his body and began to inventory his vehicle they found two body bags, an arsenal of sophisticated high powered weapons, a crossbow, knives and thousands of rounds of ammunition. He had been stalking me as evidenced by photos he had taken, along with items to indicate that he had not only planned to kill me, he had planned to torture me first.

He stated at the very first hearing, "SHE SHOULD BE DEAD, SOMEONE OTTA KILL HER AND I WILL NEVER MAKE ANY CONCESSIONS." He never did. After 32 months in the Butler County Court they never did nor did they allow me the protections available under the laws of this Commonwealth. There is no justifiable reason any one should have to live under the conditions I have. Fear and uncertainty prevailed my life, the court prolonged my misery and in the end I feel they helped kill my husband by aiding him in his madness. If the Court of Common Pleas of Butler County followed the Rules of Civil Procedure or the PA Divorce Code this could have been averted. It could have been settled if the Judge assigned to this case acted responsibly and in accordance with the laws; instead he blatantly ignored those laws which he is sworn to uphold. I will never recover the financial losses I have been forced to sustain and in time I will recover from the trauma of the last 32 months but I will never accept the fact that this is how our court system is supposed to be.

Before I turn the floor over to you, I would like to say thank you Martin J. O'Brien. Without you I would not be here today.

And thank you for listening.

CODE OF JUDICIAL CONDUCT VIOLATIONS OF CODE IN BUTLER COUNTY

Canon 1: A judge should uphold the integrity and independence of the judiciary.

I. **A.** An independent and honorable judiciary is indispensable to justice in our society. A judge should participate in establishing, maintaining and enforcing and should himself observe high standards of conduct so that the integrity and independence of the judiciary may be preserved. The provisions of this Code should be construed and applied to further that objective.

Canon 2: A judge should avoid impropriety and the appearance of impropriety in all his activities.

I. **A.** *A Judge should respect and comply with the law and should conduct himself at all times in a manner that prompts public confidence in the integrity and impartiality of the judiciary.*

II. **B.** *A Judge should not allow his family, social or other relationships to influence his judicial conduct or judgment.*

Canon 3: A judge should perform the duties of his office impartially and diligently.

I. **A.** ADJUDICATIVE RESPONSIBILITIES

II. 1. *A judge should be faithful to the law and maintain professional competence in it.* He should be unswayed by partisan interests, public clamor or fear of criticism.

III. 2. *A judge should maintain order and decorum in proceedings before him.*

IV. 3. *A judge should be patient, dignified and courteous to litigants,* jurors, witnesses, lawyers and others with whom he deals in his official capacity, of his staff, court officials and others subject to his direction and control.

V. 4. *A judge should accord to every person who is legally interested in a proceeding, or his lawyer, full right to be heard according to law,* except as authorized by law, *must not consider ex-parte communications concerning pending proceedings.*

VI.   5. *A judge should dispose promptly of the business of the court.*

VII.   **B.** ADMINISTRATIVE RESPONSIBILITIES

VIII.   3. *A judge should take or initiate appropriate disciplinary measures against a judge or lawyer for unprofessional conduct of which the judge may become aware.*

IX.   **C.** DISQUALIFICATION

X.   1. *A judge should disqualify himself in a proceeding in which his impartiality might reasonably be questioned, including but not limited to instances where:*

XI.   **a.** *he has a personal bias or prejudice concerning a party or personal knowledge of disputed evidentiary facts concerning the proceedings.*

APPENDIX IV

List of States That Have
Conducted Gender Bias Studies

Gender bias task force investigations have been conducted by the state supreme courts of the following states:

Alaska
Arizona
Arkansas
California
Colorado
Connecticut
District of Columbia
Florida
Georgia
Hawaii
Idaho
Illinois
Indiana
Iowa
Kansas
Kentucky
Louisiana
Maine
Maryland

Massachusetts
Michigan
Minnesota
Missouri
Montana
Nebraska
Nevada
New Jersey
New Mexico
New York
North Dakota
Ohio
Rhode Island
Texas
Utah
Vermont
Washington
Wisconsin

APPENDIX V

Chart of the Types of Judicial Misconduct

Below is a partial listing contained in the *Judicial Discipline and Disability Digest* (1989–1991 supplement, edited by Sara Mathias) that is published by the American Judicature Society in Chicago, Illinois. The table of contents shows the various categories for discipline and "disability" (alcoholism and substance and drug abuse):

abuse of authority
abuse of prestige of office
appearance of impropriety
bad faith, malice, or moral turpitude
bias
conduct prejudicial to the effective and expeditious administration of
    business
conduct unbecoming a judge
conflict of interest
corruption in office
disability
extrajudicial acts
gross misconduct
gross partiality
habitual intemperance
incompetence
judicial temperament
neglect of duties, failure or refusal to perform duties
neglect, delay of caseload
misuse of appointive papers
excessive absenteeism
indecorous and discourteous behavior

harassment and retaliation
abuse of authority, misuse of judicial power
falsely or improperly certifying documents
ignoring procedures and formalities intended to protect litigants' rights
interference with attorney-client relationship
misappropriation of records or evidence
coercing dispositions
denying litigant rights
failing to inform litigants of their rights
ex parte communication (one-sided communication)
failure to disqualify or disclose potential or actual conflict of interest
    (including personal bias, family relationship or political relationship)
improper personal conduct
undignified, offensive speech
criminal conduct, indictment or conviction, violence
sexual offenses, drug offenses
negligence
nepotism
patterns of misconduct in the practice of law
prejudicial conduct
unfitness for judicial office

APPENDIX VI

The following opinion was issued by Kentucky Court of Appeals Judge Michael O. McDonald (now retired).

Rendered: MARCH 17, 1995; 2:00 p.m.
Commonwealth of Kentucky Court of Appeals
No. 92-CA–002962-MR
Christy S. Halloran   APPELLANT
v.
APPEAL FROM HARDIN CIRCUIT COURT
HONORABLE LARRY RAIKES JUDGE
ACTION NO. 85-CI–1359
Roger T. Rigney   APPELLEE

MCDONALD, JUDGE, DISSENTING. The only portion of the majority opinion in which I find myself in agreement is its observation that the child has suffered abuse that in all likelihood will leave him scarred for life. In the celebrated case, Morgan v. Foretich, 546 A. 2d 407, 413 (D.C. 1988),* the court recited the Kikuyu proverb: "when elephants fight, it is the grass that suffers." That the child has suffered and will continue to suffer, whether because of actual sexual abuse or the constant litigation resulting from the allegations of such abuse, is crystal clear from this record.

I would reverse the judgment of the trial court for two reasons: the trial court erred in the first instance in entertaining Roger's motion to

---

* The *Morgan v. Foretich* case, supra, is remarkably similar to the instant case both proceduarlly and factually. Morgan, a surgeon, believed Foretich was sexually abusing their young daughter, Hilary, of whom she had custody. Although she had medical evidence of vaginal scarring and other evidence of abuse, the trial court denied her motions to restrict Foretich's visitation rights. Morgan hid her child in New Zealand and spent more than two years in jail for civil contempt when she refused to reveal the child's whereabouts. It took an act of Congress to secure her release. She and her child remain in exile.

modify custody; and the trial judge erred in failing to recuse himself from the fray when he was so obviously biased against the appellant. I note, however, that Christy has raised other allegations of error with merit, particularly the ruling of the trial court's enhancing her burden of proof.

In my opinion there was no sufficient legal justification for a modification of custody hearing. For the purpose of establishing stability and consistency in the lives of young children, once a trial court has entered an order of custody in its finalized form, such determination becomes fixed as a matter of law and is not to be disturbed. It is the policy of the statutory scheme to let those affected, particuarly the children, get on with their lives and make the necessary adjustments under, at best, very difficult circumstances. KRS 403.340 is written restrictively and in no way encourages modification of custody decrees except in very limited and exceptional circumstances. The sole circumstance applicable to this case is subsection (c) of the statute which provides:

The child's present environment endangers seriously his physical, mental, moral, or emotional health, and the harm likely to be caused by a change of environment is outweighed by its advantage to him.

Quisenberry v. Quisenberry, Ky., 785 S.W. 2d 485 (1990), artfully prescribes that the legislative intent of the statute is to stabilize the child's custodial condition and to inhibit further litigation over custody unless the child is seriously endangered. The status quo is to be maintained unless there is a proven need for change authorized by the statute. See *Dexter v. Spainhoward*, Ky. App., 563 S.W.2d 474 (1978); *West v. West,* Ky. App., 664 S.W. 2d 948 (1984); and Graham & Keller, *Kentucky Domestic Relations Law,* Sec. T21. 08 (b). It is apparent that the wisdom of the statutory law is to cautiously grant modifications and this wisdom was enacted in KRS 403.350, as the procedural vehicle to effectuate a modified decree. It provides in pertinent part:

A party seeking a . . . modificiation of a custody decree *shall submit* together with his moving papers an affidavit setting forth facts supporting the requested . . . modificiation and shall give notice, together with a copy of his affidavit, to other parties to the proceeding, who may file opposing affidavits. *The court shall deny the motion unless it finds that adequate cause for hearing the motion is established by the affidavits,* in which case it shall set a date for hearing on an order to show cause why the requested . . . modification should not be granted. [Emphasis added].

Keeping in mind the precedental admonitions to keep the custodial status quo unless the status quo is overcome by compelling reasons otherwise, a review of the affidavits will show their shortcomings.

The affidavit of Roger Rigney alleges the following, and I quote all of the pertinent statements which the trial court had at its disposal to cause a hearing under KRS 403.350:

4. That the Respondent [Christy] has continued to attempt to alienate my son from me because my son has, on different occasions, told me that his mother, the Respondent, does not like me and has told him to say bad things about me.

[Comment: Statement contains no factual basis to believe that the child was endangered by present environment with Christy as required by the statute.]

5. When my son has been in my presence, he has appeared to be extremely happy and comfortable.

[Comment: This statement show no facts of a serious endangerment while in the custody of Christy.]

6. That at the hearing of Respondent's motion, which was heard by this Court on February 23, 1990, Christine Adams, M.D. testified that she continued to treat my son for emotional problems despite the fact that I had not seen my son for a period of nine (9) months.

[Comment: This statement bootstraps the expert testimony of Dr. Adams, which was offered in the first case against Roger and suggests that if the child is still having problems, as alleged by Dr. Adams, it must be because of his present environment with Christy as the custodian. This is a creative attempt to extrapolate inferences from testimony offered on behalf of and in support of Christy. However the statement contains no facts as required by the statute.]

7. Due to the delay of this Court entering its order of June 12, 1990 and the Respondent's efforts to thwart the aforesaid order, I did not see my son for a total of sixteen (16) months except for approximately seven (7) hours at a court appointed evaluator's office in Louisville, Kentucky.

[Comment: This statement , if true, contains an egregious circumstance obviously committed against Roger; however, it does not contain any factual basis to form a belief of serious endangerment to the child resulting from his present custodial arrangement.]

8. There has been a finding by the Court that the child, has been subject to emotional abuse by his mother in the form of brainwashing.

[Comment: This brainwashing statement is a non sequitur, because it was a fact previously found by the trial court, yet it was not sufficient to cause in the trial court's order a change of custody. Therefore, it has been a fact already found not to be of serious endangerment.

9. Based upon the foregoing I believe that my son's mental and emotional condition is deteriorating because of Respondent's increased mental and emotional abuse designed to utilize the child as a weapon in her ongoing attempt to punish me for divorcing her.

[Comment: This is a statement of belief and not fact and it offers only Roger's perceptions and conclusions. It does not portray any serious endangerment.]

10. I hold this belief because of how happy and comfortable the child is with me, and because Respondent and Dr. Adams continue to report that his emotional condition deteriorates after visitation periods with me, and because of Respondent's past threats to ruin me. Attached are a letter and affidavit from Dr. Adams and the Court's prior Findings of Fact.

[Comment: This statement contains nothing other than conclusory mattters without factual basis.]

11. I believe it is clear that the child's deteriorating condition is caused by the Respondent's mental and emotional abuse, which totally disregards the welfare of the child.

[Comment: This statement contains nothing but conclusory matters and basically parrots statutory language.]

12. Based upon the foregoing, this affiant believes that the child's present environment with the Respondent seriously endangers the child's mental and emotional well-being and custody should be changed because, under the current situation, Respondent has shown that the child must either have no relationship with his father or suffer continued mental and emotional abuse by Respondent.

[Comment; This statement is nothing more than a litigant's hyperbole and merely parrots the statute.]

The second affidavit in support of the cause for a modification hearing was filed by Gladys Rigney, Roger's mother. Like Roger's affidavit, Gladys' affidavit asserts no substantive facts.

Being without a factual underpinning, which is required to trigger the activation of the statute for modification, Roger's motion for a hearing should have been denied as a matter of law. This Court held in *Gladish v. Gladish*, Ky. App., 741 S.W. 2d 658 (1987), and *West v. West, supra*, that the affidavits cannot be vague and conclusory, nor should they merely parrot statutory language. No party nor child should be subjected to a continuous custody battle unless, as the statue requires, the present circumstances *seriously endanger* the child in some way. Any subsequent modification proceedings should not commence without strict application of KRS 403.350 and KRS 403.340. See *Betzer v. Betzer*, Ky., App., 749 S.W. 2d 694 (1988).

The majority recognizes the stringent requirements to effect a custody change and admits the affidavits were less than ideal in terms of factual content. The majority is extremely critical of both parties' for causing "pain and misery on their child by continually litigating the same issue time and time again." *Infra*, at 12. Nevertheless, it concludes that "the long and bellicose history" is "precisely the sort of situation that demands a hearing." *Id.* The majority's reasoning in this regard is seriously flawed and inconsistent. It makes numerous negative references to the "incessant' battle waged by the parties and the resulting emotional harm to the child, while finding no abuse of discretion by the trial court in making it possible for the parties to continue the battle. I believe the trial court was clearly wrong and abused its discretion in granting Roger's motion for yet another round of hearings on affidavits that were far less than compelling in content. I strongly disagree with the majority's use of the "history" of the case to bolster the inadequate affidavits as KRS 403.350 requires "cause" to be established by the affidavits, not by extraneous facts or the independent knowledge of the trial court. And finally, I disagree with the averments, taken alone or considered cumulative, come close to reaching the threshold contemplated by KRS 403.350. There was nothing in these affidavits that was not already considered by the trial court in reaching its decision to leave custody with the appellant in 1990. Accordingly, I would reverse the judgment which awards custody of the child to the

---

* I am at a loss to understand why Roger's zealotry is any "less pernicious" than Christy's. p. 12, *infra*.

appellee, and would restore the parties to the status quo at the time of Roger's motion for modification.

More serious than my disagreement with the majority's resolution of the issue concerning the affidavits is my opinion that, at a minimum, the appellant is entitled to have the matter remanded and heard by an impartial fact finder. I understand the majority's reluctance to accept Christy's arguments that the trial judge erred by refusing to recuse himself. However, one cannot review this record without gleaning the obvious fact, that Judge Raikes developed such a settled aversion toward the appellant that his objectivity was seriously undermined.

While impartiality or the appearance thereof, is not defined in a precise manner, I know that implicitly the concept included adjudication without bias, prejudice, or personal interest, all coupled with the absence of any prejudgment by the fact finder. Judge Raikes is very conscientious in his work and dedicated to his office and its oath. He found himself in a dilemma when he was again confronted with this case. Good trial judges do not walk away from their sworn duty. They make every effort, as did Judge Raikes, "to bury their own dead." Several other judges had already been removed from this case, and I surmise Judge Raikes felt compelled out of a sense of duty to see this case through to the end. Nevertheless, the record is replete with indications that Judge Raikes' impartiality was affected to the extent that it might reasonably be questioned. See *Poorman v. Commonwealth*, Ky., 782 S.W. 2d 603 (1989).

Evidence of the trial court's bias is clearly evident in its written orders. In its original judgment of June 12, 1990, the court found that Christy is "an extremely manipulative, calculating, and vindictive individual." The trial court refused to give any value to the opinions of Dr. Christine Adams, the child's treating psychiatrist who first raised the possibility of sexual abuse to Christy due to symptoms the child was experiencing, or to those of Dr. Philip Lichtenstein, a forensic pediatrician, who after examining the child's anus and finding significant scarring concluded the child had been sexually abused, because their opinions had been based in part on information provided by Christy. Although the court continued custody with Christy at that time, it strongly warned her not to raise similar allegations again.

In summary, this Court believes, and so finds, that as a result of the nature and extent of the litigation surrounding the child the past two (2) years, *albeit the result of Christy's vindictive and manipulative efforts,* the harm which would likely be caused by changing his custody at this point in time would outweigh any advantages to him by doing so. KRS 403.340 (2) (c).

As a caveat to Christy, she is cautioned that this Court could, and probably would, reconsider this stance if she continues to react to Roger's relationship with the child as she has in the past. [Emphasis added].

In its order of March 8, 1991, the court stated:

This Court has previously indicated its opinion that the charges of sex abuse levied by Christy against Roger are groundless; *motivated by Christy's vindictive motive to punish and ruin Roger.* It has further indicated, albeit subtly, [sic], that Dr. Adam's support of Christy is professionally atypical.

This Court still remains highly suspect of Christy and Dr. Adams charges against Roger. In light of this Court's findings made in support of its June 12, 1990 judgment, *Christy has a substantial burden of convincing this Court of the efficacy of her most* recent charges against Roger, as set forth in Dr. Adams' January 3, 1991 affidavit.[*] [Emphasis added].

The court stated it believed the child, then only four years old, had been "brainwashed" into repeating the instances of abuse to his psychiatrist and refused to entertain Christy's request for relief. Only after Christy sought emergency relief in the Hardin District Court, which found there to be clear and convincing evidence that the child had been sexually abused by Roger, did the trial court address Christy's renewed concerns. It gave her no relief, however, but it vacated the district court's order that Roger have no further contact with the child. The court articulated the following two reasons for dismissing the district court's findings: (1) it opined that "common sense" dictated that

---

[*] This order is in response to Christy's motion to restrict Roger's visitation supported by Dr. Adams' affidavit that provided in part: "[The child] told and demonstrated that he was touched on his penis by his father; that he was told to pull his pants down to his feet; that his father was naked with his penis 'going up'; that his father pinched the child's arm and held him by his neck to insure his cooperation. The child said this occurred at his father's house in his father's bedroom. . . ."

Roger would be an "idiot" to sexually abuse his child;[*] and (2) allowing visitation was sanctioned by Dr. Riddick, the psychologist appointed by the district court to evaluate the child.[†]

In addition to his written findings demonstrating bias, the trial court engaged in other conduct that places his partiality in question. Specifically, he *sua sponte* ordered that custody be placed with the grandparents, non-parties, pending the hearing on Roger's change of custody. He appointed a campaign contributor as guardian ad litem for the child who had a professional relationship with Roger's good friend and the godfather of the child, Mark Mathis. He allowed Mr. Hubbard, the guardian ad litem, to use precious time set aside for the hearing on the merits, to question Christy about her failure to pay his fees.[‡] The trial court engaged in numerous ex parte conversations with James Ladd, the special prosecutor appointed to conduct the grand jury investigation of Roger, Mr. Hubbard, detective investigating the case and Dr. Riddick.[#] The court, upon Mr. Hubbard's ex parte urgings, ordered that the child be released from Ten Broeck Hospital where he had been placed by his treating physician and further ordered that the child's physician be restrained from having any contact with the child. The trial court appointed Elaine Brown Yarbrough, who evaluated the child prior to the

---

[*] Either Judge Raikes had lost all patience at this point or his observation in this regard reflects his lack of appreciation for the complexity and inherent difficulty in deciding the truth in cases involving child sexual abuse allegations. The horror experienced by abused children and the revulsion one experiences in hearing about it make it easy to deny that such behavior exists. However, whether Roger, is or is not, and "idiot" has no relevance to whether he sexually abused his child. Pedophiles cannot be identified by their intellectual capabilities, or by other mental or physical characteristics.

[†] Actually, Dr. Riddick's bottom line was that it was "simply impossible to determine, with any acceptable degree of factual accuracy, whether or not the child was sexually abused by his father."

[‡] Mr. Hubbard began advocating for a position on behalf of the child prior to having any opportunity to review the record or discuss the case with the experts involved. This is evident from comparing the date of his court appearance to those on his itemized bill that he had personal knowledge of the case and was lined up with the appellee from the time of his appointment should have been apparent to the trial court. That the trial court allowed Mr. Hubbard to needlessly berate and demand the appellant in his questioning of her, particularly over the issue of his fees, a collateral issue, constituted a shocking display of favoritism by the trial court.

[#] That these ex parte communications took place are set forth by the court in its order of March 15, 1991.

original custody litigation, to update her evaluation despite its knowledge that a complaint filed by Christy was pending against Yarbrough before her professional board.*

One of the most striking examples of the trial court's extra-judicial conduct and of the procedural irregularities abounding in this case concerns his ex parte communications with Mr. Ladd.* The latter read to the court the contents of the special grand jury report.† How Mr. Ladd became involved in the civil custody suit is not explained; nor are we aware of Mr Ladd's role in the preparation of the 4-½ page, single-space report. What is of record, however, is the fact that the trial court not only garnered information from Mr. Ladd but ordered that the report be disseminated to several of the professional witnesses and to the law enforcement officers investigating the criminal aspects of the case. While the majority may be correct that Judge Raikes did not rely on the report in making his ultimate decision to change custody, the fact that he directed Ladd to mail copies of the report to others and *sua sponte* filed the report of record shows that he had lost his non-adversarial stance.††

The above recitation of facts which I believe supports the appellant's claim that she was deprived of a fair hearing is not exhaustive. I have set forth matters which, in my opinion, are sufficient to show that the trial court had lost its objectivity in this case long before Roger moved for a chage of custody. I am disappointed that the majority

---

* As the majority mentions, it was primarily Yarbrough's testimony in 1990 that supported the trial court's finding that Christy was vindictive and manipulative. Thus it is not insignificant that the State Board of Examiners of Social Work of Kentucky wrote to Yarbrough on July 10, 1991, after investigating Christy's complaint that it felt Yarbrough needed "additional training and supervision in child custody evaluations," cautioned her that her "role must be unbiased" and suggested that she seek "supervision" in cases where she was "losing [her] objectivity due to countertransference toward a client." The trial court related the substance of this conversation in its order of April 23, 1991.

† In an unprecedented and unauthorized move, the grand jury actually offered recommendations to Judge Raikes in making his "King Solomon" decision! Not surprisingly, it recommended that custody be given to Roger.

†† While perhaps not of direct relevance in this matter, Mr. Ladd was temporarily suspended from the Kentucy Bar Association and ultimately was allowed to resign from the Bar Association after pleading guilty to criminal possession of a forged instrument, theft by unlawful taking (concerning a client's funds) and failure to file federal income tax returns. *See Kentucky Bar Association v. Ladd,* Ky., 845 S.W. 2d 533 (1993) and *Kentucky Bar Association v. Ladd Ky.,* 824 S.W. 2d 430 (1992). Ladd was sentenced to serve time in federal prison on the tax evasion charge *Id.*

opinion did not more fully develop its holding in this regard. Its statement that "[t]he facts simply contradict Christy's assertion that Judge Raikes could not fairly and impartially decide the case," *infra*, at 16, is merely conclusory. I would agree that the "facts" recited by the majority would lead one to find no lack of partiality, but its conclusion is reached by ignoring the many procedural irregularities, ex parte communications, bizarre and unauthorized intrusion into the matter by non-parties (grandparents, grand jury members, the special prosecutor in a separate proceeding), most of which were not mentioned or much less discusssed by the majority. It is not enough to say that this was a "highly charged" case, or to dismiss Christy's arguments by labeling her in perjorative terms. The substance of her argument deserves closer scrutiny than the majority has given it.

I can think of no case more in need of an impartial fact finder than one involving alleged sexual abuse of a young child. These cases are difficult for many reasons, not the least of which included the difficulty in believing that one would exploit his own child for sexual gratification. Another theme repeated throughout this case is the difficulty in conclusively proving whether the alleged abuse actually occurred. And, as the majority mentions, emotions can replace detached consideration.

Children of divorce are vulnerable to begin with. Children involved in a dispute over custody are even more at risk to suffer emotional trauma. However, those most in need of the protection of our legal system are the victims of abuse. Because there is rarely a witness to sexual abuse, because children are not always articulate or truthful, because there is so much at stake for the parents (protecting one's child from actual or perceived abuse or avoiding the stigma of fabricated allegations and loss of the companionship of one's child), these cases must be heard by one whose impartiality and objectivity are above reproach. As our highest court stated in *Colley v. Colley*, Ky., 460 S.W. 2d 821, 827 (1970):

As long as the adversary system of justice is used as the vehicle to resolve and adjust the disputes that arise from the dissolution of a marital partnership, the heart, soul, and conscience of the system must rest in *the imparital, objective, perceptive, and sympathetic figure* who makes the system work and respond to changing human needs—the trial judge. [Emphasis added].

I am uncomfortable with the majority's closing thoughts. That the "system" cannot "require certainty" does not excuse the manner in which this case was allowed to proceed. In my opinion, we have not only failed the appellant and the child, but every other custodial parent who may not be able to convince the trial court that his or her child is the victim of abuse.

Accordingly, in my opinion, the case should be reversed.

NOTES

INTRODUCTION

1. "Family Disruption and Economic Hardship: The Short-Run Picture for Children," survey of Income & Program Participation, U.S. Bureau of the Census, March 1991, P–70, No. 23. Greg J. Duncan and Saul D. Hoffman, "What are the Economic Consequences of Divorce?," *Demography,* 25, no. 4 (Nov, 1988): 641. The 30 percent income drop cited for women is a conservative figure, and other respected researchers have found an even greater magnitude in the drop of income for divorced women. Arizona State University Professor Sanford Braver, for example, studied the psychological effects of economic hardship on mothers after divorce. Professor Braver found in a random-sample study that the mothers' income dropped 42 percent after separation and divorce. (See "Economic Hardship and Psychological Distress in Custodial Mothers" by Sanford Braver et al, *Journal of Divorce* 12[4], 1989, page 19.)

2. Philip Stern in his book *Lawyers on Trial,* published in 1980, described an American legal scene in which only the top strata of society could afford lawyer fees. His comment "justice is for sale" is still apt twenty-six years later.

3. "Fee-For-All: Savvy Lawyers Find Way to Make Millions: Win Pro Bono Cases" by Amy Stevens, *Wall Street Journal,* November 29, 1995, pages A1 and A6.

4. A few states technically require itemized billing, but these rules are typically not enforced unless the client brings another suit in court.

5. A notable and recent exception to this practice is New York. This will be explained in a later chapter.

6. *The Wit and Wisdom of Abraham Lincoln: An A–Z Compendium of Quotes from the Most Eloquent of American Presidents,* edited by Alex Ayes, New York: Penguin, 1992, page 113.

7. These figures are not complete, because Michigan and Montana did not report.

8. These figures were provided in 1995 by the American Bar Association's standing Committee on Professionalism.

9. Telephone interview, June 2, 1994.

10. New York State Assembly Standing Committee on Judiciary, Public Hearing: Legislative Proposals Arising out of Recommendations of the Committee to Examine Lawyer Conduct in Matrimonial Actions. Sept. 23, 1993.

11. Telephone interviews, February 12, 1994 and January 19, 1996. Schafran is head of the National Judicial Education Program to Promote Equality for Women and Men in the Courts. This ambitious national educational program for judges, started more than a decade ago, was designed to eliminate judicial bias against women.

12. 60 U.S. L.W. 4532 (June 15, 1992). While the court unanimously ruled that two children could bring a federal lawsuit against their father, the majority accepted the existence of a "domestic relations exception" and held that it only applies to cases involving divorce, alimony, or child custody. For more on this entire subject, see "'Naturally' Without Gender: Women, Jurisdiction, and the Federal Courts" by Judith Resnik, *New York University Law Review* 66(1682), December 1991.

13. Public Law 103–322, Sept. 13, 1994. 42 USC 13981.

14. Duchesne v. Sugarman 566 F2d 817 (2d Cir. 1977). Santosky v. Kramer 455. U.S. 745 (1982).

15. The professor said he did not want his name used because he was embarrassed by the crime, even though he could not have detected Erdheim's criminal behavior, which was hidden under a professional persona. In fact, five other former Erdheim clients had also complained to the disciplinary authorities of being bilked of large sums, according to "Disciplinary Proceedings Appellate Division First Department," *New York Law Journal,* July 6, 1993.

16. *A People's History of the United States* by Howard Zinn, New York: Harper & Row, 1980, page 89.

17. *Crain's New York Business,* June 8, 1992, page 37.

18. Ibid., page 37.

19. "They Want a Divorce" by Nina Bernstein, *Newsday,* March 10, 1992, page 7.

20. "N.Y. Divorce Lawyers Slammed," *ABA Journal,* June 1992, page 30.

21. The Report of the New Jersey Ethics Commission was issued by a sixteen-member blue ribbon commission that was established by the Chief Judge of New Jersey to look into problems consumers have with the lawyer disciplinary system. Recommendation No. 18, Matrimonial Practice (page 178), reads: "A special committee, with a significant percentage of non-attorney members, should be appointed to review the entire practice of matrimonial law, with particular emphasis on fee practices and other related issues."

22. *The National Law Journal,* "Divorce Bar Needs an Added Level of Checks" by John Elson, June 20, 1994, pages A19–A20.

23. The unanticipated consequences of the new laws were first documented by Lenore Weitzman, a sociologist, whose 1985 book, *The Divorce Revolution,* studied the California matrimonial courts.

24. Whitney North Seymour Jr., telephone interview February 15, 1996.

CHAPTER 1

1. Wives are more likely than husbands to initiate divorce proceedings, and approximately 61 percent of all divorces in 1988 were petitioned by the wife. Husbands initiated 32 percent of divorce proceedings, according to data supplied by the National Center for Health Statistics, in the "Monthly Vital Statistics Report" 39(12), Suppl. 2, May 21, 1991.

2. A total of 29,227 malpractice claims were analyzed, based on data reported by lawyers' malpractice insurance companies to the National Legal Malpractice Data Center of the American Bar Association. Results were tabulated from claims that were opened from 1981 through September 30, 1985. The sample size for the number of family law claims was 454. See Table 15FAM, pages 271–273.

3. These are some of the reasons cited for women's lack of pensions, according to the Pension Rights Center, Washington, D.C.

4. "The Economic Status of Divorced Older Women" by William H. Crown, Phyllis H. Mutschler, James H. Schulz, and Rebecca Loew, Policy Center on Aging, Heller School, Brandeis University, Waltham, MA, 1993. The authors write (on page 10) that according to the 1990

Current Population Survey, "more than one in ten of the 41 million American women age 45 and older are either divorced (9%) or separated (2%)." On page 3, the authors note, "the median income of older divorcées (adjusted to reflect 1990 dollars) increased from $7,475, in 1976 to $9,068 in 1990—an average of less than one and one-half percent per year."

5. *Our Turn,* pages 90–91.

6. Psychology Professor Sanford Braver, in the article "Economic Hardship and Psychological Distress in Custodial Mothers," cautioned that "loss of status and self-definitions involving the former standard of living should not be underestimated." *Journal of Divorce* 12(4), 1989, page 31.

7. Figures provided by Saul Hoffman, Economics Professor at the University of Delaware, and U.S. Department of Commerce, Bureau of the Census, "Family Disruption and Economic Hardship: The Short-Run Picture for Children," Series P-70, No.23.

8. From the U.S. House of Representatives Committee on Ways and Means, "Overview of Entitlement Programs," known as the Green Book, 1992. See Table 37—AFDC Families By Reason for Deprivation of the Youngest Child, pages 683–684.

9. From HBO's "Comic Relief 1994," which broadcasts annual celebrity specials to raise money for the homeless.

10. According to statistics compiled by My Sister's Place, a New York battered women's center, 2,000 to 4,000 women are killed each year by their male partners and 500 to 800 men are killed by their female partners, usually in self-defense.

11. "Legal Issue and Legal Options," page 11. The authors cite the figure in a study by the Research Unit of the Association of Family and Conciliation Courts.

12. Ibid., page 62: "The constant flow of calls for help in these kinds of cases that comes to the National Center on Women and Family Law attests to the fact that the problem does not merely involve a few biased judges or a few 'horror story' cases. These cases present a pervasive pattern of failure to protect children from sexual abuse. Protective parents are in a Catch-22 situation. Mothers are charged as criminals if they fail to protect a child from harm and are charged as criminals if they try to protect their chilren by hiding them from harm."

13. U.S. House of Representatives 1992 Green Book, page 714.

14. Ibid., page 747. The problem isn't that fathers can't afford to support their children. On page 748 the authors cite one major study of divorces between 1968 and 1981, which found that poor children did not necessarily have poor fathers.

15. "Maternal Feelings: Myth, Taboo, and Child Custody" by Mary Becker, *Review of Law and Women's Studies,* 1992, Vol. 1:133, page 177.

16. *Our Turn,* page 96.

17. Interview May 25, 1995, Baton Rouge, Louisiana.

18. Newsletter of the Women's Bar Association of the State of New York, Nassau County Women's Bar Association, President's Message, February/March 1991.

CHAPTER 2

1. Virginia uses commissioners—divorce lawyers who are appointed to quasi-judicial roles—to hear divorce cases and then make recommendations to a judge in a written report. Commissioners are not to be confused with mediators. They do not mediate the dispute. They function in the same role as judges, except that divorcing couples are required to pay hourly fees to commissioners, unlike other areas of law in which citizens have the benefit of a publicly funded judge.

2. Ginger won an appeal on January 10, 1995. The appellate judges found: "As wife contends, there is no indication in the record that the commissioner or chancellor segregated corporate assets and liabilities from marital assets and liabilities. . . . Furthermore, the court's failure to differentiate between marital and non-marital assets led to 'double-dipping.'. . . Any monetary award and spousal support are contingent upon the proper classification and valuation of the parties' assets." In October 1995, a judge ordered that Ginger's attorney could look into Henry's business records.

3. Miller's lawyer's explanations for why he didn't try to get the child support enforced were quoted in the New York City Department of Consumer Affairs 1992 report, *Women in Divorce: Lawyers, Ethics, Fees, and Fairness.* He said he was waiting for the arrears to add up rather than having to repeatedly go to court to collect. For more on this story see *The Reporter Dispatch,* Gannett Suburban Newspapers, Sunday, January 24, 1993, page 1.

CHAPTER 3

1. *Women and the Law,* page 15.

2. Ibid., page xv.

3. *In the Eyes,* page 17.

4. In the book *Unequal Protection* (page 39), Judge Lois G. Forer writes: "Women, children, and the mentally handicapped . . . were bracketed together under the common law as a group that had no personal or legal rights. . . . The difference in legal status was based upon the presumption of their incapacity to understand and obey as full-grown men. Married women had no separate legal identity. A married couple was one person, and that was the husband."

5. Ibid., pages 33–34.

6. "Maternal Feelings: Myth, Taboo, and Child Custody" by Mary Becker, *Review of Law and Women's Studies,* 1992, Vol. 1:133, pages 167, 168.

7. *Patterns of Culture* by Ruth Benedict, Boston: Houghton Mifflin, 1934, page 75.

8. *Women and the Law,* page 61.

9. *Law of Domestic Relations,* page 283.

10. *Women and the Law,* page 59.

11. Ibid., page 62.

12. *Law of Domestic Relations,* page 327.

13. Ibid., page 343.

14. *Eugenics, Nature's Secrets Revealed: Scientific Knowledge of the Laws of Sex Life and Heredity* by Professor T. W. Shannon, A.M., Marietta, OH: S.A. Mullikin Co., 1914, pages 99–100.

15. *Divorce Revolution,* page 14.

16. Ibid., page 13.

17. Ibid., page 14.

18. *From Father's Property to Children's Rights* by Mary Ann Mason, Columbia University Press, 1994, page 61.

19. Divorce Revolution, page 15.

20. Ibid., page 41.

21. According to *Funk & Wagnalls Standard Reference Encyclopedia,* Vol. 8, Readers Digest Books, 1970, and the U.N. figures (see below).

22. *1990 Demographic Yearbook,* pages 746, 748, 750. The actual figure for the number of U.S. divorces might even be higher because it represented less than 90 percent of the information collected on divorce that year, according to the U.N.

23. William J. Goode, author of the 1956 book *Women in Divorce* (originally published as *After Divorce*), cited figures showing that in the late 1800s, Japan had approximately 367 divorces per 1,000 marriages. Russia and Egypt also had higher rates than the United States in the year 1938. During this time in Russia after the Revolution, divorces were extremely easy to obtain and required little more than an official recording of the facts, according to *Funk & Wagnalls Standard Reference Encyclopedia*, Vol. 8, by Reader's Digest Books, 1970, page 2795.

24. *Divorce Revolution*, page 20.

25. *Family Law in a Nutshell* by Harry Krause, ed. 2, St. Paul, MN: West Publishing Co., 1986, page 374.

26. *Business Week*, December 7, 1992, page 22.

27. Telephone interview with author, February 12, 1995.

28. *Divorce Revolution*, page 33.

29. Ibid., page 34.

30. Ibid.

31. "Marital Partnership and the Case for Permanent Alimony," by Sally Goldfarb, from *Alimony: New Strategies for Pursuit and Defense*, Section of Family Law, American Bar Association, 1988, page 45.

32. *Family Law in a Nutshell*, pages 349–350.

33. Telephone interview with the author, February 12, 1995.

34. *No-Fault Divorce*, Michael Wheeler, 1974, pages 126, 127

35. Page 138.

36. *Orr* v. *Orr*, 440 US 268 99 Supreme Court 1102 59 L.Ed 2nd 306 1979.

37. Issued in March 1986, this report resulted from a twenty-two-month investigation of the state of New York and represented the opinions of 2,000 legal professionals.

38. *Divorce Revolution*, page 31.

39. Susan Clabault's story received coverage in "Divorce-Law Crusade Backfires" by Stacey Singer, *Chicago Tribune*, November 2, 1995, pages 1–2. The judge blamed Clabault for losing her home because she demanded a costly trial rather than conceding to a settlement for which her lawyers had pushed. Pushing for settlement—any settlement—when an attorney has used up all of the client's money is a usual procedure, and often it is these same attorneys who have created the expectations of a better settlement in order to induce the client to

retain them and to justify their churning of the case to drive up fees. Upon making his decision, Judge Kenneth Abraham was quoted as warning Clabault: "I am cautioning you not to become a martyr to what now can only be characterized as a self-inflicted wound. . . ."

40. Telephone interview with author, May 10, 1994.

41. "Divorce Costs Rise Under New Law," *New York Times*, February 2, 1981, Sec A., page 1.

42. From a transcript of the Hearings before the Committee on the Judiciary, United States Senate, 101st Congress, on S. 2027 and S. 2648, Serial No. J–101–61, March 6 and June 26, 1990, page 127.

43. Ibid., page 1.

44. The bill was signed into law on June 19, 1980, with an accompanying memo. But thirteen days later, after the bill was already law, then-Assemblyman Gordan Burrows, now a judge, amended the memo. Both memos were circulated causing judicial confusion according to an article by Isabel Marcus that appeared in the *Buffalo Law Review*, Spring 1988–89 (volume 37), pages 445, 446.

45. *New York Daily News* article, January 13, 1980, quoted from The New York City Department of Consumer Affairs Report: *Women in Divorce: Lawyers, Ethics, Fees and Fairness.*

46. *The Litigation Explosion*, book jacket.

47. *Family Law in a Nutshell*, page 252.

48. "Are Fathers Winning the Custody Wars?" by Debi Martin-Morris, *McCall's*, March 1995, page 68.

49. See: Gender Bias Study of the Court System in Massachussetts, Supreme Judicial Court, 1989 Page 59.

50. On page 249, the book *Family Law in a Nutshell* cites UMDA § 402, which lists the following factors to determine the child's best interest: "(1) the wishes of the child's parent or parents as to his custody; (2) the wishes of the child as to his custodian; (3) the interaction and interrelationship of the child with his parent or parents, his siblings and any other person who may significantly affect the child's best interest; (4) the child's adjustment to his home, school and commmunity; (5) the mental and physical health of all individuals involved. The court shall not consider conduct of a present or proposed custodian that does not affect his relationship to the child."

51. In one quantitative study cited by University of Chicago Law

Professor Mary Becker, fathers spent five hours a week on primary child care activities compared to seventeen hours per week that mothers spent.

52. "Judicial Discretion in Child Custody: The Wisdom of Solomon?" by Mary Becker, *Illinois Bar Journal*, Vol. 81, December 1993, p. 651.

53. *Justice for Women,* Nevada Supreme Court Gender Bias Task Force, 1988, page 42.

54. Ibid., page 77.

55. *Child Custody: Practice and Procedure,* 1994 Cumulative Supplement, by Linda D. Elrod, Professor of Law, Washburn University, Clark Boardman Callaghan (Rochester, N.Y., Deerfield, Il., New York, N.Y.), May 1994, chapter 4, page 5.

56. *Family Law,* page 249.

57. *Unequal Protection: Women, Children & the Elderly in Court* by Lois G. Forer, 1991, page 66.

58. "Maternal Feelings: Myth, Taboo, and Child Custody," *Review of Law and Women's Studies* 1:133, 1991, page 140.

59. Ibid., page 137.

60. Ibid., page 158.

61. Author Sylvia Ann Hewlett, in the book *When the Bough Breaks* (page 142), points out the study that Judith Wallerstein conducted, tracking a group of upper-middle-class youngsters for ten to fifteen years after the divorce. Hewlett writes: "Two-thirds of divorced fathers in the Wallerstein study offered no help whatsoever for college, despite the fact that they are a well-heeled group. In the words of one successful engineer, 'I don't care whether my son goes to college. I couldn't care less. My responsibility is to get my life together.'. . . Mothers are often willing to contribute voluntarily to the cost of college, but since they typically have few resources, their generosity rarely amounts to much."

62. "Achieving Equal Justice for Women and Men in the Courts," The Draft Report of the Judicial Council Advisory Committee on Gender Bias in the Courts, March 23, 1990, Tab 5, page 23. by Lois G. Forer, 1991, page 66.

63. American Academy of Matrimonial Lawyers, "Bounds of Advocacy," Chicago: AAML, 1991, page 26.

64. *Unfair Tactics,* page 139.

65. "The Primary Caretaker Parent Rule: Child Custody and the Dynamics of Greed," *Yale Law & Policy Review*, Vol. 3, No. 1, pages 177–178, 1984.

66. Ibid., page 179.

CHAPTER 4

1. "Report of the Committee to Examine Lawyer Conduct in Matrimonial Actions," Hon. E. Leo Milonas, Chair, Appellate Division First Department, May 4th, 1993, New York, N.Y., page 32.

2. "Bounds of Advocacy" (page 29, unbound version) states: "Overzealous, discourteous, abrasive, 'hard ball' conduct by matrimonial lawyers is inconsistent with both their obligation to effectively represent their clients and their duty to improve the process of dispute resolution."

3. "Ethical Issues for the Matrimonial Practitioner," a seminar held October 16, 1991, at the Association of the Bar of the City of New York.

4. Telephone interview with author, January 10, 1994

5. *Mothers on Trial*, page 199.

6. The position that a mother's anger is a justifiable response to being threatened was the subject of an Amicus Curiae brief in the New York case of *Ron Brawer* v. *Tonya Pinkins*, "Maternal anger as a disqualifying element in determining child custody." The Steinem reference appeared as an ad in the New York City subways that was printed by the New School for Social Research.

7. *Unfair Tactics*, page 133.

8. The decision was upheld on appeal.

9. Telephone interview with author, March 26, 1996.

10. The article, "Testilying," by Joe Sexton, Metro Section, pages 25–26, stated that "Mr. Rossi's conviction, say prosecutors and investigators looking into police corruption fear is and example of what they fear is the most widespread form of police misconduct facing the criminal justice system. They say perjury—nicknamed 'testilying' within the department—is rarely prosecuted, often condoned by superiors and an instrinsic part of the police culture."

11. *How to Divorce Your Wife* by Forden Athearn, Garden City: Doubleday, 1976, page 18.

12. "Bounds of Advocacy," page 19.

13. See "Report of the Committee to Examine Lawyer Conduct in Matrimonial Actions," page 39 and Appendix R, West Virginia Statute Divorce, Annulment and Separate Maintenance § 48–2–33.

14. Interview May 7, 1994.

15. The Committee on the Judiciary, U.S. Senate, 101st Congress, Serial No. J–101–61, March 6 and June 26, 1990, page 96. A copy of the hearing showed: "The *most* important cause of high transaction costs or delays that increase these costs is perceived to be lawyers who abuse the discovery process. . . . Lawyers who 'over-discover' cases rather than focus on controlling issues and lawyers and litigants who use discovery as an adversarial tool or tactic to 'raise the stakes' for their opponents are the most frequently cited causes across all segments."

16. *Mothers on Trial,* page 199.

17. The letter was on exhibit presented from Charlotte Bogart to the House Judiciary Committee, Pennsylvania House of Representatives for the public hearing: *Domestic Relations Injustices in the Pennsylvania Legal System*, held September 12, 1991.

18. U.S. Senate, The Committee on the Judiciary Hearings.

19. See *Mothers on Trial.*

CHAPTER 5

1. Professor Lisa Lerman provides an excellent understanding of this in the law journal article "Lying to Clients."

2. See *Women in Divorce: Lawyers, Ethics, Fees, and Fairness*, published by the New York City Department of Consumer Affairs, March 1992.

3. Northwestern University Law Professor John Elson has written about this practice, which he documented as occurring in Illinois, in "Divorce Bar Needs an Added Level of Checks," *The National Law Journal,* June 20, 1994, page A19.

4. *The Wall Street Journal,* Oct. 28, 1991, page A16.

5. Telephone interview with author, May 9, 1995.

6. *Gitlin* v. *Hartmann,* 175 Ill.App.3d 805, 811 (2d Dist 1988).

7. "Value Billing—Matrimonial Attorney's Fees in the 90's," by Barbara A. Stark, *Journal of the American Academy of Matrimonial Lawyers,* Vol. 7, 1991, page 83.

8. "The Rodent: The Official Underground Publication for Associates," Rodent Publications, 2531 Sawtelle Blvd. No. 30, Los Angeles, California. The article, "Webster Hubbell Gives Double Billing a Bad Name," appeared in the *Illinois Legal Times,* March 1995, page 6.

9. Interview October 27, 1994.

10. Interview December 21, 1995.

11. "Lying to Clients," page 717.

12. Ibid.

13. Telephone interview with author, November 27, 1993.

14. Telephone interview with author, February 15, 1996.

15. Commissioners are divorce lawyers who act as quasi-judges in Virginia.

16. See the New York State Bar Association Professional Ethics Committee's Ethics Opinion 599 (3/16/89).

17. "*R. Brandes, P.C.* v *Zingmond,* Nassau County Supreme Court," *New York Law Journal,* June 17, 1991, page 27.

18. Matter of Edward M. Cooperman, 187 A.D. 2d 56 (2d Dep't 1993) aff'd 83 N.Y. 2d 465 (1994).

19. The use of nonrefundable retainers was discussed at length in the report of a judicial panel, the New York Committee to Examine Lawyer Conduct in Matrimonial Actions, May 4, 1993, pages 16–18, the findings of which were presented to Chief Judge Kaye.

20. "Client Self-Protection," Letter to the Editor, *New York Times,* January 17, 1992.

21. "Matter of Bailey, Marshall and Hoegniger (Merzon)," *New York Law Journal,* June 23, 1993, page 30.

22. "Divorce Lawyers Often Shortchange, Overcharge Women Clients, Study Finds" by Ellen Joan Pollock, *Wall Street Journal,* March 13, 1992, Page B3.

23. "Report of the Committee to Examine Lawyer Conduct in Matrimonial Actions," May 4, 1993, page 19.

24. Ibid., page 20.

25. Professional Ethics Committee of Board of Overseers of the Maine Bar Opinion 97 (5/3/89), ABA/BNA Lawyers' Manual on Professional Conduct at 901:4208.

26. Bennett, 131 Ill. App. 3d at 1055–56, and In re Marriage of

Landon, Rule 23 Order, July 26, 1985, First District Appellate Court, No. 85–0040.

27. The marriage of Bennett, 476 N.E. 2d 1297 (2d District 1985), was reported in the *Chicago Daily Law Bulletin* by H. Joseph Gitlin in the column "Lawyer's Forum: Family Law," under the heading "Wife entitled to hearing on attorney fees."

28. The litigant requested anonymity.

29. The lawyer had billed her $9,670 for *one month* of work. After a year, her lawyer demanded an additional $30,000 on top of this.

30. "Report of the Committee to Examine Lawyer Conduct in Matrimonial Actions," May 4, 1993, page 22, reports that the use of retaining liens is a legally accepted practice, established by common law as far back as 1915.

31. "Matter of Bailey," page 30.

32. Telephone interview conducted by author with woman who requested anonymity, Jan 10, 1994.

33. Official Wisconsin Reports 122 Wis. 2d 94 *Jeanette Helmbrecht* v. *St. Paul Insurance Company and Raymond Colwin,* decided January 31, 1985.

34. Telephone interview conducted by author with litigant who requested anonymity, May 8, 1994.

35. Pollack is one of the former members of the Committee to Examine Lawyer Conduct in Matrimonial Actions, a blue-ribbon panel of lawyers and judges that reviewed the Consumer Affairs *Women in Divorce* report, conducted public hearings, and subsequently made recommendations to curb many of the abuses described in this chapter.

CHAPTER 6

1. The figure of one third is an underestimate because state courts often consolidate related cases involving the family into one case and reopen cases rather than file new ones when subsequent orders are needed, according to *State Court Caseload Statistics: Annual Report 1992,* published by the National Center for State Courts, 1994. The courts divide domestic relations caseloads into six main case types with the majority falling into three main categories: marriage dissolution (comprising 44 percent); support/custody (comprising 19 percent); and

domestic violence (comprising 12 percent). The miscellaneous, pater-
nity, adoption and URESA (Uniform Reciprocal Enforcement of support Act) categories together comprise 25 percent.

2. As of December 1993, according to Bob Wolf of the Marketing
Department at the American Bar Association.

3. *Meyer* v. *Meyer* Vol 441 NW 2nd Series, page 544. Minnesota
Court of Appeals Judge Daniel Foley wrote in his decision: "It does not
ennoble a great profession to perpetuate a fee system that places upon the
backs of ordinary wage earners and people of modest means the burden
of oppressive debt. . . . the system is wrong and must be corrected."

4. Ginger Martin's case was discussed in Chapter 2.

5. "In the Spirit of Public Service," page 15. It is interesting to note
that the ABA cautioned on the front cover of the report that the views
of the Commission "should not be construed as representing the policy
of the Association."

6. Telephone interview with author, January 10, 1994.

7. See "Report of the Gender Bias Study of the Supreme Judicial
Court," issued by the Massachusetts Supreme Judicial Court, Boston,
1989, page 21.

8. "The Breakdown of the Monopoly of the Bar Card: *The Game
Is Over,*" The Section of Litigation, ABA, William A. Brewer, Jennifer
L. Martin, Bickel & Brewer, "Value Billing and Gaining Competitive
Advantage in the Legal Marketplace," 1992 ABA Annual Meeting, San
Francisco, Ca., August 10, 1992.

9. "Value Billing: Reforming the Lawyer-Corporate Client Relationship," Zoë Baird, The Section of Litigation, ABA, "Value Billing
and Gaining Competitive Advantage in the Legal Marketplace," 1992
ABA Annual Meeting, San Francisco, August 10, 1992.

10. See "Revolution in Lawyers' Fees: The Meter Is Being Shut
Off" by Margot Slade, *New York Times,* October 22, 1993, page 1.

11. "Straight Talk on Fees," by Ray DeLong, *Family Advocate* 11(2),
Fall 1988, page 38.

12. *Lawyers on Trial,* page 52.

13. *Using a Lawyer,* page 67.

14. *Lawyers on Trial,* page 52–53.

15. *Using a Lawyer,* page 67.

16. California Senator Robert Presley (D-Riverside) introduced a

bill to remove the disciplinary system from the control of the bar in January 1986. The bill was amended to let the bar keep the disciplinary system, but it created an oversight position called bar monitor, which was established in January 1987. The monitor, Robert Fellmeth, issued a scathing report on his initial findings. He wrote: "I would be shirking my duties as assigned by law to contend that the system now in place, or as it is evolving, approaches a minimum level of acceptability" ("The Discipline System of the California State Bar: An Initial Report," by Robert C. Fellmeth, *The California Regulatory Law Report; Reporter,* 7[3], Summer 1987, page 28). In the next three years, Fellmeth issued eight more progress reports, which resulted in more reforms. In his last report, Fellmeth said that while the system was much better, more reforms were needed.

17. Telephone conversation with author.

18. Report of the Commission on Evaluation of Disciplinary Enforcement to the ABA, May 1991, Appendix A: Implementation of Clark Committee Recommendation, Page 63–93.

19. Deborah Rhode, page 940.

20. "Report of the New Jersey Ethics Commission of the Supreme Court of New Jersey," Richard J. Hughes Justice Complex, Trenton, N.J., Appendix A–12. Figures compiled September 1, 1992.

21. Executive Summary, "Final Report of the State Bar Discipline Monitor" by Robert Fellmeth, Center for Public Interest Law, University of San Diego, Alcala Park, San Diego, California, September 20, 1991, page 14.

22. The National Law Journal, *Divorce Bar Needs an Added Level of Checks,* June 20, 1994, page A19-A20.

23. "Achieving Equal Justice for Women and Men in the Courts: The Draft Report of the Judicial Council Advisory Committee on Gender Bias in the Courts," Administrative Office Judicial Council of the Courts of California, San Francisco, 1990, page 746.

24. See "New Guidelines for New York Divorce Lawyers Ignite Acrimonious Debate" by Jan Hoffman, *New York Times,* November 8, 1993, pages B1–B2.

25. "The Highest Incomes," *American Demographics,* October 1992, page 10. Nassau's median household income is $54,283.

26. *Criminology,* page 377. This definition was excerpted from

"The Nature, Impact, and Prosecution of White-Collar Crime," published by the U.S. Government in 1970 and written by Herbert Edelhertz, former chief of the Fraud Section of the Criminal Division of the U.S. Department of Justice.

27. "Lying to Clients," page 692. See this article for a fuller discussion of lawyer deception and the lack of strong rules.

28. Ibid., page 687.

29. "Report of the Commission on Evaluation of Disciplinary Enforcement" (also known as the McKay Commission), presented to the American Bar Association in May 1991, pages 37–38. The use of the phrase *irreparable harm* is in Model Rule 20 A. The McKay Commission was created by the ABA in 1989.

30. Ibid. According to the "Report of the New Jersey Ethics Commission" (the Supreme Court of New Jersey, 1993, page 149), New Jersey has procedures in place for prompt removal of attorneys whose conduct could seriously harm clients.

31. "Report of the New Jersey Ethics Commission," page 149.

32. "Lying to Clients," page 696.

33. Deborah Rhode and David Luban, *Legal Ethics, 2d ed.* Foundation Press, Westbury, N.Y., 1995, page 860.

34. McKay Commission report, page 9.

35. Ibid., page 10. The National Organization of Bar Counsel represents 400 lawyer disciplinary counsels representing 60 jurisdictions in the United States and Canada.

36. Ibid.

37. Executive Summary, "Final Report," page 14.

38. "Lying to Clients," page 693.

39. In his book on white-collar crime, *Power, Crime and Mystification* (page 52), author Steven Box quotes from an article in the *University of Pennsylvania Law Review* (1966): "A trusted cashier committing embezzlement, a minister who evades payment of his taxes, a teacher making sexual advances toward minors and a civil servant who accepts bribes have a fear of detection which is more closely linked with the dread of public scandal and subsequent social ruin than with apprehensions of legal punishment."

40. "Report of the New Jersey Ethics Commission," page 64. Investigators invited New Jersey's Deputy Attorney General Douglas

Harper, who oversaw jurisdiction for regulating occupationally licensed businesses such as shorthand reporters, plumbers, electricians, and the Board of Medical Examiners. Harper testified that no profession, including the medical profession, had absolute confidentiality over proceedings, as lawyers do. Since then, New Jersey has changed its policy and enacted reforms so that all lawyer punishments are disclosed, including when lawyers are privately admonished by the grievance agency.

41. "Report of the New Jersey Ethics Commission," page 61.

42. The extent to which lawyers oppose even partially opening the system was evident in 1993 when lawyers turned out in droves at a New York State legislative committee hearing to protest the proposal to lift the secrecy. As a result of lawyer lobbying efforts, the New York legislature decided to allow the system to continue in complete secrecy. This means that lawyers being investigated for criminal conduct can keep doing business and obtaining unsuspecting clients.

43. McKay Commission report, page 23.

44. Telephone interview with author, December 15, 1995.

45. *The National Law Journal*, "Anti-Lawyer Attitude Up," by Randall Samborn, pages 13–17.

46. *American Bar Journal*, Vox Populi, "The Public Perception of Lawyers: ABA Poll," by Gary A. Hengstler, September 1993.

CHAPTER 7

1. "Achieving Equal Justice for Women and Men in the Courts: Draft Report of the Judicial Council Advisory Committee on Gender Bias in the Courts," pages 57–60.

2. "In the Spirit of Public Service," page 44.

3. Page 243.

4. Page 98.

5. Achieving Equal Justice for Women and Men in the Courts (Draft), Issued by the Judicial Council of California, Administrative office of the Courts, Tab 5, pp. 57–62.

6. "Report of the Florida Supreme Court Gender Bias Study Commission," the Supreme Court of Florida, Tallahassee, 1990, pages 53–54, 77.

7. Ibid., 212–213.

8. "Gender and Justice: Report of the Vermont Task Force on Gender Bias in the Legal System. A project by the Vermont Supreme Court and Vermont Bar Association," January 1991, page 65.

9. "Achieving Equal Justice for Women and Men in the Courts: The Draft Report of the Judicial Council Advisory Committee on Gender Bias in the Courts," Administrative Office of the Judicial Council of the Courts of California, San Francisco, 1990, Tab 5, page 60.

10. "New York State Commission on Judicial Conduct Report," 1993, page 43. These particular rules are the same for judges in all fifty states and the District of Columbia.

11. "A Top Judge in Connecticut Is Suspended" by David Margolick, *New York Times*, February 19, 1994, page 21.

12. Data from the American Judicature Society publication *Judicial Conduct Reporter* 16(3), Fall 1994, page 2.

13. *Judicial Conduct Reporter* 15(3), Fall 1993, page 2. The total does not include Virginia, Wyoming, Vermont, South Dakota, Montana, Massachusetts, Idaho, and Oregon, because those states did not supply figures. The total number of complaints represents pending complaints and complaints received. The number of complaints exceeded the number of judges nationwide, but this is due to multiple complaints filed against individual judges.

14. *Judicial Conduct Reporter* 16(3), Fall 1994, front page.

15. Interview with Cynthia Gray, director of the American Judicature Society, March 6, 1995.

16. "Is Judicial Discipline in New York State a Threat to Judicial Independence?" *Pace Law Review* 7, page 304. "Legal error" sometimes connotes genuine error, but it has also become a euphemism the commissions use to describe situations where laws are overlooked.

17. "An Overview of Judicial Immunity," reprinted from the *State Court Journal*, by Samuel P. Stafford, published by the National Center for State Courts (Research Essay Series Number E001), Summer 1977.

18. Ibid.

19. *Legal Focus* 1(1), January 1995, page 1.

20. There seems to be confusion within the profession as to whether judicial rulings in and of themselves can constitute official judicial misconduct. While the official word is that rulings are not subject to investigation, Pat Hall, a former Colorado judge and

member of her home state's judicial conduct commission, said in an interview (March 14, 1995) that if the judge repeatedly ignores the law and a pattern can be determined, then the rulings will be treated as misconduct. But her view contradicted the response of Rick Wehmhoefer, the director of the Colorado Judicial Ethics Commission. Wehmhoefer said his agency does not look at judicial rulings in and of themselves.

21. Judicial Conduct and Ethics panel at the American Bar Association Annual Meeting, New York Hilton Hotel, New York City, August 7, 1993.

22. Ibid.

23. Ibid.

24. *Hard Copy,* from the segment "The Marrying Judge," CBS Television, July 17, 1995.

25. *Judicial Discretion*, published by the National Judicial College, 1991, page 8.

26. "Is Judicial Discipline in New York State a Threat to Judicial Independence?," *Pace Law Review* Vol. 7, No. 2, Winter 1987 page 302.

27. *Discretionary Justice: A Preliminary Inquiry,* by Kenneth Culp Davis, University of Illinois Press, Bloomington, Ill., 1971, page 3.

28. "Achieving Equal Justice for Women and Men in the Courts," Draft report Administrative Office of the Judicial Council of the Courts of California, Tab 5, pages 36–37.

29. Interview March 2, 1995.

30. *The Judges Journal,* Summer 1985, page 5.

31. Taped telephone interview with Justice Thompson, January 4, 1994.

32. See "Judicial Discipline," *Pace Law Review* 7(2), Winter 1987, pages 339–345.

33. "Utah Task Force on Gender and Justice: Report to the Utah Judicial council," March 1990, page 15.

34. Quote from a Butte County Regional Meeting, "Achieving Equal Justice for Women and Men in the Courts," Draft report published by Administrative Office of Judicial Council of the Courts of California, Tab 4, Introduction.

35. "Utah Task Force on Gender and Justice: Report to the Utah Judicial council," March 1990, page 33.

36. "Concerning the Plight of Children in Cases of Parental Abuse," memo to U.S. Attorney General Reno, November 29, 1993. Authors were lawyers Randal Burton and Sherry Quirk and researcher/victim Amy Neustein.

37. Case 21, 1988, the Alabama Judicial Inquiry Commission.

38. "Benchmark" 13(4), Winter 1990.

39. Telephone interview with author, March 10, 1995.

40. *William David Johnston* v. *Mary Sue Johnston*, No. 1985–2787 before Senior Judge Edward L. Snyder, Armstrong County Court House, Kittanning, PA, August 15, 1994.

CHAPTER 8

1. In *The Bohemian Grove*, page 9. Sociologist William Domhoff says, "Group-dynamics research suggests that members of socially cohesive groups are more open to the opinions of other members and more likely to change their views to those of fellow members."

2. According to the *Barron's Dictionary of Legal Terms,* by Steven H. Gifis, ed. 2 (Barron's Educational Services, Hauppauge, N.Y., 1993) the Latin definition of *ex parte* is "in behalf of or on the application of one party; by or for one party."

3. From The Commonwealth of Kentucky Court of Appeals, March 17, 1995. No 92-CA-002962-M.R.

4. "In the Spirit of Public Service: A Blueprint for the Rekindling of Lawyer Professionalism," 1986, page 44.

5. See *The Bohemian Grove.*

6. *Legal Ethics* by Deborah Rhode and David Luban (Draft), 1992, page 947.

7. According to the appellate brief, the judge justified the low child support award by saying that Laura "spends too much on her child."

8. "Plaintiff will execute a Deed. . . to defendant. . . . Each party waives any right of alimony. . . ."

9. This case was documented in the *Women in Divorce* report, page 31.

10. Gender & Justice in the Colorado Courts," Colorado Task Force on Gender Bias in the Courts, 1990, page 64.

11. "Report of the Florida Supreme Court Gender Bias Study Commission," 1990, page 72.

12. *Justice for Women,* Nevada Supreme Court Gender Bias Task Force, January 31, 1988, page 51.

13. Page 712.

14. Telephone interview with author, December 28, 1995.

CHAPTER 9

1. See "Moving from the Village to Harlem" by Tracie Rozhon, *New York Times,* Sunday, June 11, 1995, Section 9, Real Estate, page 6.

2. According to handwritten notes of Peggy's attorney Squire N. Bozorth on January 17, 1988.

3. 141 Ill. App. 3d 956, 96 Ill. Dec. 276 in re the Marriage of Joanne Pitulla v. Samuel Pitulla Nos. 84-0271, 84-1299. March 19, 1986. Rehearing denied April 16, 1986.

4. "Rinellas upholding a family tradition," *Chicago Daily Law Bulletin,* July 30, 1986, page 1.

5. Letter to Georgina M. Mahoney, Counsel for the Attorney Registration and Disciplinary Commission (ARDC), from Joanne Pitulla, dated June 1, 1988.

6. "Rinella firm charged excessive fee: court," *Chicago Daily Law Bulletin*, August 9, 1990, page 1.

7. Testimony before the Illinois Task force on Gender Bias in the Courts, public hearing in Chicago, Illinois, February 9, 1989.

8. In June 1994, when I contacted Richard Rinella to get his side of the story, he had more nasty words for his former client. "She's an obsessed, maniacal woman who is out of her mind. . . . She's a liar. She's an absolute liar. She agreed to pay the fees. She knew it was $8,500 at the prove-up. She agreed to it."

When I reminded him that Illinois's highest court, the Illinois State Supreme Court, had ruled in Joanne Pitulla's favor, he exclaimed: "I don't agree with that [decision]. I think the case was crazy. I think it was an outrageous decision. It was a stupid, ridiculous decision that allowed somebody to come back three years later to open up the judgment where she agreed to everything. . . ."

9. "Court sets 3-year suspension for divorce lawyer," *Chicago Law Bulletin,* September 23, 1993. The decision—623 N.E. 2d 300 (Ill. 1993)— stated that Timpone had engaged in the following acts of misconduct: "comingling client funds, conversion of client funds, failing to maintain

complete records of client funds, disregarding a tribunal's orders, deceit in handling his client fund account, misrepresenting a matter in a written statement submitted during an ARDC investigation, failing to promptly pay client funds, and neglecting several clients' proceedings."

CHAPTER 10

1. *Helmbrecht* v. *St. Paul Ins. Co.* 122 Wis 2d 94. Official Wisconsin Reports, page 106.

2. June 30, 1992, letter to President Judge Warren G. Morgan, Court of Common Pleas, Harrisburg, Pa. Eventually, the Pennsylvania House of Representatives held six days of public hearings, and Representative Pesci eventually garnered support from thirty-four legislators for the proposed legislation, which would have formed a task force to investigate the injustices in divorce court. The proposal died in the House of Representatives' Judiciary Committee.

3. Telephone interview with author.

4. . . . *In the Spirit of Public Service: A Blueprint for the Rekindling of Lawyer Professionalism*, American Bar Association Commission on Professionalism, 1986, Page VII.

5. Telephone interview with author, June 2, 1994.

6. "Mothers Stage Hunger Strike in Houston," *Alternatives for Protective Parents* 1(2), Spring 1993. Published by the National Center for Protective Parents in Civil Child Sexual Abuse Cases. (See Appendix II.)

7. Swarthmore College Bulletin, "Courting Disaster" by Elizabeth Bennett, August 1989, page 9.

8. *In the Eyes*, page 136.

9. "Legal Focus," published by Citizens' Project of Judicial and Court Reform, Box 1233, Wilkes-Barre, Pennsylvania 18703.

10. *AntiShyster* 2(1), January 1992.

11. "Achieving Equal Justice for Women and Men in the Courts: Draft Report of the Judicial Council Advisory Committee on Gender Bias in the Courts," published by the Judicial Council of the Court of California, March 23, 1990, Tab 5, page 74.

12. Telephone conversation with author, June 2, 1994.

13. "Feminists Say Kaye's Sold Out" by John Camer, *Albany Times Union*, May 6, 1995, page A2.

14. "Coercive Harmony," *California Lawyer*, May 1995, page 37.

15. Telephone interview with author, August 1995.

16. *New York Times,* "Divorced Fathers Makes Gain in Battles to Increase Rights," by Jan Hoffman, April 26, 1995, pages A1 and B5.

CHAPTER 11

1. According to the proposed New York Assembly bill, 4199–A: "The court shall seek to assure that each party shall be equally represented and that where fees and expenses are to be awarded, they shall be awarded on a timely basis, pendente lite, so as to enable adequate representation from the commencement of the proceeding. Applications for the award of fees and expenses may be made at any time or times prior to final judgment. Both parties to the action or proceeding and their respective attorneys shall file an affidavit with the court detailing the financial agreement between the party and the attorney. . . ."

2. Professor Becker's article in the *Illinois Bar Journal,* "Judicial Discretion in Child Custody: The Wisdom of Solomon?" (Vol 81, December 1993) provides an excellent understanding of the problem of judicial discretion.

3. *The Divorce Decision: The Legal and Human Consequences of Ending a Marriage* by Richard Neely, New York: McGraw-Hill, 1984, page 79.

4. Ibid., page 80.

5. Telephone interview with author, August 1995.

6. The McKay Report is formally known as the "Report of the Commission on Evaluation of Disciplinary Enforcement," presented to the ABA in May of 1991, page 23. The Commission was created by the ABA in 1989.

7. "Crooked Lawyers Protected" by Nina Bernstein, *Newsday,* January 21, 1992, pages 4 and 83. By the time he was disbarred by Manhattan's disciplinary committee, Cohn was on his deathbed (from AIDS) and could harm no more clients.

8. "Nonlawyer Practice in the United States," Discussion Draft for Comment, ABA Commission on Nonlawyer Practice, April 1994, page 11.

9. Ibid., page A.AZ–3.

10. As Professor Lisa Lerman wrote in *Lying to Clients* (page 746): "The absence of specific rules concerning deception of clients amounts to tacit permission for lawyers to continue to use deception."

11. "Lawyers Face Consumer Law" by John H. Kennedy, *Boston Globe,* October 4, 1991, page 69.

12. *Aponte* v. *Leo Raychuk,* 140 Misc. 2d 864, 531 N.Y.S. 2d 689, and 60 A.D. 2d636, 559 N.Y.S. 2d 255.

13. "Cheaper, Faster Civil Justice" by Whitney North Seymour Jr., *New York Times,* January 7, 1992.

14. "Report of the Committee to Examine Lawyer Conduct in Matrimonial Actions," otherwise known as the Milonas Report, New York, May 4, 1993, page 41.

15. Section 474, Item C of the law requires that judges ensure "compliance with appropriate requested discovery in a timely fashion; and (D) setting, at the earliest practicable time, deadlines for filing motions and a time framework for their disposition."

16. Telephone interview with author, June 2, 1994.

17. *The Essential Talmud,* by Adin Steinsaltz, translated from the Hebrew by Chaya Galai, Basic Books, 1976, pp. 131–32.

18. Ibid., page 132.

CHAPTER 12

1. Part 1400.2, "Statement of Client's Rights and Responsibilities," Title 22, Official Compilation of Codes, Rules and Regulations of the State of New York.

2. *New York Law Journal,* "Uniform Client Disclosure Forms Required," by Gary Spencer, pp. 1–2.

3. Note: Consumers would be well advised to eliminate from the written retainer any language allowing the lawyer to take a lien on the client's property.

4. Check with your local bar association to see if mediation in fee disputes is mandatory in your state.

5. A New York report by the Committee on the Profession and the Courts Chairman Louis A. Craco (November 1995, page 39) that evaluated the legal profession found that the Suffolk County Bar Association in New York has established standards for lawyers participating in a referral bank. In order to join, the lawyer must sign a grievance release waiver that authorizes the association's executive committee to examine the lawyer's grievance files and the lawyer must carry at least $100,000 in malpractice insurance.

```
3•00 2
3•00 ST
3•00 CA
0•00 CG


    1 #
 05-20-13
0889#01-06@
```

6. Committee to Examine Lawyer Conduct in Matrimonial Actions Report, L.A.W. Guidelines for a Retainer Agreement May 4, 1993, Appendix J.

7. Page 71.

8. Telephone interview with author, August 10, 1993.

9. *AARP Bulletin,* October 1991, Vol. XXXII, No. 9. *In My Opinion: Steps to ensure divorced women get fair share* by Anne E. Moss.

BIBLIOGRAPHY

The Bohemian Grove and Other Retreats
G. William Domhoff
New York: Harper & Row
1974

Criminology: Crime and Criminality, ed. 3
Martin R. Haskell and Lewis Yablonsky
Boston: Houghton Mifflin
1983

Discretionary Justice: a Preliminary Inquiry
Kenneth Culp Davis
Bloomington: University of Illinois Press
1971, 1969

The Divorce Revolution
Lenore Weitzman
New York: The Free Press
1985

The Finest Judges Money Can Buy
Charles R. Ashman
Los Angeles: Nash Publishing
1973

*From Father's Property to Children's Rights: The History of Child Custody
in the United States*
Mary Ann Mason

New York: Columbia University Press
1994

Getting Your Share: A Woman's Guide to Successful Divorce Strategies
Lois Brenner and Robert Stein
New York: Crown Publishers
1989

The Hardest Case: Custody and Incest
H. Joan Pennington, Esq.
Trenton, NJ: National Center for Protective Parents
February 1993

How to Sue Your Lawyer: The Consumer Guide to Legal Malpractice
Hilton Stein
Legal Malpractice Institute
103 Washington Street, Department 158
Morristown, NJ 07960
1989

In the Eyes of the Law
Norma Basch
Ithaca: Cornell University Press
1982

*". . . In the Spirit of Public Service:" A Blueprint for the Rekindling of
Lawyer Professionalism*
ABA Commission on Professionalism
Chicago: American Bar Association
1986

Law of Domestic Relations
Homer H. Clark, Jr.
St. Paul, MN: West Publishers
1968

Lawyers on Trial
Philip Stern
New York: Times Books
1980

Legal Issues and Legal Options in Civil Child Sexual Abuse Cases: Representing the Protective Parent
H. Joan Pennington and Laurie Woods
New York: National Center on Women and Family Law
1990

The Litigation Explosion: What Happened When America Unleashed the Lawsuit
Walter K. Olson
New York: Penguin
1991

"Lying to Clients"
Lisa Lerman
University of Pennsylvania Law Review 138(3)
January 1990

"Making Courts Safe for Children"
Charles B. Schudson
reprint from *Journal of Interpersonal Violence*
Beverly Hills, CA: SAGE Publications
March 1987

American Bar Association Model Code of Judicial Conduct
Chicago: American Bar Association Center for Professional Responsibility
1990

1995 Edition of the Model Rules of Professional Conduct
(national ethics guideline for lawyers)
Chicago: American Bar Association Center for Professional Responsibility
1995

Mothers on Trial
Phyllis Chesler
Orlando: Harcourt Brace Jovanovich
1991, 1987, 1986

1990 Demographic Yearbook, 42nd issue
New York: United Nations
1992

No-Fault Divorce
Michael Wheeler
Boston: Beacon Press
1974

On Trial: America's Courts and Their Treatment of Sexually Abused Children
Billie Wright Dziech and Judge Charles B. Schudson
Boston: Beacon Press
1991, 1989

Our Turn: Women Who Triumph in the Face of Divorce
Christopher L. Hayes, Deborah Anderson, Melinda Blau
New York: Pocket Books
1993

Power, Crime and Mystification
Steven Box
London and NY: Routledge Publishers
reprint 1989

Unequal Protection: Women, Children, and the Elderly in Court
Lois G. Forer
New York: W.W. Norton
1991

Unfair Tactics in Matrimonial Cases
Lawrence A. Moskowitz

New York: John Wiley and Sons
1990

*Using a Lawyer. . . and What to Do If Things Go Wrong: A Step-by-Step
Guide*
Kay Ostberg in association with HALT (Help Abolish Lawyer Tyranny)
New York: Random House
1990

When the Bough Breaks: The Cost of Neglecting Our Children
Sylvia Ann Hewlett
New York: Harper Perennial
1991

With Justice for None
Gerry Spence
New York: Penguin Books
1989

Women and the Law of Property in Early America
Marylynn Salmon
Chapel Hill: University of North Carolina Press
1986

Your Pension Rights at Divorce: What Women Need to Know
Ann E. Moss
Washington, DC: Pension Rights Center
1991

INDEX